Mathieu Kassovitz

Manchester University Press

DIANA HOLMES and ROBERT INGRAM *series editors*
DUDLEY ANDREW *series consultant*

Jean-Jacques Beineix PHIL POWRIE

Luc Besson SUSAN HAYWARD

Bertrand Blier SUE HARRIS

Robert Bresson KEITH READER

Leos Carax GARIN DOWD AND FERGUS DALEY

Claude Chabrol GUY AUSTIN

Jean Cocteau JAMES WILLIAMS

Claire Denis MARTINE BEUGNET

Marguerite Duras RENATE GÜNTHER

Georges Franju KATE INCE

Jean-Luc Godard DOUGLAS MORREY

Diane Kurys CARRIE TARR

Patrice Leconte LISA DOWNING

Louis Malle HUGO FREY

Georges Méliès ELIZABETH EZRA

Maurice Pialat MARJA WAREHIME

Jean Renoir MARTIN O'SHAUGHNESSY

Alain Resnais EMMA WILSON

Coline Serreau BRIGITTE ROLLET

François Truffaut DIANA HOLMES AND ROBERT INGRAM

Agnès Varda ALISON SMITH

Jean Vigo MICHAEL TEMPLE

FRENCH FILM DIRECTORS

Mathieu Kassovitz

WILL HIGBEE

Manchester University Press

MANCHESTER AND NEW YORK

distributed exclusively in the USA by Palgrave

Published by Manchester University Press
Oxford Road, Manchester M13 9NR, UK
and Room 400, 175 Fifth Avenue, New York, NY 10010, USA
www.manchesteruniversitypress.co.uk

Distributed exclusively in the USA by
Palgrave, 175 Fifth Avenue, New York, NY 10010, USA

Distributed exclusively in Canada by
UBC Press, University of British Columbia, 2029 West Mall, Vancouver,
BC, Canada V6T 1Z2

British Library Cataloguing-in-Publication Data
A catalogue record for this book is available from the British Library

Library of Congress Cataloging-in-Publication Data applied for

ISBN 0 7190 7146 1 *hardback*
EAN   978 0 7190 7146 1

ISBN 0 7190 7147 X *paperback*
EAN   978 0 7190 7147 8

First published 2006

15 14 13 12 11 10 09 08 07 06   10 9 8 7 6 5 4 3 2 1

Typeset in Scala with Meta display
by Koinonia, Manchester
Printed in Great Britain
by Biddles Ltd, King's Lynn

Contents

List of plates

All stills reproduced courtesy of BFI Stills, Posters and Designs.

Series editors' foreword

To an anglophone audience, the combination of the words 'French' and 'cinema' evokes a particular kind of film: elegant and wordy, sexy but serious – an image as dependent on national stereotypes as is that of the crudely commercial Hollywood blockbuster, which is not to say that either image is without foundation. Over the past two decades, this generalised sense of a significant relationship between French identity and film has been explored in scholarly books and articles, and has entered the curriculum at university level and, in Britain, at A-level. The study of film as an art-form and (to a lesser extent) as industry, has become a popular and widespread element of French Studies, and French cinema has acquired an important place within Film Studies. Meanwhile, the growth in multi-screen and 'art-house' cinemas, together with the development of the video industry, has led to the greater availability of foreign-language films to an English-speaking audience. Responding to these developments, this series is designed for students and teachers seeking information and accessible but rigorous critical study of French cinema, and for the enthusiastic filmgoer who wants to know more.

The adoption of a director-based approach raises questions about auteurism. A series that categorises films not according to period or to genre (for example), but to the person who directed them, runs the risk of espousing a romantic view of film as the product of solitary inspiration. On this model, the critic's role might seem to be that of discovering continuities, revealing a necessarily coherent set of themes and motifs which correspond to the particular genius of the individual. This is not our aim: the auteur perspective on film, itself most clearly articulated in France in the early 1950s, will be interrogated in certain volumes of the series, and, throughout, the director will be treated as one highly significant element in a complex process of film production and reception which includes socio-economic and political determinants, the work of a large and highly skilled team of artists and technicians, the mechanisms of production and distribution, and the complex and multiply determined responses of spectators.

The work of some of the directors in the series is already known outside France, that of others is less so – the aim is both to provide informative and original English-language studies of established figures, and to extend the range of French directors known to anglophone students of cinema. We intend the series to contribute to the promotion of the informal and formal study of French films, and to the pleasure of those who watch them.

DIANA HOLMES
ROBERT INGRAM

Acknowledgements

I want to express my sincere thanks to the various friends, family and colleagues who have offered encouragement, support and practical help during the writing of this book. First to the AHRC for granting me a six-month research award to complete the writing-up of this book. To the University of Exeter for providing a matching period of leave which allowed the necessary space and time for my ideas to develop. Also to Phil Powrie and Keith Reader for their initial support with this project in relation to the AHRC study-leave bid.

I am grateful to members of the Centre for Research in Film Studies (CR-IFS) at Exeter University, who offered very helpful initial feedback on earlier drafts of my work on Kassovitz. Special thanks go to Saër Maty Bâ and Bridget Birchall for their generous and incisive comments on later drafts of specific chapters. I would also like to acknowledge a considerable debt of gratitude to my very good friend and colleague Susan Hayward for her invaluable support, enthusiasm and advice throughout this project. Friends and family in the UK, Spain and France have, in various ways (and sometimes without even knowing it) offered vital support throughout this project, for which I am extremely grateful.

My final thanks are reserved for my wife, Isali Gómez de Toro, without whose love, patience and support (both practical and emotional) I could not have finished this book – and also our son Tom, who puts everything in perspective.

For Isali and Tom. With love.

Introduction

Looking at his filmography to date, there is a temptation to divide Mathieu Kassovitz's career into two distinct phases. The first, comprising his short films and feature films up to and including *Assassin*(s) (1997), engages in an often provocative way with socio-political debates in contemporary France through an aesthetic mode of address designed to appeal primarily to a youth audience. The second phase, post-*Assassin(s)*, appears to be marked by a conscious shift towards bigger-budget, more unashamedly commercial, genre productions. (This trend would seem to be continuing with Kassovitz's current project, an ambitious, French-produced, English-language science-fiction film entitled *Babylon AD*, due to be shot in 2006.) Nevertheless, in both phases of his career, Kassovitz has remained consistent in his commitment to the 'popular', in terms of his use of genre, visual spectacle and a conscious targeting of a youth audience.

As a young director, Kassovitz first came to the attention of the wider French public with the release of his second feature, *La Haine* (1995); a controversial and visually seductive depiction of a day in the life of a multiethnic trio of male youths from a disadvantaged housing estate on the outskirts of Paris. Released in a presidential election year dominated by discussions of *fracture sociale* (the disintegration of the social fabric and widening gap between the haves and have-nots of French society), *La Haine*'s controversial subject matter and confrontational approach (the title means 'hate' in English) seemed to strike a raw nerve with French audiences, attracting almost two million spectators in France.

La Haine instantly established not only Kassovitz's directorial career, but also that of one of its lead actors, Vincent Cassel. It was, furthermore, identified by critics as one of a growing number of films by mostly young directors that, in choosing to engage directly with socio-political issues, marked French cinema's 'return to the political' after a decade (the 1980s) that had been dominated by the postmodern play of the *cinéma du look* and the lavishly staged retro-nostalgia of the heritage film. The film was also seen as the most prominent example of a 'new' sub-genre in French cinema: the *banlieue* film. Finally, *La Haine* sparked extensive (some might say excessive) debate due to its controversial representation of *fracture sociale* and, in particular, police violence against young male inhabitants of the working-class estates of the Paris suburbs. These debates continue today on campuses in both the UK and the USA, where *La Haine* is taught extensively on French and film studies syllabuses.

For these reasons *La Haine* has become seen as, arguably, one of the key films to emerge from 1990s French cinema. However, it is not where Kassovitz begins and ends as a filmmaker. Thus, while not seeking to deny *La Haine*'s significance to either Kassovitz's career or, more generally, developments in French cinema of the 1990s, the aim of this book is to redress the balance somewhat by considering Kassovitz's entire output as both director and actor.

The director of five shorts and five features to date, Kassovitz enjoyed critical and commercial success in France with *La Haine*, followed by spectacular failure with his next feature *Assassin(s)* (1997); an experience that led to a period of self-imposed exile in Hollywood towards the end of the decade, from which he returned to France to direct the decidedly mainstream thriller *Les Rivières pourpres* (2000). This more direct engagement with American-influenced genre cinema led eventually to his first Hollywood feature, the psychological horror-thriller, *Gothika* (2003). In addition to his career as a director, Kassovitz has made a name for himself as an actor – appearing in twenty features and six short films to date (and sometimes in his own films), gaining critical acclaim, including two César nominations for *Métisse* (Kassovitz, 1993) and *Amen* (Costa-Gavras, 2002) and one award for his performances in *Regarde les hommes tomber* (Audiard, 1994) as well as enjoying box-office success as the male-lead in *Le Fabuleux destin d'Amélie Poulain* (Jeunet, 2001).

In both France and abroad, Kassovitz has therefore made a considerable impact as director and actor in a relatively short period of time – one of the reasons for writing this book at what is still a relatively early stage in his career. He has also gained a reputation in France as an uncompromising and outspoken personality. First, because of the polemics that surround the subject matter of some of his films. Second, for his often confrontational attitude towards, on the one hand, the political establishment in France, and, on the other, the French cinematic establishment – including the CNC and the heavyweights of French film criticism, *Positif* and *Cahiers du cinéma*, whom Kassovitz sees as largely dismissive of his particular brand of popular filmmaking.

Looking beyond the more sensational and controversial headlines garnered by the outspoken opinions of 'Kasso' the public personality and (largely) self-styled rebel of France's Seventh Art, this book intends to locate Kassovitz's cinema in relation to key cultural and cinematic developments that have taken place in France during the 1990s. On the one hand, it will address the effects of the shifting configurations of French popular culture that began in the 1980s under the auspices of Lang's *le tout culturel*, which have seen the legitimising of mass cultural forms such as television, advertising and pop music (Dauncey 2003: 12–14). This, in turn, has led to an increasingly prominent place being accorded to an Americanised, multiethnic youth culture in France, which forms a central reference point for Kassovitz's cinema. On the other hand, Kassovitz's films can also be used to understand key shifts and trends in French cinema since the early 1990s, such as new realism, the so-called *jeune cinéma*, as well as the emergence of what we might term a 'post-look' spectacular genre cinema – a popular French cinema that looks to Besson and Beineix, Hollywood genres and South-East Asian cinema for its inspiration and modes of production, rather than the more traditional reference points of French realism, the *auteur* and European art-house cinema.

The book begins in Chapter 1 with a consideration of the origins and influences that have shaped Kassovitz's development as a director, but also the cultural context within which he emerges as a filmmaker: arguing that his particular brand of popular cinema is entirely consistent with the tastes and consumption practices of youth audiences in France. Chapter 2 focuses on *Métisse* and *La Haine*, which, it will be argued, use the arena of popular culture as a space of 'constant contestation' (Hall 1981: 239), in which the discourses and modes of representation employed by hegemony in relation to issues such as race, ethnicity, youth and exclusion are actively challenged. In this context,

Chapter 2 also considers French hip-hop as a structuring iconography within Kassovitz's early films.

Chapter 3 moves on to analyse *Assassin(s)*, Kassovitz's third feature and the final instalment of what shall be termed his *fracture sociale* trilogy. A far less accessible film than either *Métisse* or *La Haine*, the sprawling polemical narrative of *Assassin(s)* was roundly rejected by contemporary French critics at the time of its release. One of the principal aims of this chapter, then, is to revisit a much maligned and, I believe, largely misunderstood film. Instead, it will be argued that *Assassin(s)* represents Kassovitz's most challenging and sophisticated film to date, a bold attempt to explore the recourse to violence by an alienated youth class in contemporary France – and the media's role in both influencing and perpetuating this social crisis.

Chapter 4 examines the American influences (both from mainstream Hollywood and independent, exploitation cinema) evident in all of Kassovitz's films to date as a director. It also analyses, and with particular reference to his two most recent films (*Les Rivières pourpres* and *Gothika*), the various ways in which Kassovitz 'interfaces' with Hollywood, and thus occupies something of a bridging position between American and French film cultures. Equally, Chapter 4 explores how the cultural myth of Hollywood finds increasing resonance and immediacy with contemporary French audiences and a new generation of post-look filmmakers, such as Kassovitz. The fifth and final chapter considers Kassovitz's acting career to date, exploring the continuity and difference between his films as actor and director, his attempts to conspire against a star trajectory, and how issues of authorship come into play when he appears on both sides of the camera in his own films.

As this book will argue, Kassovitz's work as both actor and director 'matters' because his films pose important questions about the place and the function of the 'popular' in contemporary French cinema. What does popular cinema actually mean in the context of contemporary French cinema? How does it function in relation to representations of ethnicity, class and age?[1] Who or what qualifies as 'popular'? How does the notion of popular cinema in a national context fit within what is essentially a transnational medium (cinema) operating in what Shohat and Stam (2000: 381–401) refer to as the

1 I have deliberately not included gender and sexuality in this list because, as we shall see, these are significant blind-spots in Kassovitz's cinema.

age of the 'posts': post-structuralist; postmodern; postcolonial; even post-celluloid? Finally, what is the purpose of the popular in contemporary French cinema and culture? Does the arena of popular culture represent a hegemonic space in which the ideas, values and representations of minority or marginal groups are merely appropriated and exploited by the mainstream, or can it function as a viable site of resistance that is at once cultural, political and social?

All of the above questions will be addressed in detail in the chapters that follow through an analysis of Kassovitz's output as both actor and director since the early 1990s. (Kassovitz's latest film as an actor, *Munich* (Spielberg, 2006) will, unfortunately, not feature as part of this analysis, since, at the time of completion of the monography (December, 2005) the film had still not been released.) Let us begin, then, by framing the debates around the popular as they relate to Kassovitz's cinema and the cultural context of the period from which he emerged as a filmmaker: the 1980s and early 1990s.

References

Dauncey, Hugh (ed.) (2003), *French Popular Culture: An Introduction*, London: Arnold

Hall, Stuart (1981), 'Notes on deconstructing the popular', *People's History and Socialist Theory*, in Raphael Samuel (ed.), *People's History and socialist theory*, London: Routledge, 227–40

Shohat, Elia Habiba and Stam, Robert (2000), 'Film theory and spectatorship in the age of the posts' in *Reinventing Film Studies*, Christine Gledhill and Linda Williams, London: Routledge, 381–401

1

The popular polemicist

When questioned in interviews as to why he chose to become a film-maker, Kassovitz has routinely offered the following answer: 'Mes parents travaillent dans le cinéma. S'ils avaient été boulangers, j'aurais été boulanger. Ils étaient cinéastes, je suis devenu cinéaste' (Bourguignon and Yann 1995: 8).[1] Although this is indeed an accurate statement – his father, Peter Kassovitz, is a director working in both film and television and his mother, Chantal Rémy, a film editor – such a prosaic response seems at odds with a filmmaker who emerged in the 1990s as one of French cinema's most vital new talents.

It is, first of all, a pedestrian description from a director whose work is anything but – characterised as it is by a seductive visual style that combines fluid, restless camerawork with an exacting control of an often spectacular *mise en scène*. Secondly, such a pragmatic explanation implies a distinct lack of engagement: whereas Kassovitz is a filmmaker who is both passionate about cinema as a popular cultural form and, in his earlier films at least, a director who shows a keen awareness of cinema's potential to engage a mainstream audience with controversial contemporary socio-political issues. Finally, his reply: 'my parents are filmmakers so I'll become a filmmaker' suggests a parochial outlook, entirely at odds with the international ambition Kassovitz has for his films. It implies a fatalistic acceptance of the status quo, belying the fact that he emerged as one of the most outspoken critics of the French film industry in the 1990s – viewed by Kassovitz (1998) as a restrictive cultural industry that resists the

1 'My parents worked in cinema. If they'd been bakers, I'd have been a baker. They were filmmakers, so I became a filmmaker.'

possibilities of the popular by narrowly defining itself in relation to an intellectualised, art-house identity and taking the French New Wave as its seemingly fixed reference point.

In order to understand Kassovitz the filmmaker, we need therefore to appreciate not only the background that led him into the industry but also the network of local, national and global influences which have shaped and continue to inform his particular type of cinema. Moreover, given the emphasis Kassovitz places on his own work as popular cinema, it is necessary to locate his films within the context of the 'popular' in contemporary French cinema; and French culture more generally. This chapter will therefore explore the cultural context within which Kassovitz emerged to direct his first three short films, concentrating in the second half on key transformations relating to youth culture that have taken place in relation to French popular culture since the early 1980s.

Origins and influences: 'a different way of looking at cinema'

Born in Paris on 3 August 1967, Kassovitz grew up in Ménilmontant – a relatively cosmopolitan district of the twentieth *arrondissement* made up of artists, immigrants and (prior to its gentrification in the 1990s) working-class families. His father, Peter Kassovitz, is a Hungarian Jew who, after fleeing the Soviet invasion of Hungary in 1956 as a student journalist, eventually arrived in Paris, where he began a career shortly after as a filmmaker. The artistic and creative traditions continue with Mathieu's Hungarian grandparents. His grandmother, Elise Kassovitz (also known as Bözsi) was a sculptor and painter, while his grandfather, Félix Kassovitz, was a cartoonist and anarchist. Both grandparents were Holocaust survivors, having been interned in separate Nazi concentration camps during the Second World War.[2] This family history can, perhaps, help to explain Kassovitz's decision to enter a creative medium such as film, as well as his apparent predisposition – inherited from his grandfather it would seem – to reject and challenge authority in all its forms.

The family home where Mathieu grew up in Paris during the late 1960s and 1970s was located in a converted warehouse of

2 For more details on Peter Kassovitz and the family history in Hungary see Mérigeau (2004).

Ménilmontant, in what might broadly be described as a left-wing intellectual milieu: artist Kiki Picasso and filmmaker Chris Marker both lived in the same apartment block; while director Costa-Gavras – *the* iconic *auteur* of 1970s civic cinema – was also a regular visitor (Aubel 2003: 19). Kassovitz's parents appear, therefore, to have been part of the increasingly politicised intellectual and artistic scene found in Paris during the late 1960s and 1970s; though the extent to which they were actively involved in such movements is unclear. For example, Peter Kassovitz is known to have participated in the May '68 demonstrations, including making a number of short documentary films.[3] However, his subsequent work in film and television has shown little evidence of the radical or politically committed artist, and is more concerned with exploring his own history as an Eastern-European Jewish immigrant.[4]

In interviews, Kassovitz barely comments on the intellectual and political circles in which his parents moved when he was growing up during the 1970s. Instead he concentrates on the immersion in cinema (on both sides of the camera) permitted by his family background. From an early age Kassovitz frequented the editing suites, film and television sets where his parents worked. At 11 he appeared in his father's first feature film *Au bout du bout du banc* (Peter Kassovitz, 1979) acting alongside Jane Birkin and Victor Lanoux. While these experiences undoubtedly taught Kassovitz much about the industry that he would eventually work in, just as important for him were the family trips to the cinema that soon became a regular feature of his childhood. He considers these outings to the movies, particularly those taken with his father, as formative experiences in the sense that they instilled a passion for cinema while at the same time equipping him with a keener understanding of film techniques and the mechanics of the moving image: 'Quand on allait au cinéma, il y avait une façon de regarder les films qui était un peu différente ... Ça m'a

3 According to Tarr (2005: 63), he was even in the *maquis* in Nicaragua.
4 During the 1970s, Peter Kassovitz directed dramas for French television, including, most notably, episodes for the series *Médecin de nuit*. In 1979, he directed his first feature film *Au bout du bout du banc* the story of four generations of a Jewish immigrant family who gather for a ninetieth birthday celebration in Paris. Since then he has directed three more feature films, including most recently *Jakob the Liar* (1999) a Hollywood feature starring Robin Williams, that tells the tale of Nazi oppression of Jews in the Warsaw ghetto during the Second World War.

appris à essayer de voir des choses différentes au cinéma' (Bourguignon and Yann 1995: 8).[5]

As film practitioners, his mother and father were able to explain to
their son how and why image and narrative were constructed on screen
in the way that they were, introducing him to the effect/affect of *mise
en scène*, editing and narrative construction. One of the most important of these trips to the cinema came in the mid-1970s when Kassovitz was about 10 and his father took him to the Paris Cinémathèque
to see *Duel* (Spielberg, 1971). The young Kassovitz was immediately
struck by Spielberg's directorial style – accurately described by Kolker
(2000: 257) as a proficient (if ideologically problematic) structuring
of narrative and control of *mise en scène* that encourages the spectator
to surrender themselves to the narrative. Kassovitz has since claimed
(Tirard 2000) that his greatest lessons in filmmaking have come from
Spielberg, and that it is the 'physicality' and 'efficiency' of Spielberg's
mise en scène that so impresses him. By this, he refers not only to the
way that Spielberg allows the camera to physically navigate through
the on-screen space inhabited by his characters (effectively making
the camera an independent protagonist within the diegesis), but also
to the effect this has in suturing the spectator into the narrative: elements Kassovitz has undoubtedly integrated into his own brand of
youth-orientated popular cinema.[6]

Alongside these family outings to the cinema in the late 1970s
and early 1980s, where, in addition to Spielberg, he had 'discovered' contemporary directors such as Beineix, Lucas, Scorsese and
Besson, Kassovitz supplemented his film education in other ways.
Taking advantage of the greater freedom from his parents that came
with adolescence, as well as the variety of programming offered by
cinemas in Paris, the teenager was able to indulge his increasingly
eclectic tastes: frequenting the independent *art et essais* film theatres
of the Latin Quarter (he mentions in particular the Rue des Écoles),
where he describes seeing many French 'classics' of the 1950s; while
also developing a love of American science-fiction blockbusters (Spielberg, Lucas) and horror cinema (Craven, Argento and Romero) from
the late 1970s and early 1980s (Kassovitz 1998).

5 'When we used to go to the cinema, we had a way of watching films which was a
  bit different ... which taught me to try and see different things at the cinema.'
6 See Chapter 4 for a more detailed discussion of Spielberg's influence on Kassovitz.

The young Kassovitz was, however, less enthusiastic about French cinema of the same period, as comments made during an interview in the late 1990s prove:

> Il y a aussi le cinéma français des années 30/40/50. Ca s'arrête avec Melville. Après, c'est le trou. Il y les films d'Yves Robert : *Le Grand Blond, Un Eléphant ça Trompe Enormément, Nous irons tous au Paradis* qui sont pour moi des chefs-d'œuvre. Après, il ne se passe plus rien pendant des années, jusqu'à Beineix, Besson. (Kassovitz 1998)[7]

At first glance, this rather random coupling of two such different directors (Robert and Melville) seems to reveal little more than an illustration of Kassovitz's own eclectic tastes. Although more recently associated with the heritage film as a result of his Pagnolian diptych *La Gloire de mon père* (1989) and *Le Chateau de ma mère* (1989), Robert had enjoyed considerable box-office success in the 1970s with comedies such as *Un Éléphant ça trompe énormément* (1976) and *Nous irons tous au paradis* (1977), films dealing with the lives and loves of a group of middle-aged Parisian men. While it is difficult to envisage Kassovitz as a fan of his later work, he considers Robert's earlier films to be comic masterpieces (a further indication of his instinctively popular tastes). Despite the obvious differences between Kassovitz and Robert's films, not least the fact that they play to different generations and are located in virtually opposing socio-economic milieus, elements of Robert's comedy – focused as it is around a type of male-centred 'buddy' humour – can nonetheless be detected in both *Métisse* and the moments of comedy in *La Haine* that emerge from the interplay between the central trio of Vinz, Saïd and Hubert. The possible influence of Robert's comedy does, however, point to potential limitations in Kassovitz's own cinema; namely the relatively marginalised position occupied by female protagonists in the narratives of his films.

With regard to Melville, the link is perhaps more obvious. It is hardly surprising that Kassovitz should align himself with this particular French *auteur*, whose love of Americana and preference for offering a French reinterpretation of Hollywood genres (the gangster film, *film noir*, detective thriller) resonates with Kassovitz's own

7 'There's also French cinema of the 1930s, 1940s and 1950s. That stops with Melville. Then there's a gap. There are the films of Yves Robert *Le Grand Blond, Un Eléphant ça trompe énormément, Nous irons tous au paradis* which for me are masterpieces. After that nothing happens for years until Beineix and Besson'.

fascination and engagement with popular American cinema. One final and important influence from 1970s French cinema is Costa-Gavras. A regular visitor to the apartment block where Kassovitz grew up – his son lived in the same building – Costa-Gavras was another of the filmmakers Kassovitz discovered through his parents: 'Môme, mon père m'a montré ses films et ce que j'ai fait a été influencé par des films comme Z où L'Aveu. Des films forts, profonds, où l'on touche à des sujets importants, primordiaux' (Kassovitz 1998).[8] The connection felt by Kassovitz to Costa-Gavras's films of the 1970s (a director with whom Kassovitz would eventually work as an actor in the early 2000s) is entirely logical, given that many of his own feature films attempt to engage popular audiences with contemporary socio-political issues in a similar way to the so-called civic or political cinema of that period with which Costa-Gavras is so closely associated. Moreover, the criticism levelled at directors of civic cinema such as Costa-Gavras and Boisset in the 1970s for effecting a spectacularisation of politics (Hayward 1993: 241–2) is remarkably similar to that directed towards Kassovitz for the supposedly 'designer visions' of exclusion found in La Haine.

With the exception of the few directors named above, Kassovitz generally views the 1970s and early 1980s as rather barren years for French cinema; professing to find little of interest within his own national film culture during this period until the arrival of Beineix and Besson and the cinéma du look, and thus turning beyond France for inspiration. In addition to his avid consumption of mainstream Hollywood and various cinema 'classics' such as Citizen Kane on video and laser disc (the more cumbersome pre-cursor to DVD), Kassovitz further satisfied his taste for genre and exploitation cinema by attending Sunday morning screenings, arranged by the underground Paris-based film magazine Starfix, which promoted cult directors, genre and exploitation cinema from America and South-East Asia to a French audience.[9] By his early teens, Kassovitz was a devoted subscriber to the French horror and fantasy film magazine Mad Movies,

---

8 'As a child, my father showed me his films, and what I have done has been influenced by films such as Z or L'Aveu. Powerful, profound films that deal with important, essential subjects.'

9 Starfix was established in 1983 by film journalists Christophe Gans (the future director of Le Pacte des loups (2001) and Nicholas Boukhrief, co-author of the screenplay for Kassovitz's third film, Assassin(s) who would also pursue a career as a director in the late 1990s.

exhibiting the excessive (obsessive) passions of a cult cinema enthu-
siast: writing fake reviews and creating fanzines for his favourite films
and directors; visiting the same Parisian cinema to watch repeated
screenings of *American Graffiti* (Lucas 1973) every Saturday for almost
a year (Kassovitz 1998). This enthusiasm for cult cinema was, moreover, combined with his own desire to make films. At the age of 13,
Kassovitz was already shooting his own no-budget horror films with
his parents' Super-8 camera, imitating the shock and gore found in
films such as *Evil Dead* (Raimi, 1981) with home-made props such as
limbs from shop-store mannequins covered in red paint (*ibid.*). He was
also spending an increasing amount of time on the film and television
sets and in edit suites where his parents worked, keenly observing the
practices and techniques of actors and crew around him.

Despite his love of American cinema – mainstream genre cinema,
blockbusters and exploitation movies – it was, in fact, the work of a
French director, *not* that of Scorsese, Spielberg or Lucas that proved
to be the '*film-déclic*': the film that opened Kassovitz's eyes to the possibilities of a career as a director. Aged 17, he accompanied his father
to see Besson's debut feature, *Le Dernier combat* (1983); a low-budget
science-fiction film shot in black and white and with virtually no dialogue about human survival in a post-apocalyptic world. According to
Kassovitz (*ibid.*) it was not only Besson's imaginative and assured control of *mise en scène* that proved such an inspiration, but also the fact
that a young, unknown French director working with a limited budget
had excelled in making a convincing science-fiction film – a genre
which received wisdom within the French film industry considered
the exclusive domain of Hollywood. Kassovitz therefore took Besson's
film as proof that he could make a career for himself directing the
type of cinema he loved (horror, science-fiction) even within a national
cinema which at that time – with the notable exceptions of comedy
and the *policier* (crime thriller) – largely eschewed the possibilities of
popular genre and exploitation cinema.

Suitably inspired by the innovation and ambition of Besson's
Le Dernier combat, Kassovitz decided almost immediately after the
screening to drop out of school a year before completing his *bacca-
lauréat*; the required qualification for entry into the French university
system (and, just as importantly, France's national Film School, the
Fémis). While on the face of it this may have seemed like a brave
decision, Kassovitz was, by his own admission, an unenthusiastic

student at school who rarely excelled in academic pursuits. Indeed, in the summer vacation prior to his penultimate year at school, he had already been working as an unpaid assistant for a Parisian production company, who then offered him another placement the following winter (*ibid.*). This offer, combined with the encouragement gained from seeing Besson's debut feature thus gave Kassovitz the confidence to terminate his studies and launch himself into a career in the film industry.

Apprenticeship and short films

Having dropped out of secondary education, Kassovitz spent the second half of the 1980s working on a variety of film productions, with responsibilities ranging from runner to assistant director. He also found work during this period on a number of advert shoots, music videos and *films industriels* (a catchall term used in French to describe all manner of technical, instructive or promotional short films commissioned by organisations and corporations). Kassovitz's attitude towards this time spent filling what might have otherwise been seen as a series of dead-end jobs, gives an insight into his approach to filmmaking:

> Quand j'étais stagiaire, par exemple, je n'avais pas grand chose d'autre à faire que bloquer la rue, ça me laissait donc pas mal de temps pour observer la façon dont le metteur en scène travaillait. J'avais le scénario entre les mains, et quand je regardais où le réalisateur posait sa caméra, j'essayais de comprendre pourquoi.
> (Kassovitz quoted in Tirard 2000)[10]

For Kassovitz, the menial task of blocking the street for a location shoot was transformed into an opportunity to learn about framing, camera placement and directing actors. In many ways, this represented a natural extension of the days spent on set with his father, or in editing suites with his mother; echoing the approach of Besson, who, like Kassovitz, learned his craft as a filmmaker largely by observing the cast and crew of the film sets on which he assisted in

10 'When I was a trainee, for example, I didn't have much to do other than to block the street [for shooting], which left me a fair bit of time to observe how the director worked. I had the script to hand, and when I looked at where the director was placing his camera, I tried to work out why.'

the early years (Hayward 1998: 11). Kassovitz has, moreover, extended this strategy for learning onsite to his acting career, accepting cameo roles in film by directors whom he admires (Besson, Jeunet, Blier and Spielberg) in order to better understand the working practices of these filmmakers.

The emphasis placed by Kassovitz on the practical – on 'doing' rather than merely thinking or theorising about cinema – was combined with a strong element of autodidacticism. As a teenager, Kassovitz would spend hours at home (re-)viewing videos and laserdiscs of films by his favourite directors in order to discern not only *how* they were made but also but also *why* – with regard to narrative structure, visual spectacle and audience identification – they worked; and, in the case of those less successful films, why not. As Kassovitz puts it: 'c'est comme ça que j'apprends. En étant spectateur' (Tirard 2000).[11] His use of video as a tool of instruction for the aspiring filmmaker learning his craft is further evidence of Kassovitz's place amongst a new generation of youthful spectators who – through repeated, selective and fragmented viewings of films on video and now DVD – consume, understand and construct cinema in a different way to their predecessors. It is precisely because he was immersed in such cinema as both spectator and aspiring filmmaker that Kassovitz's films display an implicit understanding of the tastes and modes of consumption of a contemporary (youth) audience for films that grab the attention of the spectator in ever more arresting and immediate ways.

After five years in the industry, gleaning as much practical experience as he could from the various films he had been involved in, and having worked his way up to assistant director on the largely forgotten comedy *Moitié-moitié* (Boujenah, 1989), Kassovitz decided it was time to advance his career as a director. Following his father's advice to make what he could with what he had, Kassovitz invested all his savings developing a short film that he would write, direct and star in. Beyond his own modest investment of FF20,000, the majority of which would have to be spent on post-production and transferring to a print that could be exhibited at festivals, there was virtually no money for the film. Kassovitz thus called in favours from friends and associates within the industry to assemble a skeletal crew for the shoot. In an attempt to minimise costs, he even resorted to borrowing an 8mm

11 'That's how I learn. By being a spectator.'

Bolex camera from his neighbour – who, in return, became the film's director of photography (Kassovitz 1998).

The title of the resulting short film, *Fierrot le pou* (1990), is an obvious play on Godard's *Pierrot le fou* (1965). While this playful inversion may well display a youthful irreverence similar to that found in the early work of Godard or Truffaut, Kassovitz's first seven-minute short film is far removed from the self-reflexive, and, at times, intellectual preoccupations of the French New Wave *auteurs*. Instead, through its combination of hip-hop style and an instinctively popular aesthetic, *Fierrot le pou*, examines issues of ethnicity and stereotyping via a comic encounter on a basketball court between an attractive woman of mixed race and an unathletic, white nerd/aspiring B-Boy (played by Kassovitz). The two characters train at separate ends of the court, the young man failing to impress with a string of uncoordinated moves, and shots that, in more ways than one, completely miss the target. As Kassovitz's character makes one final play for the young woman's attentions, shots of the slight, bespectacled figure are intercut with images of a muscular black basketball player who executes the slam-dunk with athletic precision. Having finally secured the desired acknowledgement from the young woman that he craves, the film ends with a smug-looking Kassovitz being brought down to earth as an attempt to repeat his success with a long-range shot ends up with the ball wedged between the hoop and backboard – an act that brings howls of laughter from a non-diegetic chorus of voices as the credits roll.

Kassovitz's first short film thus becomes a statement of intent from the ambitious young director. The title itself suggests irreverence towards the central position of the French New Wave in the history and critical appraisal of French cinema since the late 1950s. Kassovitz is quite literally turning Godard upside down; breaking with the legacy and myths of the French New Wave in search of inspiration from other, more mainstream, cinematic reference points (in particular Besson and Spielberg). The film also announces a clear affinity with contemporary, urban, multicultural and transnational forms of popular culture found in Kassovitz's subsequent films – both in relation to French hip-hop and African-American popular culture more generally. To suggest that the fascination with African-American culture found in *Fierrot le pou* can be read as a desire to 'be black' (Tarr 2005: 63) seems a little excessive, although it does draw attention to the important issue of the white appropriation of black and beur (Maghrebi-French) culture addressed by the film. In fact *Fierrot le pou* does not present itself as a wish-fulfilment narrative for Kassovitz/the white B-boy to inhabit the body and thus 'be' the African-American or French postcolonial other (the film's self-mocking tone puts pay to that idea). Rather, *Fierrot le pou* acknowledges the complex network of local and global influences that now inform postcolonial youth culture in France, while at the same time warning of the dangers for white French youth of merely investing in empty signifiers of racial or ethnic difference. The film ends, then, with a joke at the expense of the aspiring white B-boy, who, Kassovitz seems to be suggesting, should simply try and be himself instead of attempting to inhabit stereotypical fantasies of the black 'other'.

Fierrot le pou thus establishes a number of recurring stylistic and thematic features in Kassovitz's filmmaking: the use of black and white images; references to French hip-hop culture and issues of postcolonial identities in France; as well as announcing Kassovitz's presence on both sides of the camera (playing a character in *Fierrot* – the nerdish white B-boy – that would resurface in *Métisse* as Félix and, to a lesser extent, in the character of Max from *Assassin(s)*). The film also introduces what has become possibly the most recognisable stylistic signature in Kassovitz's *mise en scène*: the use of highly mobile camerawork and the elaborate long take. The fact that this type of camerawork appears at all in Kassovitz's first short film is remarkable given the technical constraints under which he was operating. As we have already noted, *Fierrot le pou* was filmed on a wind-up 8mm Bolex camera, which meant that each shot could last no more than 30 seconds (Kassovitz 1998). Faced with such technical restrictions, the obvious solution for Kassovitz would have been to construct the film around series of rapidly edited shots to compensate for the restricted shooting time offered by the Bolex. However, the young filmmaker refused to compromise his aesthetic vision for *Fierrot le pou*. Instead, by combining a limited number of rapidly edited sequences with longer single takes (in which the camera was allowed to run to its thirty second maximum), and relying on engaging composition, fluid camera movement and action within the frame, Kassovitz was able to produce the sense of energy and spectacle he desired for his audience.

Having completed a rough edit of *Fierrot le pou*, Kassovitz considered how best to find an audience for his (still incomplete) short.

Ignoring the advice of friends to incorporate the film's modish hip-hop style into a music video, he took a copy of the rough edit – a video recorded from the screen of the Steinbeck editing desk on which *Fierrot le pou* had been cut – to various independent production companies in search of additional investment to produce a more polished edit (with sound) and a print which could then be shown on the short-film festival circuit. After numerous rejections, Kassovitz arrived at the offices of Lazennec, an independent production company led by a team of youthful producers who had recently established their reputation with the success of Eric Rochant's *Un monde sans pitié* (1989). Here he was greeted by Christophe Rossignon, who had himself only recently been employed as part of the company's expansion into short film production, Lazennec Tout Court. From what seemed like an unlikely pairing – Rossignon is ten years older than Kassovitz and, as the son of a farmer from Nord-Pas-de-Calais, his origins could not be more further removed from Kassovitz's urban Parisian roots – a firm professional and personal friendship was established. Rossignon and Kassovitz struck up an instant rapport, forming a close-knit partnership that lasted for seven years, three shorts and three features, including Kassovitz's breakthrough *La Haine*.

This collaboration with Rossignon and Lazennec was crucial for Kassovitz's career in that in that it offered the young director a considerable amount of freedom to develop his own particular brand of popular youth-orientated cinema. In the 1990s, the majority of independent producers continued to see their role as primarily artisanal, tending to rely on state-derived funding from the Centre National de la Cinématographie (CNC). They therefore tended to promote films fitting the profile of projects traditionally supported by the selective aid from the CNC, which in the early 1990s essentially meant either *auteur* films or heritage cinema. In contrast to the dominant trends in production and funding, Lazennec initiated a more progressive approach; forging professional alliances with co-producers, TV networks and distributors in order to establish what might best be described as a partially integrated mini-major which looked as much to private investment as it did to state aid to fund short and feature-length film production. For a director such as Kassovitz, who, by this point, had had every project submitted to the CNC for selective funding rejected, the support of Lazennec and Rossignon proved something of a lifeline.

Under the auspices of Lazennec Tout Court, Kassovitz completed the required post-production on *Fierrot le pou*. A more tightly edited version of the film (complete with sound) was circulated on the festival circuit, to a decidedly mixed reception. Despite winning minor awards and a degree of public praise, Kassovitz felt that the film was not really appreciated by those within the industry (filmmakers, producers and critics), primarily because its unashamedly popular appeal clashed with the prevailing view in France of the short film as the territory of emerging *auteur* or avant-garde cinema (Kassovitz 1998).[12] In this respect, Kassovitz established the pattern that would mark the reception of his films in France to date; whereby success with French audiences would be contrasted with ambivalence or indifference from the critical establishment of France's more high-brow film journals such as *Positif* and *Cahiers du cinéma*.

After *Fierrot le pou*, Kassovitz and Rossignon turned their attention to a second short, *Cauchemar blanc* (1991); also shot in black and white, but this time with dialogue. *Cauchemar blanc* confirmed Kassovitz's talent as a *metteur en scène*, benefiting from a more experienced technical crew and a cast of professional actors including Jean-Pierre Daroussin and Yvan Attal. Kassovitz's second short is also marked by its more overtly political content. In *Fierrot le Pou*, issues of race, ethnicity and representation are largely secondary concerns in what is essentially a comic short intended to showcase the young director's talent. *Cauchemar blanc*, on the other hand, deals more directly with the realities of racism in contemporary France, albeit in a way that was far removed from the more naturalistic realism found in French films from the 1980s such as *Laisse béton* (Le Péron, 1984) or *Le Thé au harem d'Archimède* (Cahref, 1985).

As in the original *bande déssiné* (comic book, or BD) storyline from which it was adapted,[13] *Cauchemar blanc* centres on the issue of *ratonnades* (anti-Arab violence in France). A gang of far right-thugs – a football hooligan, his dim-witted accomplice and two 'respectable' middle-aged men – wait in a car for their intended victim, a lone

---

12 '*Fierrot le Pou* n'a pas été si apprécié que cela. Ça rentre pas trop dans le cadre des courts-métrages que l'on eût trouver dans un festival' / '*Fierrot le pou* really wasn't really appreciated all that much. It didn't really fit into the framework of the short film that you'd expect to find at a festival.'

13 *Cauchemar blanc* originally appeared as a story by legendary French BD artist Moebius (Jean Giraud), who later worked on designing the futuristic décor for Besson's *Le Cinquième élément* (1997).

Algerian immigrant, to leave work. What follows is a surreal rendering of the *ratonnade*, in which the would-be thugs eliminate themselves one by one through their own incompetence. One drives into a phonebox while attempting to run over his victim; another is shot accidentally; a third is knocked out by a stray blow from a nunchucker, intended for the immigrant. Kassovitz thus employs surreal comedy to transform the far-right vigilantes from menacingly powerful figures into objects of ridicule. Just as importantly, in the dream the Arab immigrant faces up to his attackers with the support of local residents from the housing estate, whose number includes a black police chief; thereby inverting the stereotype of the ethnic other as the excluded, helpless victim of racism.

However, any satisfaction the spectator may derive from seeing the vigilantes' plans backfire so spectacularly is short-lived, as Kassovitz reveals the 'white nightmare' of the film's title. In the final sequence we return to the starting-point of the narrative, only to find that what we have witnessed was merely the 'bad dream' of one of the attackers dozing in the car. As the Arab immigrant worker returns home for real, the gang of racist thugs successfully execute their attack. And this time local residents switch off their lights, preferring to ignore the racist violence rather than offering any form of communal resistance. Significantly, we hear, but do not see, the attack taking place. Instead, Kassovitz chooses to hold the camera on the neighbouring flats rather than on the gang themselves. The implication here is that, like the local residents who turn away, by failing to take a stand against similar violence in society, we are all guilty of colluding with the racist attackers.

The impact of the 'real' violence played out in the final moments of *Cauchemar blanc* is all the more powerful given the surreal and comic events that come before. The surreal *ratonnade* that takes place at the start of the film therefore functions as an allegory for the way in which racist violence is perceived as a 'fantasy' by those who dismiss such attacks as the work of a handful of extremists – a throwback to the 'Arab-bashing' of 1960s and 1970s – thus refusing to acknowledge the extent to which organised racist violence persists in contemporary French society. What *Cauchemar blanc* forces us to confront in its final image – a medium long shot of the immigrant victim's motionless body lying in front of the housing estate – is the uncomfortable *reality* of contemporary French racism, at a time in the early 1990s when the far-right's popularity was on the increase in both local and national elections in France. *Cauchemar blanc* thus provides an indication of the political direction Kassovitz would take in his first three feature films. Moreover, the unorthodox approach to the representation of socio-political realities found in *Cauchemar blanc*, which contrasts considerably with the anticipated naturalism of French social realism, hints at how, in subsequent films such as *Métisse* and *La Haine*, Kassovitz would entertain and engage his French audience before forcing them to confront uncomfortable truths about the society in which they live.

With *Cauchemar blanc* receiving a favourable response from both critics and audiences on the festival circuit (and being included in the 'Perspectives du Cinéma' section at the 1991 Cannes festival) a certain momentum was building behind Kassovitz's career. Keen to make the transition from short film to feature production, Kassovitz presented Rossignon with the proposal for what would eventually become his first feature film, *Métisse*, which he would write, direct and star in. Before embarking on such a demanding project – not only in the sense that it was the debut feature film for both director and producer, but also because *Métisse* would occupy Kassovitz on both sides of the camera – it was decided that he should make one more short film, allowing him to gain further experience of the pressures of simultaneously performing/directing as well as building up a working relationship with the technical crew that would be used on *Métisse*. As Kassovitz described it the aim was 'de voir comment je me débrouillerais sur un film beaucoup plus structuré, dans un huis clos, sans véritable histoire. Un exercice de style en fait' (Kassovitz 1998).[14]

However, if Rossignon was expecting the young director to simply use the short as a technical test-run for *Métisse*, he was to be somewhat surprised when presented with the treatment for the film. Simply entitled *Assassins* (1992), the 10–minute short showed a professional killer offering his new assistant a 'lesson in murder' – the germ of an idea that would eventually become the sprawling, polemic narrative of Kassovitz's third and most controversial film to date, *Assassin(s)* (1997). The film attracted negative attention for its amoral premise and decontextualised depiction of violence, was prohibited to spectators under 16, and harshly criticised by the French ministry of

14 'To see how I handled myself with a more structured film, in a contained environment, without any real storyline. An exercise in style, in fact'.

culture. Kassovitz (*ibid.*) even claims to have received a letter signed by the incumbent socialist culture minister, Jack Lang, denouncing the film as 'un appel au meurtre'.[15] The ensuing controversy – the first of many in Kassovitz's career – ensured that *Assassins* would only be seen by a very limited audience. Accorded minor distribution on the festival circuit, *Assassins* remains the least easily obtainable of Kassovitz's three short films. Unlike *Fierrot le pou* and *Cauchemar blanc*, which are included as extras on the French DVD releases of *Métisse* and *La Haine* respectively, *Assassins* (the short film) does not appear on the DVD of Kassovitz's 1997 feature film *Assassin(s)*. This decision could, perhaps, be read as a later admission by the director that the original short was an ill-judged 'exercise in style' – particularly when it is considered that the restrictive format of a 10–minute short film would render problematic any detailed, meaningful analysis of the cultural, economic and political origins of violence in society.

In France the short film has traditionally been viewed as the classic means for aspiring *auteurs* – typically filmmakers from the independent sector learning their craft, or recent graduates of film schools such as the Fémis – to establish a fledgling reputation within the industry before embarking on a career directing feature length films. More recently, the changing audiovisual landscape in France – and above all, the increasing importance of television's funding of cinema production – has allowed directors from non-traditional backgrounds in advertising, music video or even digital-effects design (such as Pitof) whose ambitions are located more directly within the spheres of the youth market or mainstream genre cinema to effectively bypass the apprenticeship of the short film altogether. Though Kassovitz undoubtedly used the short film circuit as a traditional means of self-promotion and exposure within the French film industry, the references to popular youth culture (hip-hop, BD, Besson) found in his short films, as well as their technical ambition far in excess of the meagre budgets with which he was working, are indicative of a new type of director. Moreover, by approaching controversial social subject matter in a way that replaced the more muted naturalism traditionally associated with French social realism with a visual style and thematic concerns that acknowledged the demands and tastes of a youth audience, Kassovitz determined the approach that would inform his first three features: *Métisse*, *La Haine* and *Assassin(s)*.

15 'a call to murder'.

Le tout culturel: legitimising youth in contemporary popular culture

Kassovitz's early years as a movie fan and apprenticeship within the French industry during the late 1980s and early 1990s, reveal a taste for popular cinema (largely, but not exclusively informed by America) combined with a keen sense of autodidacticism and a desire to address contemporary socio-political issues concerning French youth – of which the young filmmaker in the early 1990s felt very much a part. As a director he has remained faithful to the films and filmmakers that so attracted him as an adolescent – in particular Spielberg and Besson, but also Beineix, Scorsese and Raimi. This predilection for the popular has emerged as a key characteristic in Kassovitz's work. In more general terms, it also points to an important cultural shift taking place in France during the 1980s and 1990s: namely the legitimising of American-influenced mass cultural industries within the sphere of the popular and the reconfiguring of youth at the centre of French popular culture.

As Stuart Hall (1981: 232–3) reminds us, popular culture is not a fixed or monolithic entity. Rather, it is constantly evolving and must be read in the specific context of the socio-political, economic and historical conditions in which it emerges. Thus, in the context of a western capitalist society, the 'popular' in popular culture refers (amongst other things) both to the market (that which is commercially successful) as well as the cultural practices and experiences that represent the thoughts and values of the people – which, although they may seem so, are not always one and the same thing. In the case of cinema, any attempt to distinguish between the commercial and the anthropological characteristics of the popular is further complicated by the fact that popular film has only ever existed in the market economy (Dyer and Vincendeau 1992: 4). Kassovitz's films exhibit an understanding that such commercial imperatives are virtually indissociable from popular cinema. He openly admits, for example, that part of the reason behind accepting to direct commissioned films features such as *Les Rivières pourpres* and *Gothika* was to secure box-office success that would allow him to work with greater financial and artistic freedom on subsequent, more personal, projects (Tirard 2000).

As sociologist Ulf Hannerz argues (1996: 81–90), in the most recent phase of globalisation, driven by technologies that condense and, in some cases, remove longstanding spatial and temporal boundaries between previously distant communities and cultures, national understandings of culture have become insufficient. In this context, the relationship between popular culture and national culture is unstable, as transnational or global cultural forms (particularly the audiovisual) acquire an increasing resonance within local or national cultural configurations. Viewed more negatively, such changes have facilitated a form of global mass culture dominated by the image that offers an essentially Americanised conception of the world (Hall 1995: 29): broadening our horizons only to limit and homogenise the scope of the popular. Clearly, then, popular culture can no longer be contained within national boundaries. Instead, it is increasingly predicated on the shifting configurations of the global and the local – something that, as we shall see, is readily apparent in Kassovitz's films.

In the French context, the notion of *culture populaire* (popular culture; a culture of the people) was originally applied to rural or folk culture. With the progressive shift to industrialisation and urbanisation from the mid-nineteenth century, however, the popular came increasingly to be associated with the tastes and consumption practices of modern urban society – specifically, the working class (Rigby 1991: 9–11). This association of the working classes with popular culture in the discourse of French politicians and intellectuals was, for many years, largely idealised and highly selective. From the time of the Popular Front government in 1936 through to Malraux's *Maisons de la Culture* of the 1950s and 1960s, the intention had been to forge a truly 'popular' culture that would bring high culture (*la culture cultivée* or *grande culture*) to the people. French popular culture in the aftermath of the Second World War was thus seen by certain intellectuals as 'a battlefield for the working-class, who were in danger of being seduced by American style-consumerism and corrupted by mass media' (Rigby 1991: 68). Such notions of popular culture were, however, hopelessly out of touch with the reality of socio-economic and cultural change occurring in post-war France. During the *trente glorieuses* (the thirty years of modernisation and economic prosperity post-1945) France emerged as a fully-fledged consumer society, increasingly drawn to Americanised mass culture – records, cinema, radio and, later, television – and one that 'operated according to a free-market philosophy rather than the humanist principles which had inspired the democratisers and popular educators' (Looseley 1995: 26)

And yet, paradoxically, there was a clear refusal on the part of many politicians and intellectuals to equate mass culture with popular culture – a situation that continued in France until at least the late 1970s. Rigby (1991: 159–62) explains this stance both as resistance to the growth of a superficial, materialistic, consumer culture in post-war France (of which mass cultural forms were considered to be an integral part) and evidence of a continued and deep-seated hostility towards the influence of American popular culture 'traditionally seen as the home of capitalist mass culture in all its vulgarity and exploit-ativeness'. Significantly, such attitudes towards mass culture and espe-cially cultural imports from the United States were not shared by the majority of the French population; and above all young people, who proved enthusiastic consumers of American films, music, fashion (and later TV). Born in the late 1960s, Kassovitz thus emerged from a new generation of cultural consumers for whom Americanised mass culture was not considered an alien or guilty cultural pleasure to be resisted, but rather as an integral part of French popular culture.

By the early 1980s, with the election of the Fifth Republic's first socialist government, it appeared that politicians were at last begin-ning to acknowledge the attitudes and tastes expressed by the majority of the French population with regard to popular culture. A radical shift in cultural policy was announced by the new culture minister, the charismatic and dynamic Jack Lang, which became known as *le tout culturel*. A succession of reforms during Lang's two periods in office (1981–86; 1988–93) were introduced, leading to 'developments in the economics and organisation of (popular) culture and ... far reaching changes to the ways in which the state conceived of culture as an object of policy' (Dauncey 2003: 12). The effect of these reforms was threefold. Firstly they allowed for the legitimisation of a range of mass cultural forms such as fashion, advertising, BD, pop music and television through government recognition leading to partial state subsidy of these 'cultural industries'. Second, audiovisual media (television and cinema) was identified as the primary focus of debates over popular culture and French cultural identity – in other words placing the image at the centre of popular culture. Finally, and most importantly in relation to a filmmaker such as Kassovitz, by simul-taneously challenging longstanding hostility towards the validity of mass cultural forms, while breaking down the perceived barriers between high culture (*la culture cultivée*) and popular or mass culture, Lang's reforms arguably placed youth at the centre of discourses sur-rounding popular culture.

As has already been suggested in the introduction to this book, through his cultural references and influences Kassovitz makes a conscious effort to place his films in the realm of mass popular culture. He does so in order for them to engage with as wide an audience as possible (both in France and abroad). Nevertheless, his cinematic style and cultural frame of reference makes a youth audience Kassovitz's natural demographic. The position occupied by Kassovitz in relation to the popular mirrors the broader cultural shifts taking place in France at that time. Just as mass culture was rejected by most politicians and intellectuals prior to the 1980s as vacuous and impoverished in comparison to the great works of art and literature found in high culture, so youth culture had, until this point, either been dismissed as moronic or else stigmatised as 'false and alienated' due to its imitation of American popular cultural forms (Rigby 1991: 168). Such criticisms can also be read as an attempt by an older generation to exert a degree of control over the cultural practices of young people. Rejecting youth pop culture as moronic or artistically impoverished thus becomes a strategy for limiting its broader impact amid concerns about the 'corruption' (moral, cultural, ethical) of French youth by Americanised mass culture. Moreover, when read as a commentary on the significance of young people's contribution to culture and society more generally, such attacks also serve to play down the influence and activities of more militant counterculture youth movements. In this way, the more militant and politicised content and social commentary of certain French rap groups such as Assassin and NTM can be dismissed as having little relevance beyond its modish youth audience.

Sociologist Edgar Morin was one of the few French intellectuals to counter this position before the 1980s. As early as 1962 Morin observed how mass culture in France was increasingly concerned with promoting 'youth values' over those of an older generation, suggesting that youth culture would have an increasing role to play in shaping the content and direction of mass culture, and, by extension, that of French popular culture (Galland 1997: 52). However, while youth culture had formed an increasingly visible and influential element within French popular culture since the 1960s, it was not until the legitimisation of those cultural industries most closely associated with youth by a socialist government twenty years later, that France's youth class began to be taken seriously by politicians and intellectuals as an integral part of contemporary popular culture. Crucially, at

the same time as this foregrounding of youth in relation to the popular occurred, a further key social transformation was taking place;
namely the dissolution of a clearly defined political consciousness or
cultural identity within the working class (Forbes and Hewlett 1994:
388).[16] In many ways, then, there was a reconfiguration of the popular
in France during the 1980s, whereby youth was coming to replace
the working class as the social category most readily associated with
popular culture.

Of course, this notion of a homogenised youth 'class' is problematic, mainly because it masks important differences within
France's youth population; of which ethnicity, gender, sexuality and
socio-economic background are the most obvious. And yet, in other
ways – and above all through representation and cultural discourse
– youth dœs present itself as a viable social category. France's disparate youth 'class' therefore exists as social grouping (real and/or
imagined) through which cultural and socio-political change can be
read and onto which the aspirations or, more frequently, anxieties
surrounding such change can be projected. Thus in the 1950s youth
became, according to Jobs (2003: 689), 'an icon of rejuvenation ... the
reconstruction's motivating spirit ... as France sought to remake itself
after the calamities of The Second World War'. More typically though,
youth and youthfulness have been identified with social malaise and
crisis: witness in the 1990s how young male inhabitants (often of
immigrant origin) from the rundown working-class estates of the
French urban periphery came to symbolise in both media representation and political rhetoric the social malaise of *insécurité* and *fracture
sociale* affecting France. Indeed, it is precisely this notion of youth in
crisis and 'youth in trouble/youth *as* trouble' (to paraphrase Hebdige
(1988: 19)) that Kassovitz chooses to explore in his earlier social films,
by focusing on the experiences of this alienated youth class and their
(mis-)representation by the mainstream media in France.

The position of youth as central to contemporary French popular

16 This change resulted largely from post-war economic restructuring, that led
away from heavy industry towards the tertiary sector and the '*moyennisation*' of
this new working class emerging from the service industries population. INSEE
figures show a steady decline for the working class as a recognisable socio-
economic group. In 1946 *ouvriers* represented 38 per cent of the workforce, a
figure which had fallen to 29 per cent by the 1990s and as low as 14 per cent
by the 2000s (for the most recent statistics, see www.insee.fr site last accessed
12/5/05).

culture can be further explained by the way in which technology and commerce have been 'the driving forces of popular culture' in France since the early 1980s to a greater extent than ever before (Dauncey 2003: 13). Popular culture is increasingly experienced via new digital or audiovisual media. Such technology is best understood and most enthusiastically embraced by younger consumers; further aligning popular culture with youth. As such, young people become not only the target market, but also the means of marketing these cultural forms and new technologies. Advertising – another of the cultural industries 'legitimised' by Lang and the deregulation of French television in the 1980s – thus fetishises the cult and desirability of youth in its attempts to sell these new technologies. Such a strategy can be seen as further evidence of the desire in France (as in other western societies) to hold on to this position as youthful consumer for as long as possible – hence the emergence of the so-called *vieux jeunes* in France during the 1990s as the tastes, values and consumption practices of youth are now seen to extend to individuals in their thirties and forties.

Recent innovations in audiovisual technology have given rise to new mass or popular cultural forms – such as the video game and the music video. They have, moreover, significantly transformed consumption and production of the image in popular culture. The shift in patterns of audiovisual consumption in France first became apparent in the 1980s, prompted, on the one hand, by the increasing dominance of television over cinema, and, on the other, by the emergence of a video-clip culture ('*le clip*') associated with music video, advertising and experimental video art. More recently, the growing popularity of DVD, reality TV, video games and the internet, as well as the availability of relatively cheap DV technology (cameras and desktop editing software) have further expanded the possibilities for production and consumption of audiovisual and digital media.

These changes have had a profound effect on contemporary cinema: engendering a reciprocal relationship in which new audiovisual forms borrow from film aesthetics and technology, and, in doing so, redefine cinematic codes and conventions (Lalanne 2000: 62–3). The music video, for example, borrows from cinema in various ways – from its adaptation of cinematic codes of *mise en scène* and narrative construction and recycling of iconic screen images to its use of film technology such as scope cinematography and special effects.

However, restricted as it is by the usual 3 to 5-minute format of a pop song and necessitated by its need to make an immediate impact (the music video is, after all, essentially a means of marketing a given artist and song) the music video is required to adapt these codes and conventions to a much more rapid and intrusive editing style than traditionally found in cinema. The editing style developed by the music video has, in turn, influenced the approach of many contemporary directors and film editors; not only because its immediacy and energy have proved popular with mainstream or youth audiences, but also because an increasing number of cinema directors have emerged from a background in *le clip* – Kassovitz himself spent time early in his career working in music video production (directing a video clip for rapper Tonton David (1990)) and has more recently directed a music video for rap group Sayan Supa Crew (2000) as well as adverts for the parfumier Lancôme (2001), French department store Printemps (2000) and a public service advert for the SNCF (2004).

Kassovitz is therefore very much a part of this new generation of spectators and practitioners, whose tastes and consumption practices have been influenced by technological advances in audiovisual culture. It is hardly surprising, then, that he should incorporate such elements into his films. A number of sequences in *La Haine* – such as when Hubert smokes a joint in his room to an extra-diegetic funk soundtrack – are suggestive of the music video aesthetic. Elsewhere, the largely superfluous fight scene in *Les Rivières pourpres*, where Max Kerkerian (Vincent Cassel) takes on a band of neo-Nazis, Kassovitz makes playful references to video-gaming culture, by integrating music and commentary ('game over'; 'player 2'; Kerkerian wins!') into the soundtrack and imitating the choice of camera angles and editing style found in martial-arts video-games, such as the *Tekken* series.

And yet despite these references to new audiovisual cultural forms, Kassovitz's films still retain a strong sense of the cinematic. For, above all, his strength as a filmmaker comes from his skill as a *metteur en scène*; his eye for composition, and a highly developed understanding of camera movement and cinematic space. Indeed, Kassovitz is one of the few exponents of what we might term 'post-look' or spectacular genre cinema in France (promoted by directors such as Gans, Pitof and Kounen) who makes extensive use of the *plan séquence* in his films – seemingly the antithesis of the rapidly cut editing (*surdécoupage*) that tends to be associated with this type of Hollywood-led genre cinema. Kassovitz's consistent use of the elaborate and fluid long take – established in *Fierrot le pou* and repeated in every film to date – and its central importance to his *mise en scène* has, in many ways, been profoundly misunderstood (or overlooked) by those who choose to explain his direction in terms of 'MTV aesthetics'. Although quick cutting is a feature of his aesthetic, Kassovitz will, more often than not, opt for the elaborate long take, whenever possible. We see this both in *La Haine* – for example, the scene in the *cité* where a teenager recounts events of an episode of *Candid Camera* to Vinz, Hubert and Saïd – and, more recently, in *Gothika*, where in the confines of the cell or treatment room Kassovitz is happy to play out conversations in long single takes rather than immediately resorting to continuity style shot/counter shot editing more readily employed in Hollywood.[17]

Postcolonial identities, rap and resistance: the hip-hop generation

Along with the emergence of youth as arguably the dominant signifier of contemporary French popular culture, the promotion of difference (ethnic, cultural, sexual) has become a key component within the popular. According to Jean-Pierre Colin, who worked with Lang at the Ministry of Culture in the 1980s and early 1990s, the real living popular culture of the day – youth culture – was the only one that had fully embraced ethnic differences (Rigby 1991: 182). The acceptance of difference by French youth in the 1980s manifested itself in the creation of anti-racist movements (of which the most prominent was SOS Racisme), as well as the formation of immigrant associations and mass social protest such as the so-called *Marche des beurs* in 1983.[18] Such initiatives within the French youth class came, on the one hand, in opposition to growing electoral support for the far right in France during the early 1980s; and, on the other, in support of demands by French descendants of immigrants (particularly those from former French colonies such as Algeria) for a greater recognition of their contribution to and rightful place within French society. Alongside these forms of social protest and political mobilisation, a new cultural

17 See actress Halle Berry's comments in the cast interviews of the UK DVD release of *Gothika* on Kassovitz's reluctance to employ the standard shot/reverse shot.
18 For detailed history of anti-racist alliances and the Beur movement, see Jazouli (1992).

form emerged which would provide an outlet for political and cultural expression for France's immigrant youth, and prove a key reference point and structuring aesthetic in Kassovitz's early films: hip-hop.

Hip-hop, which comprises break-dancing, street art (graffiti and tagging) as well as music (sampling, scratching and rapping), finds its origins in the mid-to-late 1970s in the predominantly black and Hispanic housing projects of New York's south Bronx; arriving in France as early as 1984. As a cultural form 'indissociable from its urban context' (Cannon 1997: 151) it rapidly established a following in Paris and other large French cities. On the one hand, it was appropriated by disenfranchised multicultural youth, who identified with its origins in American ghettos and sought to use hip-hop as a means of articulating the alienation and exclusion experienced within the working-class housing estates of France's deprived urban periphery (the *banlieue*). On the other, it simultaneously attracted a cross-over television audience with TF1's weekly dance and music programme; simply entitled *Hip Hop*.

This drive by hip-hop into the mainstream of popular youth culture in France was further facilitated by the introduction of culturally protectionist legislation in the early 1990s aimed at ensuring French radio stations' playlists comprised a minimum of 40 per cent French-language songs. Ironically, government legislation that was expected to promote the more traditional exponents of the *chanson française* (Brel, Brassen, Gainsbourg *et al.*) in fact opened up the French air waves for youth-orientated stations (such as NRJ) to showcase new talent and promote established artists from the underground rap scene (IAM, NTM, Assassin, MC Solaar; and, more recently, Oxmo Puccino, Fonky Family and Sayan Supa Crew) thus ensuring mainstream exposure for what was, by then, an identifiably French cultural form.

During the 1990s, hip-hop style increasingly permeated mainstream youth culture; not only in relation to music – where rap now commands a multi-million Euro sector of the French record industry – but also through fashion, advertising and, to a lesser extent, cinema. Given the commercial exploitation of hip-hop culture, it is easy to forget the extent to which rap music provides a vital means of expression to young artists from disenfranchised social and ethnic minorities and, above all, those from the disadvantaged urban peripheries (the *banlieue*). In this respect, hip-hop – and especially rap music – functions as one of the few outlets for the marginalised youth from the *banlieue*, and working-class immigrant districts of the larger French cities, to articulate their own experiences: a means of informing a youth audience as well as providing an alternative social commentary on issues such as exclusion, racism, oppression and violence. On a number of occasions, this engagement with social issues has led rap artists to take a more militant stand against perceived injustice or social oppression. Paris-based crew NTM's provocative and explicit challenge to the far-right politician Jean-Marie Le Pen at a concert in Toulon, caused a considerable media storm in 1996 and led to the group's prosecution by the local Front National-dominated council. More recently in 2004, Hamé (Mohamed Boroukba) a young Maghrebi-French rapper with the group La Rumeur was taken to court by the French minister of the interior for material distributed at concerts, in which the rapper condemned alleged police brutality against ethnic minorities in the *banlieue*.

Unsurprisingly, given that the majority of French hip-hop artists are descendants of immigrants from former French colonies, much of the social commentary contained within these rap songs is concerned with issues of racism, ethnic difference and identity; in short, the urgent and important issues facing an increasingly multicultural, postcolonial French society. Indeed, beyond the obvious linguistic differences, what marks French hip-hop as distinctive from that produced in the United States is its treatment of issues of race and ethnicity within a more fluid, postcolonial framework. Though including a disproportionately high number of black artists of African and Afro-Caribbean origins, the French hip-hop scene – in contrast to the fixed urban and racial identities of an increasingly nihilistic American 'gangsta' rap scene – comprises a far greater ethnic diversity, where identity is articulated within a more fluid network of local, national and transnational positionings.

Take, for example, the leading French rap star of the past decade, MC Solaar, who was born in Senegal to parents originally from Chad, but raised from a young age in a working-class immigrant neighbourhood of northern Paris. Though based – as virtually all rap music is – on the system of beats and samples pioneered by African-American artists from the United States, his music is clearly influenced, sonically and lyrically, by French and West African culture (as well as on his most recent album, *Mach 6*, the music of the Indian subcontinent). Similarly, the Marseilles-based crew IAM, one of the most successful French rap groups of the 1990s, comprises members of Italian, Spanish, Maghrebi and Madagascan descent. Their music accordingly articulates a network of local and global influences: negotiated, on the one hand, by a strong sense of belonging in relation to cosmopolitan working-class *cités* of Marseilles – dubbed 'La Planète Mars' by the group – and, on the other, through an awareness of the group's individual diasporic origins that incorporate elements of Afrocentrisim and Egyptology (IAM apparently stands for 'International Asiatic Man') into the lyrical content of their music.

The real significance of hip-hop for contemporary French popular culture, therefore, comes not only from the fact that these rap artists – many of whom are the descendants of immigrant parents from former French colonies – engage with less rigid notions of ethnicity and identity than their American counterparts but also that their music is now very much located at the heart of popular youth culture. As such, it is able to connect with a sizeable mainstream audience. It is no coincidence that French hip-hop emerged in France during the early 1980s at the time when a number of high-profile, youth-led, multiethnic anti-racist associations such as SOS Racisme were establishing themselves as influential actors within broader debates surrounding questions of integration, racism and immigration. French rap, in particular, now represents one of the most significant and vital arenas for popular debate around the postcolonial (issues of racism, integration, diaspora and national identity) in contemporary French culture. In this context, hip-hop is a popular cultural form that has given a voice to marginalised youth from within France's ethnic minorities and has, in turn, been enthusiastically embraced by a mainstream youth market who, in addition to desiring the American-influenced style of hip-hop, identify with the values and attitude espoused by the music and culture.

Though not a rapper, dancer or graffiti artist, Kassovitz nonetheless immersed himself in the emergent hip-hop culture of the eighteenth and twentieth *arrondissements* and neighbouring *banlieues* to the east of Paris during the 1980s and early 1990s. The extent of his affiliation to the Parisian hip-hop scene before its cross-over into the mainstream can be gauged by the collaboration of original 'underground' artists in his earlier films and shorts. The a-cappella rap performed over the credits of *Fierrot le pou* by Rockin Squat (at that time relatively unknown beyond the underground Parisian rap scene, but now, along with his crew, Assassin, one of French rap's longest standing and most respected militant rap stars) identifies the colonial origins of contemporary racism while calling for unity amongst all oppressed peoples.[19] Similarly, Assassin's 'Peur du métissage' – an attack on the far right's depiction of multiculturalism and the non-European immigrant 'invasion' of France as a threat to national and cultural identity – accompanies both the opening and closing credits of *Métisse*. The rap soundtrack of Rockin Squat and Assassins was, therefore, the obvious choice for those films by Kassovitz dealing with questions of race, identity and belonging in contemporary French society.

The association of Kassovitz's cinema with French hip-hop culture was further cemented by *La Haine*. The success of the film and its association with hip-hop style was such that a compilation album was released of music 'inspired by' the film that included virtually all the most important rap acts of the mid-1990s (IAM, Assassins, Ministère Amer).[20] In broader cultural terms, the popularity and influence of *La Haine* also marked a point in the mid-1990s when hip-hop culture and rap in particular established itself as possibly the most important and marketable popular cultural reference for France's youth class.

Through his early shorts and first three features Kassovitz thus emerges as the emblematic filmmaker of France's hip-hop generation. His use of hip-hop style in these films – not just rap music, but also fashion, art and dance – allows him to address a series of social issues (exclusion in the *banlieue*, racism, integration and violence) in a way that speaks directly to a youth audience. In this respect his films are clearly linked to the role of subcultural style as social commentary found in much French hip-hop. This, beyond any stylistic concern, is the central importance of hip-hop's influence on Kassovitz's cinema – a point that will be examined in detail in the next chapter.

The principal position occupied by hip-hop in French contemporary popular music points to a further series of notable transformations relating to the configuration of popular culture in France since

19 'que tu sois noir ou blanc le problème est le même – tous sur la même scène – meme si l'homme blanc a l'exploitation qui coule dans ses veines.' / 'whether you're black or white the problems are the same, we're all on the same stage even if exploitation courses in the white man's veins'.

20 Interestingly, there is, in fact little rap music in the original soundtrack of *La Haine*. The majority of music that appears in the film is soul and funk – the music that has traditionally formed the basis for rap's breakbeats and samples.

the early 1980s. Hip-hop's phenomenal success in France with a cross-over youth audience is evidence of how the boundaries between margin–centre, global–local, militant–commercial are increasingly blurred within the contemporary sphere of the popular. French Hip-hop is, after all, a cultural form imported from the African-American ghettos of Harlem and the Bronx, and seen as offering an authentic voice of resistance to ethnic minority youth from the deprived estates of the *banlieue*, but which is now also a mainstream genre and multi-million Euro business concern in France. Similarly, most observers of the French hip-hop scene note that the emerging popularity of rapping, tagging and break-dancing in France during the early-1980s owed as much to exposure through mainstream media such as TF1 weekly 'Hip-Hop' program as it did to the underground movement of pirate-radio stations and hip-hop club nights (Cannon 1997: 152–3).

The evolution of French hip-hop has thus been shaped by a two-way cultural exchange between the margin and centre, at the same time as it has been informed by external cultural references (most significantly, but not exclusively, the African-American urban diaspora). Representations, experiences and meanings of hip-hop style in France function through a network of global and local cultural references, throwing into question any previously fixed or sealed notions of popular culture as contained purely within the framework of the national.

Hall suggests (1995: 29–30) that in our current epoch of globalisation, mass global culture – filtered through American sensibilities and cultural politics – exerts an increasingly powerful pull on the characteristics of localised (national) popular cultures. This seems a particularly accurate description of the processes at work in relation to French hip-hop outlined above. However, it can also be seen at work in French cinema – as the industry struggles to define itself against Hollywood, while an increasing number of young filmmakers are happy to assimilate influences of American mass culture into their own films (an argument that will be developed in detail in Chapter 4). This acceptance of the global and the local as a natural part of contemporary popular culture is apparent in Kassovitz's own tastes and practices as a filmmaker: not only the influence of mainstream Hollywood, American independent exploitation cinema and Hong Kong martial arts movies but also the references in his films (most notably *Fierrot le pou, Métisse* and *La Haine*) to the transatlantic, urban and diasopric identities of hip-hop culture.

In his analysis of cultural discourses surrounding the popular in modern France, Rigby (1991: 22) proposes that popular culture – be it in the urban or rural context – has traditionally been seen to 'bind communities together by the practice of human relationships'. In its relation to the French working-class, the popular has therefore been understood primarily within a specifically urban context (think for example of the representation of working class culture in French poetic realism of the 1930s). In a more contemporary context – where beyond any immediate local ties, 'community' can also be created via internet connection or satellite receiver – technology becomes a key binding agent within French popular culture, allowing cultural consumers (and above all youth) to tap into a new form of global mass culture 'dominated by image which crosses and re-crosses linguistic frontiers much more rapidly and more easily, and which speaks across languages in a much more immediate way' (Hall 1995: 29). This is precisely the form of contemporary popular culture found in Kassovitz's films. He understands the power of the image and the fact that the popular cannot be limited by national boundaries. A film such as *La Haine* thus presents a cross-over mainstream audience with issues of exclusion and social fracture amongst the alienated youth of the deprived *banlieue* through a visual idiom that not only assimilates the iconography of American directors such as Scorsese, Spielberg and Spike Lee, but which also draws on the look and style of African-American hip-hop culture as it has been transposed to the disadvantaged estates of the Parisian urban periphery.

A popular youth aesthetic: the *Cinéma du look*

So far we have discussed in detail the influence of Americanised mass-cultural forms and French youth culture (hip-hop, Hollywood and BD) on Kassovitz's development as a filmmaker. But what of the influence of French cinema? While Kassovitz's short films identified him as a director in tune with the broader developments taking place in French popular culture during the 1980s, in many ways their focus (both aesthetic and thematic) ensured his position as something of an outsider in relation to production trends in French cinema of the early 1990s, in an industry still dominated by popular comedy and the heritage film on one side, and the *auteur* film on the other (Powrie 1999: 2–10).

Though clearly part of the audiovisual cultural industries that were at the centre of much of Lang's policies for *le tout culturel* (the others being television and popular music) French cinema was in a peculiar position in that it had begun a process of cultural legitimisation way before the reforms and rhetoric of the 1980s. Cinema had been identified as the seventh art in France since the 1920s, and, in many ways, had always sought to maintain this association with 'high' rather than mass or popular culture. This position is reflected by the fact that the CNC's selective funding (first introduced in the 1960s) has traditionally been directed towards heritage or *auteur*-led productions, often at the expense of French comedy,[21] but also the way that, in their analysis of French national cinema, French academics, critics and film historians have tended to promote the *auteur*, avant-garde or the state prescribed 'quality and culture' of the heritage film over directors associated with popular cinema.

Contrary to the established position of the French film industry as an art form somehow distanced from other mass-cultural forms, Kassovitz has chosen to align himself with cinema as a commercial 'industry', embracing the popular potential of cinema as a mass cultural-medium. Consequently, he has often found himself positioned as a relative outsider in the French film industry, despite the commercial (popular) success of a number of his films – a situation that has been compounded in recent years by his decision to work in Hollywood.

Despite such strong resistance from certain sectors of the French film industry towards a certain type of youth-orientated, American-influenced popular cinema, there is in fact a clear precursor to the style of cinema promoted by Kassovitz (and other young directors such as Gans, Pitof and Kounen) within French cinema of the 1980s: namely, the *cinéma du look*. This stylistic trend is associated in particular with the trio of Luc Besson, Jean-Jacques Beineix and Léos Carax. Though the three directors did not intentionally set out to forge a new cinematic movement, their films shared common thematic and above all stylistic qualities which led them to be described collectively

21 See, for example, Poiré's interview with *Cahiers du cinéma* (Nevers and Strauss 1993) in which the director of *Les Visiteurs* (1993), one of the most successful French comedies of all time, contrasted the difficulties in funding French comedy with the considerable assistance offered to the heritage film via direct government aid, CNC grants and foreign sales.

as the *cinéma du look*, or look cinema. Essentially the *cinéma du look* is characterised by the primacy of the image over narrative; a spectacular visual style which manifests itself through a highly stylised *mise en scène* (elaborate framing as well as a preoccupation with colour and décor); a cinephile tendency to reference and recycle from other films; and a focus on youthful protagonists who are often marginal or romantic figures.

With its emphasis on bold colour, seductive cinematic spectacle, playful postmodern pastiche of existing genres and styles, and, crucially, youth-centred narratives, the *cinéma du look* attracted large audiences, particularly those from the coveted market of 18 to 25-year-olds. More specifically, these films found a connection with a disenchanted youth class who, in the 1980s, as a result of economic recession, spiralling youth unemployment and the failure of the recently elected socialist government to deliver on its bold programme of social reforms, viewed itself as increasingly marginalised. In this context, Luc Besson's *Subway* (1985) is not only a visually arresting, playful example of postmodern cinema, which in its opening scenes cites Socrates alongside Sinatra before embarking on a spectacular chase through a studio recreation of the Paris Metro, it is also a film that foregrounds the alienation felt by a marginalised youth class inhabiting this underground world outside the limits of the societal norm.

Unsurprisingly, given his age and tastes, Kassovitz was instantly attracted to the *cinéma du look*; stating a preference for the films of Beineix and Besson over Carax. This distinction is significant, since Beineix and Besson, like Kassovitz, were largely self-taught practitioners who had worked their way up through the film industry. They were also instinctively popular directors; associated far more closely than Carax with the 'negative' connotations of the *cinéma du look* – advertising,[22] video-clip aesthetics and a depoliticised youth culture. In contrast, Carax, who had studied cinema at Paris III University and written for *Cahiers du cinéma* before moving into directing, was more enthusiastically received by critics from high-brow French film journals who felt comfortable with his background as a cinema critic, as well as the references to the French New Wave – and, above all, Godard – that appear in his films (Austin 1996: 132)

22 Like Beineix, Kassovitz has worked in advertising as a director. Interestingly, though Kassovitz has chosen to enter the world of advertising after having established himself as a high-profile cinema director, not before.

Equally significant was that the *cinéma du look*, more attuned to a cinema of attractions than the concerns of *auteur* cinema, acknowledged the significant shift taking place amongst young French audiences in relation to the tastes, practices and patterns of audiovisual and cultural consumption. As Powrie (2001: 10–26) makes clear, beyond its stylistic innovation, the *cinéma du look* served as a point of intersection for various socio-cultural phenomena appearing in France during the 1980s with broader philosophical debates concerning the value, power and circulation of images within an advanced capitalist economy.

On the one hand, films such as *Diva* (Beineix, 1980) and *Subway* were evidence of what cultural critics were beginning to refer to as a postmodern aesthetic: a playful recycling of texts and images and breaking down of distinctions between high and low art. On the other, the amorality, violence and rejection of society offered by the marginalised youthful protagonists in look cinema spoke not only of the alienation felt by the youth class in 1980s France, but also more generally of a collapse in the faith of master narratives (as they relate to political, ethical or philosophical systems) found in the postmodern age: a notion most closely associated with the work of French philosopher François Lyotard. Finally, the reproduction and seemingly endless circulation of images in the films of Beineix and Besson, as well as their fragmentation of narrative and fascination with surface image, allowed the *cinéma du look* to be discussed in the context of the burgeoning advertising culture found in France during the 1980s, but also in relation to Baudrillard's reading of postmodern culture as one of simulation, based on the communication and circulation of signs, whereby all objects are reproduced or endlessly disseminated and end up referring only to themselves (not any reality external to representation).

In particular, the influence of advertising and new audiovisual technologies (such as video) and the dominance of a televisual mode of reception – whereby spectators 'zap' between channels, consuming an increasingly fragmented series of decontextualised narratives and only the most arresting surface images – was seen as threatening to push cinema towards a creative crisis of 'tout à l'image': the image and nothing else. Filmmakers such as Besson and Beineix (the main exponents of the *cinéma du look*) were thus seen by high-brow film critics such as those writing for *Cahiers du cinéma* as propagating a cinema that was all style and no substance – and that took its inspiration from superficial contemporary popular cultural forms such as advertising, video, pop music and BD rather than the more 'classical' influences of literature, theatre and painting. Beineix memorably defended his films against such attacks, describing how the advertising aesthetic with which his type of cinema had been so negatively associated had appropriated the beauty rejected by the New Wave; his films dispensed with stories or histories and captivated young people whose aspirations an ageing French cinema no longer espoused, articulated or indeed understood (Austin 1996: 120). The *cinéma du look* thus spoke directly to a new type of young audience (and one that included the young Mathieu Kassovitz) in a visual cinematic language that they could both understand and relate to.

Of the handful of directors associated with the 1980s *cinéma du look*, it is Luc Besson who has had the most significant and enduring influence on Kassovitz. Beyond the inspiration offered by his debut feature *Le Dernier combat* – which, as we have already mentioned, gave Kassovitz the confidence to drop out of school at 17 and embark on his career as a filmmaker – Besson's influence on Kassovitz can also be seen both in cinematic style and production methods. Though Kassovitz routinely cites *Mean Streets* (Scorsese, 1973) as his favourite film and reiterates the lessons taught to him by Spielberg's cinema, his seductive visual style and film practice are clearly indebted to Besson as much as they are to any American filmmaker. Where he differs from Besson, perhaps, is in relation to location. Whereas Besson seeks to construct cinematic spectacle in spaces that are somehow removed from the everyday – the historical setting of *Jeanne d'Arc* (1999); the futuristic world of *Le Cinquième élément* (1997); the natural beauty of the ocean in *Le Grand bleu* (1988); the underground labyrinth of subcultural style in *Subway* – Kassovitz, in his first three features at least, locates his seductive filmic spectacle in the here and now of contemporary urban France (a point we shall return to discuss in detail in Chapter 2).

In terms of film production, Kassovitz shares with Besson a keen understanding of the technical requirements of the medium that comes from years of frequenting and working on filmsets before directing. With this understanding comes the ability to extract, cinematographically speaking, the maximum from the technology at his disposal. Both directors construct seductive cinematic spectacle through an elaborate (but always controlled) *mise en scène* that combines striking imagery with fluid camerawork. In this respect, the similarities between Kassovitz and Besson are perhaps most apparent in *La Haine* (the careful attention to composition and highly mobile camera) and *Les Rivères pourpres* (a crime thriller that tries to beat Hollywood at its own game); while the technically demanding sequences shot on the mountain glacier in the latter film brings to mind the challenges faced by Besson in capturing the natural beauty of the ocean in *Le Grand bleu*.

The legacy of the look: breaking with the New Wave

The importance of the *cinéma du look* in relation to Kassovitz's development as a filmmaker cannot, therefore, be overstated. Beyond any stylistic or thematic influence, Kassovitz sees the *cinéma du look* of the 1980s as occupying a pivotal position in contemporary French film history: 'Les deux mecs qui ont enfin cassé la Nouvelle Vague il y a dix ans, c'est Besson et Beineix. Avec eux on a tous pris conscience qu'il y avait une nouvelle cinématographie' (Les Frères K 1997: 52).[23] By identifying Besson and Beineix in this way, Kassovitz underlines his own allegiance to popular, youth-orientated cinema over the intellectual and 'artistic' concerns of French *auteur* cinema. The contribution of Beineix and Besson in the early 1980s is crucial in so much as their films suggested to a new generation of filmmakers that it was possible for French cinema to break free from the overbearing legacy of the New Wave whose myths, modes of representation and preoccupations – not least the centrality of the *auteur* to the filmic text – had had a disproportionate influence on how French cinema has defined itself since the 1960s:

le problème, c'est que ce n'est pas le cinéma français qui bouge mais des individus. Sur tous les films de cette mouvance, aucun n'a eu d'avance du C.N.C.! ... Le cinoche français a du pot d'avoir des gens comme Kounen, Noé, Dupontel... mais ce ne sont en aucun cas les institutions bureaucratiques et intellectuelles qui aident à créer ça. Faire *Dobermann* ou *La Haine*, c'est la guérilla pour trouver des sous. (Kassovitz 1998)[24]

23 'The two who finally broke from the New Wave ten years ago, were Besson and Beineix. With them, we all realised that there was a new type of cinema.'
24 'The problem is that it's not French cinema that's moving forward, but individuals. Of all the films from this "movement", none received an advance from

The '*mouvance*' (more a network of likeminded directors than a clearly defined movement or stylistic trend) to which Kassovitz refers in the above quote consists of two generations of French filmmakers. First, a new generation of what we might refer to as 'post-look' filmmakers: directors such as Jan Kounen, Christophe Gans, Nicolas Boukhrief, Pitof and Gaspar Noé who take the *cinéma du look* as a key reference point, but whose work also displays an appreciation of exploitation and cult-genre cinema from around the world, as well as being influenced by Hollywood production practices. We might also include the actor and long-time Kassovitz collaborator Vincent Cassel in this group, since he has starred in films by all of the above directors. The other part of this 'mouvance' comprises Luc Besson, Marc Caro and Jean-Pierre Jeunet: older, more established figures within contemporary French cinema, but who are nonetheless viewed as mavericks or outsiders within the industry and whose work in the 1980s and 1990s paved the way for this younger generation of post-look directors to find an audience.

Though they cannot be seen to represent a clearly defined movement, given the stylistic and thematic diversity of their work, all of the above filmmakers share a desire to embrace a broad popular mainstream audience, while maintaining a certain scepticism towards the high-brow critical appraisal of – or intellectual engagement with – their films. Moreover, given the popular appeal of their films to youth audiences and the often polemical response to their work – both in terms of its content, but also hostility to American-style production influences – these directors constitute a significant force in contemporary French cinema.

Kassovitz (Les Frères K 1997: 52) suggests that the characteristic shared by these directors (beyond the obvious fact that they are all men) is that they are all, as he puts it, '*énervés*' (agitated). What might Kassovitz mean by this rather curious description? On the one hand, these filmmakers are *énervés* in the sense that they share an excitement and enthusiasm for the possibilities offered by cinema as a medium of popular spectacle – see for example *Le Cinquième élément* and *Vidocq* (Pitof, 2001) – a trait which is also reflected in the energy

---

the CNC! French cinema is lucky to have people like Kounen, Noé, Dupontel... but, under no circumstances, is it the bureaucratic and intellectual institutions which help to create that. To find the money for films like *Dobermann* or *La Haine* is guerrilla filmmaking'.

found in the kinetic editing of *Dobermann* (Kounen, 1997) and the restless camerawork of *La Haine*. On the other hand, the directors with whom Kassovitz aligns himself are *énervés* (irritated or agitated) by what they consider the constraints and lack of ambition of the French system within which they find themselves – a factor which has led a number of them to spend time working in Hollywood. In this respect their work both reacts against and is a direct challenge to the safe parameters (somewhere between the limitations of *auteurist* art-house nombrilism and staid heritage films) within which they believe French cinema functions under the guidance of the CNC.

However, this rupture with the French New Wave, initiated by the *cinéma du look* and so enthusiastically adopted by Kassovitz, was not embraced by all young filmmakers in France. In the early 1990s, the critical and, at times, high-profile commercial success of a directors such Eric Rochant (*Un monde sans pitié*, 1990); Cyril Collard (*Les Nuits fauves*, 1992) and Arnaud Despleschin (*La Sentinelle*, 1992), led *Cahiers du cinéma* to proclaim the arrival of a new *jeune cinéma* which, despite influences from various filmmakers and 'currents' within French cinema history, retained the New Wave of the 1950s and 1960s as its 'year zero'; and the concept of the *auteur* as its central guiding principle (Jousse, Saada *et al.* 1993: 28–30). Therefore, for many French critics and directors, the 1990s was a decade concerned less with breaking from the New Wave, than with identifying with the emergence of a 'new' New Wave that would maintain the centrality of the *auteur* both as a means of differentiating French cinema from Hollywood and as a marker of supposed artistic or intellectual 'quality'.

By making a conscious decision to reject the French New Wave in favour of the *cinéma du look*, Kassovitz was doing two things. Firstly, he was refusing to endorse the patriarchy of the French New Wave or invest in its romanticised mythologies. Secondly, he was affirming his own directorial style and tastes as shaped by and in tune with those of a new and younger generation of French spectators and audiovisual consumers for whom the classical and intellectual references of the New Wave had been replaced by the pop and mass cultural forms of an Americanised youth culture found in the *cinéma du look*. Kassovitz's desire to break away from what he saw as the constraints of the New Wave were clear from the outset of his career as a director. His playful inversion of the title of one of the most celebrated New Wave master-pieces for his short *Fierrot le Pou* acts, in this respect, as a statement of intent from the young director. This sense of rebelling, cinematically speaking, against the law of the father is highly appropriate, given that intergenerational conflict emerges as a recurring theme in Kassovitz's films. Ironically, however, this act of rebellion in some ways brings him closer to the 'young Turks' of the original French New Wave of the 1950s who were also looking to forge a new type of cinema by reacting against what they saw as the staid, predictable and creatively stifling practices of a previous generation of directors, producers and scriptwriters.

We may choose to interpret this notion of the 'agitated filmmaker' (*cinéaste énervé*) in one further way; but which applies specifically to Kassovitz, in so much as his early films and shorts can be seen to embody a sense of outrage and anger at social injustices (racism, exclusion, violence and social fracture) and a desire to transfer this anger onto the screen. Here Kassovitz stands apart from the other post-look directors with whom he associates, in that he enters into a longstanding tradition in French cinema of the *auteur* as engaged social commentator. Unlike Kounen and Noé, whose portrayal of violence, racism and exclusion seems merely present in order to shock or repulse its audience, Kassovitz encourages his spectator to engage with the complex realities of the social–political issues he addresses on screen, while also (in his earlier films at least) offering an impassioned 'wake-up call' to the dominant societal norm.

This chapter has argued for Kassovitz as an instinctively popular filmmaker. His particular cinematic vision, production practices and directorial style have been informed by, and are clear examples of, key shifts within French popular culture that have taken place since the early 1980s: most significantly the legitimisation of the American-influenced mass culture industries and the reconfiguration of youth culture at the centre of the popular. Beyond any crude indication of box-office marketability, the commercial success that has accompanied much of Kassovitz's career to date demonstrates that he understands what contemporary audiences want and, just as importantly, how to deliver it to them. In this respect, Kassovitz can also be defined as a 'popular' director since his films seek to engage with a broad, cross-over audience (not a minority elite). Finally, by addressing, in his earlier films, urgent contemporary socio-political issues in an often controversial way, Kassovitz reminds us that popular culture (and cinema in particular) has the potential to be more than the site of modish and superficial diversion. Beyond any commercial imperative or simple reflection of the people's tastes, there are also key political and ideological implications that need to be taken into account in relation to popular culture. It is precisely this question of the popular as a site of social struggle – an unstable space in which society attempts to make sense of itself and in which relations of power between margin and centre are in constant contestation – to which we shall now turn our attention.

References

Aubel, François (2003), 'Kassovitz: Jusqu'ici tout va bien', *Epok* 42, (December–January), 16–25

Austin, Guy (1996), *Contemporary French Cinema*, Manchester: Manchester University Press

Bourguignon, Thomas and Tobin, Yann (1995), 'Entretien avec Mathieu Kassovitz: les cinq dernières secondes', *Positif*, June, 8–13

Cannon, Steve (1997), 'Paname city rapping: B-Boys in the *banlieues* and beyond', in Hargreaves and McKinney (eds), *Postcolonial Cultures in France*, London/New York: Routledge, 150–68

Dyer, Richard and Vincendeau, Ginette (eds) (1992), *Popular European Cinema*, London: Routledge

Dauncey, Hugh (ed.) (2003), *French Popular Culture: An Introduction*, London: Arnold

Galland, Olivier (1997), *Sociologie de la jeunesse*, Paris: Armand Colin

Forbes, Jill and Hewlett, Nick (1994), *Contemporary France: Essays and Texts on Politics, Economics and Society*, London/New York: Longman

Hall, Stuart (1981), 'Notes on deconstructing the popular', *People's History and Socialist Theory*, in Raphael Samuel (ed.), *People's History and Socialist Theory*, London: Routledge, 227–40

—— (1995), 'The local and the global', *Vertigo*, 5, autumn/winter, 28–30

Hannerz, Ulf (1996), *Transnational Connections*, London/New York, Routledge

Hayward, Susan (1993), *French National Cinema*, London/New York: Routledge

—— (1998), *Luc Besson*, Manchester: Manchester University Press

Hebdige, Dick (1988) *Hiding in the Light: On Images and Things*, London/New York: Routledge

Jobs, Richard, I. (2003), 'Tarzan under attack: youth comics and cultural reconstruction in postwar France' *French Historical Studies*, 26/4 (Fall), 687–725

Jousse, T. *et al.* (1993), 'Le cinéma nouveau est arrivé: dix places pour le jeurne cinéma', *Cahiers du cinéma*, 473, 27–30

Kassovitz (1998), 'Les aventures de Mathieu Kassovitz' interview in *Steadycam*, consulted at www.mathieukassovitz.com/itw/steadycam.htm (site last accessed 19/7/05)

Kolker, Robert (2000), *A Cinema of Loneliness*, Oxford/New York: Oxford University Press

Lalanne, Jean-Marc (2000), 'Changements à vue: vingt ans de cinéma et de clips', *Cahiers du cinéma* (*Hors-série*), April, 62–3

Looseley, David, L. (1995), *The Politics of Fun: Cultural Policy and Debate in Contemporary France*, Oxford/Washington: Berg

Les Frères K (1997), 'Kounen et Kasso se lâchent', *Première*, July, 51–4

Mérigeau, Pascal (2004), 'Je suis Français, mais toujours Hongrois' (interview with Peter Kassovitz), *Le Nouvel Observateur*, 2063, (20 May) consulted at www.nouvelobs.com/articles/p2063/a241425.html (last accessed 27/1/05)

Nevers, Camille and Strauss, Frédéric (1993), 'Entretien avec Jean-Marie Poiré et Christian Clavier', *Cahiers du cinéma*, 465, 84–9

Powrie, Phil (1999), 'Heritage history and New Realism', in Powrie (ed.) *French cinema in the 1990s: Continuity and Difference*, Oxford: Oxford University Press, 1–21

—— (2001), *Jean-Jacques Beineix*, Manchester: Manchester University Press

Rigby, Brian (1991), *Popular Culture in Modern France: A Study of Cultural Discourse*, London: Routledge

Tarr, Carrie (2005), *Reframing Difference: Beur and* Banlieue *Filmmaking in France*, Manchester: Manchester University Press

Tirard, Laurent (2000), 'Mathieu Kassovitz: la leçon de cinéma' Studio, no. 160, consulted at www.mathieukassovitz.com/rivieres/interviews/studio.htm (site last accessed 22/7/05)

1 Vincent Cassel (Vinz), Saïd Taghmaoui (Saïd) and Hubert Koundé (Hubert) in *La Haine* (1995)

2 Vincent Cassel (Kerkerian) and Jean Reno (Niémans) in *Les Rivières pourpres* (2000)

1

47

3 Kassovitz and crew shooting at altitude for *Les Rivières pourpres*

4 Mathieu Kassovitz (Johnny) and Jean-Louis Trintignant (Marx) in *Regarde les hommes tomber* (Audiard, 1996)

48

5 Mathieu Kassovitz (Albert Dehousse) in *Un héros très discret* (Audiard, 1996)

6 Mathieu Kassovitz (Riccardo Fontana) in *Amen* (Costa-Gavras, 2002)

Social struggles in the popular sphere

> Popular culture is one of the sites where ... [the] struggle for and
> against a culture of the powerful is engaged: it is also the stake to be
> won or lost *in* that struggle. It is the arena of consent and resistance ...
> that is why popular culture matters.
> (Hall 1981: 239)

The *fracture sociale* trilogy

Though Kassovitz has never explicitly defined them as such, there
are compelling reasons for identifying his first three feature films,
Métisse (1993), *La Haine* (1995) and *Assassin(s)* (1997) as a trilogy. The
three films take as their subject matter key and controversial socio-
political debates facing France during the 1990s that had already been
introduced in Kassovitz's short films, and develop them in relation
to a disenfranchised youth class. The first instalment of the trilogy,
Métisse, is a comedy that explores racism and postcolonial identities in
France through what Kassovitz describes as a 'histoire de cul': a love
triangle between a young French women of mixed race and her two
male partners; one the son of an affluent African diplomat, the other
a white Jew from the working-class suburbs of Paris. Similar issues
of racism, ethnicity and cultural identity are addressed in Kassovitz's
second film, *La Haine* but this time such themes are firmly located in
the explosive setting of the *banlieue* and explored alongside the exclusion, delinquency and violence that forms part of daily life for the
young male inhabitants of a deprived working-class housing estate
(*cité*) on the outskirts of Paris. *Assassin(s)*, the final film in the trilogy,
maintains this focus on marginalised youth, but without limiting

it exclusively to the *cité*, while also foregrounding the issue of violence and the media. The three films therefore form what might be described as Kassovitz's *'fracture sociale* trilogy'. The term *fracture sociale* refers not only to the perceived disintegration of community and civic responsibility that accompanies exclusion, violence and delinquency but also to the growing divide between rich and poor in French society, and appears to have entered the popular vernacular in France in the mid-1990s: it was repeatedly used by Chirac during the presidential campaign of 1995, the same year *La Haine* was released. As such it seems an appropriate description for Kassovitz's trilogy of social films.

Beyond their common focus on topical and often controversial social subject matter, Kassovitz's first three feature films are bound in various other ways. Firstly, by their location in the Parisian *banlieue* (and the contrast between the *cité* and city found in *La Haine* and alluded to in *Métisse*) but also through the numerous references to Americanised hip-hop culture (rap and graffiti) and their dialogue with American cinema – in particular the work of Spike Lee and Martin Scorsese. Alongside these intertextual allusions to Hollywood there are a number of recurring *intra*textual references shared between Kassovitz's own films: for example, the globe that appears in both the opening and closing credits of *Métisse* returns in *La Haine*, as the image onto which a Molotov cocktail is dropped while Hubert delivers his opening monologue. The globe resurfaces later in *La Haine* on the advertising board declaring 'Le Monde est à vous' –[1] itself a reference to *Scarface* (Hawks, 1932). It is then glimpsed briefly in *Assassin(s)*; reflected in the window of the RER carriage in which Max travels home from his first encounter with Wagner. Finally, the three films are further linked by their casting: Vincent Cassel and Hubert Koundé star in both *Métisse* and *La Haine*, while Kassovitz casts himself in all three films – with starring roles in *Métisse* and *Assassin(s)* and a not insignificant cameo as a skinhead in *La Haine*.

The fact that Kassovitz – a director who has consistently aligned himself with the aesthetics, tastes and influences of popular cinema – should choose to begin his career with an often polemical focus on social themes in his early films and shorts, reminds us that there are also key political and ideological implications that need to be taken

1 'The world is yours.'

into account in relation to the popular. For his part, Stuart Hall (1981: 232–3) suggests that there is 'no whole, authentic autonomous popular culture': not only does our notion of what constitutes popular culture change as a result of the historical and socio-political context in which it is experienced, but cultural industries have the power to rework and reshape what they represent; imposing definitions (ideological positionings or cultural representations) of ourselves and others that fit more easily with the dominant societal norm or hegemony.[2] Hall (ibid.: 231) emphatically refutes, however, that this reality makes for a society filled with subservient 'cultural dupes' who are unable to recognise or resist attempts by the dominant societal norm to control and direct representations within the popular. In this respect, the sphere of popular culture (and by extension popular film) is most usefully understood as an unstable site of 'cultural contestation' (ibid., 239). It is the arena in which a given society attempts to make sense of itself in relation to perceptions of nation, class, ethnicity, gender and sexuality through individual or collective cultural expression.

Although the dominant societal norm may attempt to shape the images and identities present within the popular sphere, such representations are not exclusively under their control and can be challenged or subverted. What is more, the popular does not necessarily equate directly to the mainstream – even though we may tend to think of it that way. For example, though focusing specifically on the experiences of the marginalised French descendants of North African immigrants and constituting only a dozen or so films that were seen for the most part by a modest number of spectators, Beur cinema of the 1980s is nonetheless seen by Bosséno (1992: 51) as reviving a French tradition of 'populist cinema' in the sense that the directors set their films in 'a real country, and one that is in crisis'. Resistance from the margins (by minorities or subcultures) to dominant forms of representation, appropriation and exploitation can, therefore, form a legitimate part of the popular sphere.

This reading of the ideological or political implications of the pop-

2 'Hegemony' is here understood in relation to Stuart Hall's use of the term, which expands on Gramsci's original notion of 'hegemony' as a form of political/ideological domination in relation to the state. Hall's understanding of 'hegemony' thus encompasses the whole domain of social and cultural life (in particular the role of the media and popular culture), enabling us to see such domination as both contested and uncertain. For more details, see Morley and Kuan-Hsing (1996).

ular has important ramifications for Kassovitz's *fracture sociale* trilogy. This chapter will, however, be concerned with the first two feature films – *Métisse* and *La Haine* – due to their unambiguous association with a popular youth-orientated audience and attempts to entertain their spectator in order to engage him or her with the social issues addressed in the film. (As we shall see in Chapter 3, in *Assassin(s)*, Kassovitz's follow up to *La Haine* and the final instalment of the *fracture sociale* trilogy, things are not so clear-cut.)

Popular culture (in this case, cinema) may indeed be the site where the most intense manifestations or representations offered by the dominant societal norm in relation to 'race', class and sexuality are to be found. And yet it is precisely for this reason that the popular is the arena in which such hegemonic forces can and should be most actively (and effectively) contested. In other words, the arena of popular culture is the space in which filmmakers such as Kassovitz can most directly challenge the political and socio-cultural influence of the dominant societal norm before a mainstream audience. It is also (and, just as importantly) the arena in which the modes and methods of representation employed by the dominant societal norm to win and shape consent – ensuring that the power of hegemony over subordinate groups appears as both legitimate and natural – can be most widely exposed to scrutiny. In this respect, Kassovitz's *fracture sociale* trilogy challenges not only the social injustices of exclusion, racism and violence experienced by France's disenfranchised youth class but also the ways in which the dominant societal norm, largely through the media, constructs its own discourses and images of marginal youth as contemporary French society's disaffected 'other'.

As we shall see, though, Kassovitz's attempts to give a voice to the marginal in the arena of popular film are not without their problems. First because of the commodification of the 'other' that inevitably takes place within popular culture (the danger of subcultural forms being appropriated and subsequently misrepresented by the mainstream for profit). And second because Kassovitz's own origins as the son of artistic professionals working in film and television are somewhat removed from those of the marginal characters he chooses to portray, which leaves him open to accusations that his films offer little more than unauthentic, 'designer' visions of *fracture sociale*.

Métisse : 'un film de rue'

Just as themes of racism, ethnicity and cultural identity are fore-grounded in two of Kassovitz's earlier short films (*Fierrot le pou* (1990) and *Cauchemar blanc* (1991)), so they loom large in the narrative of his debut feature *Métisse*. The prevalence of these themes in Kassovitz's early work can be explained by that fact that, in the 1990s, issues of racism, integration and national identity remained (as in the 1980s) key and often controversial subjects in French politics and the media. Their prominence in Kassovitz's cinema can also be explained by the young director's immersion in French hip-hop culture, with its strong anti-racist stance and emphasis on the alliance of a multi-ethnic youth audience – which itself reflects the extensive involvement of French youth in anti-racist and immigrant movements during the 1980s and 1990s.

It is, moreover, unsurprising that Kassovitz should be inclined to engage with debates surrounding ethnicity and cultural identity, given his own background as the French-born descendant of a Jewish immigrant father, who grew up in an ethnically diverse district of Paris. Félix, the name of the lead Jewish character played by Kassovitz in *Métisse* thus takes his name from Kassovitz's Hungarian-Jewish grandfather. However, as in *La Haine*, while his own Jewish ethnicity appears as an obvious marker in the film, in *Métisse* Kassovitz is, in fact, more concerned with exploring issues of a plurality of postco-lonial identities in a contemporary, multiethnic French society, that are constructed from a complex matrix of local, national and trans-national (diasporic) positionings. In this respect, his films are also different from so-called Beur cinema of the 1980s and 1990s, with its extensive (and unsurprising) focus on Maghrebi-French subjec-tivities.

Evidence of the local, national and even transnational inspiration for the film can be seen in the way that, though taking its basic narra-tive structure from Spike Lee's *She's Gotta Have It* (1986), *Métisse* also draws on both Kassovitz's own cultural identity as a white French Jew, and his own experiences in a mixed-race relationship:

> À l'époque je vivais avec la fille qui jouait dans le film et j'allais souvent aux Antilles avec elle. J'étais le seul blanc et je me suis dit : 'bon, moi ça me dérange pas mais qu'est-ce-que je ferais si ma nana me trompait

avec un black. Est ce que je dirais que c'est un sale con ou un sale nègre (Kassovitz 1998)[3]

In Spike Lee's original film, the narrative centres on Nola Darling, a young, independent African-American woman who cannot decide which of the three male partners she is dating is the one for her. In his reworking of the film, Kassovitz maintains the strong independent female protagonist in the form of Lola (the *métisse* of the title, played by Julie Maudvech), but reframes the context and focus of her dilemma: she is pregnant (and knows who the father is), but finds herself unable to choose between her two wildly contrasting male partners, Félix (a white, working-class Jew) and Jamal (the son of a wealthy African diplomat), for fear of losing one of them for good. The film is, in fact, less concerned with Lola's response to her own predicament or with revealing the narrative's central enigma (though the test results indicate Félix is the father of the baby, the spectator never finds out for certain) than it is with exploring how the two men react to the situation they find themselves in with regard to their own latent prejudices concerning 'race', class and cultural difference.

Having completed his polemical short film *Assassins*, Kassovitz began production for *Métisse* in 1992. In common with nearly all films by first-time, unknown directors Kassovitz was able to attract only limited investment – a situation compounded by the fact that the film was also Rossignon's first feature as the principal producer. As it went into production, *Métisse* had yet to obtain television investment beyond the virtually automatic funding from Canal Plus, the French satellite channel legally obliged to invest in a minimum of 80 per cent of French feature-film production according to the conditions of its broadcasting charter.[4] This precarious financial situation was exacerbated by the fact that *Métisse* had failed to obtain additional funding from the CNC. Though the film was entitled to the automatic aid provided to all French films, it was refused selective aid in the form of either the advance on exhibition profits (*avance sur recettes*)

3 'At that time I was living with the woman who acted in the film and I often went to the Antilles [French Caribbean] with her. I was the only white guy and I said to myself: "well, it doesn't bother me, but what would I do if she cheated on me with a black guy. Would I say that he was a dirty bastard or a dirty black bastard?'

4 Further television and video distribution rights to *Métisse* were eventually purchased by the Franco-German broadcaster Arte once the film had been completed.

or through the additional financing offered to certain first films (*aide sélective*). At a time in the early 1990s when funding for first films was on the increase, Kassovitz has never forgotten this 'rejection' of his brand of popular cinema by the CNC.[5] Included in *Métisse*'s final credits under the acknowledgements or thanks from Kassovitz the rather cryptic acronym 'FTCNC' appears. According to the director (Kassovitz 1998) this stands for 'Fuck The CNC' – an indication of the level of resentment felt by Kassovitz towards the organisation charged with the responsibility of protecting and promoting French cinema at all levels of production, distribution and exhibition.

Though Kassovitz had chosen to direct a comedy – historically speaking, the popular genre *par excellence* of French cinema – in many ways *Métisse* was financed, shot and marketed in the style of an underground film or '*film de rue*' (Kassovitz 1998). The prominence of hip-hop style in the film's costumes, music and locale along with the graffiti titles and credits used in *Métisse* (drawn by Kassovitz himself) enhanced the film's urban or 'street' credentials. By the early 1990s French hip-hop had established itself as part of mainstream youth culture. However, it was still seen by many (particularly the establishment) as a marginal and rather menacing cultural form. The choice of the song 'Peur de la métissage' by hard-core Parisian rap crew Assassins to accompany the film's opening credits was therefore significant in that it clearly identified *Métisse* with the more militant and politicised (which is to say non-mainstream) elements of French hip-hop from the 1980s and early 1990s . Kassovitz even extended this 'underground' approach to the film's promotion in Paris. Unhappy with the efforts of *Métisse*'s official distributors to market and promote the film, he decided to exploit alternative promotion networks: employing what he described (*ibid.*) as '*l'affichage pirate*' (illegal or unofficial fly-postering) around the streets of the capital to attract an audience.[6]

Working with an extremely limited budget – not even knowing if the production funds would last until the end of the shoot – Kassovitz completed filming for *Métisse* in thirty-two days. He was, furthermore,

5 Since the CNC's declined to grant selective aid for his second film, *La Haine*, Kassovitz has refused to apply for *aide sélective* on subsequent features.

6 According to the *Steadycam* interview with Kassovitz (1998), prior to the film's release red flyers were posted up around certain areas of Paris with the words 'Le 20 mai nous seront tous. Métisse' ('On 20 May we'll all be. Mixed.')

forced to shoot on 16mm film rather than the industry standard 35mm, affecting the quality, texture and richness of the image. For similar reasons, Kassovitz, along with his director of photography Pierre Aïm, elected to 'sacrifice light' in *Métisse* (*ibid*.), choosing to forego complex lighting set ups in certain scenes in order to allow the camera to be as mobile as possible. Ultimately, then, the mobility and energy of the camera were deemed more important than the overall quality of the image – Kassovitz's argument being, presumably, that it was better to present the spectator with engaging images of lesser quality than beautifully lit images shot unimaginatively. These decisions serve to emphasise *Métisse* as popular spectacle, a film that aims to engage its audience visually in order that they may enter into a more sustained relationship with the protagonists and subject matter. This inventive and arresting use of composition and camera movement is present throughout *Métisse*: from the title sequence in which the camera races almost at ground level through the streets of Paris, to the 4-minute continuous Steadicam shot (reminiscent of the celebrated Copacobana nightclub scene from Scorsese's *Goodfellas* (1991)) in which we follow Félix as he enters a hip-hop club with his brother, navigates his way through the dancefloor and then exits following an altercation with a friend. Similarly, in the film's opening sequence the camera restlessly pans and tracks, searching out Félix and Jamal as they arrive outside an apartment block in a relatively affluent area of central Paris. The pair are then caught in close-up as they squash into the antiquated lift that will take them to up to Lola's flat. Kassovitz undoubtedly uses the *mise en scène* here to provide a visual spectacle that will instantly engage and entertain his spectator. And yet the camerawork also functions in relation to the film's social theme (tolerance of difference in a multiethnic society) to evoke the unease and tension that exists between two individuals from different backgrounds in terms of class and ethnicity, forced together by circumstance. Kassovitz uses the fragmented close-up shots in the lift precisely to foreground the differences that are making his protagonists so uncomfortable. The pair's close physical proximity highlights the contrast between the black and white skin of the actors, while a close-up from outside the lift shot at ground level emphasises class difference: Félix sports cycling shoes – cycling traditionally seen in France as a working-class leisure activity – whereas Jamal is wearing expensive-looking, more formal footwear.

Popular comedy and postcolonial identities

If *Métisse* was alternative or underground in relation to its production methods, in other ways it was more conventional. By exploring
the lived tensions within a multicultural, postcolonial French society
through the relationship of Félix, Lola and Jamal, *Métisse* draws on
a long-established comic narrative which easily pre-dates cinema
itself: the *ménage à trois* (love triangle). Kassovitz does reserve a
modern twist for this established comic trope, however. In *Métisse* it
is the female protagonist who is playing her male suitors against one
another; leaving the man, uncharacteristically for a French comedy,
as the butt of the joke.

In addition to this use of the *ménage à trois*, the film's energetic,
witty dialogue delivered in inverted street slang *(verlan)* incorporates
the vaudeville traditions of mainstream French screen comedy (quick-
fire dialogue and wordplay) into the vernacular of contemporary urban
youth. Elsewhere, and just as importantly, *Métisse* relies extensively
on visual humour and physical comedy; such as the repeated gag in
which Félix, unable to extricate himself from the pedals of his racing
bike as it comes to a halt, crashes to the floor. Much is also made of
the physical characteristics of Félix (played by Kassovitz); his skinny
frame and oversized glasses contrasting with the beauty and physical
presence of Jamal, or the athleticism of Félix's brother, Max (Vincent
Cassel). The film also plays towards the surreal and absurd, such as
the scene in which Félix – still uncertain as to whether or not he is
the father of Lola's child – dreams of being overtaken in a cycle race
by Jamal riding in a pram and dressed as a baby, with Lola waiting at
the finish line.

Kassovitz was not, however, the first director to interrogate contemporary attitudes towards 'race', difference and cultural identity in France
through comedy. A number of postcolonial popular comedies appeared
in the 1980s and early 1990s: *Black Mic Mac* (Gilou, 1986); *L'Œil au
beur(re) noir* (Meynard, 1987) *Romuald et Juliette* (Serreau, 1989); *La
Thune* (Galland, 1991) all addressing similar issues to those found in
Métisse. In common with Kassovitz's film, the majority of these narratives are also based around the inter-ethnic couple and the wider social
tensions that such a union produces. It is, however, the manner in
which Kassovitz chooses to explore these contemporary social realities
of racism, integration and cultural identity that distinguishes *Métisse*
from other postcolonial French comedies of the early 1990s.

Comedy is usefully understood as an ideologically ambivalent genre, 'mimetic of social reality and yet distanced from it', in which potentially transgressive or taboo subjects are largely contained via three key strategies: stereotyping, the exaggerated nature of comic performance and utopian or conservative narrative resolution (Vincendeau 2001: 24). While the postcolonial comedies of the 1980s and early 1990s may well have been important in that they represented one of the few areas in which French cinema was 'positively engaging with cultural difference in a multiethnic France' (Tarr 1997: 67), the majority of these films deal with such issues precisely by employing the comic strategies of stereotyping, exaggeration and the utopian happy ending. *Black Mic Mac* thus presents the spectator with a largely clichéd portrayal of an African immigrant community living in the Goutte d'Or district of Paris and their outrageous attempts to prevent the closure of the hostel where they live by a white French health official. Elsewhere, Serreau's *Romuald et Juliette* provides a clear example of utopian resolution at work within the postcolonial comic narrative. The film focuses on the unlikely romance that develops between a black cleaner from the French Caribbean and a white French company executive. Having overcome the prejudices of those around them towards the relationship – prejudices that are based as much on class as they are on ethnic difference – Romuald and Juliette marry, Juliette falls pregnant and the couple set up a home with the children from their previous relationships.

The effect of stereotyping or utopian narrative resolution in comedies such as *Black Mic Mac* and *Romuald et Juliette* is to distance these films somewhat from the social realities they address. Audiences are thus invited to confront debates concerning racism, integration and difference, but are rarely forced to ask hard, uncomfortable questions about how they affect the society in which they live once the happy ending has been played out on screen. *Métisse*, on the other hand, displays a refreshing honesty towards the complexities of multiculturalism and racism in France. Kassovitz's film plays with preconceived notions of 'race' and ethnicity as they relate to socio-economic standing and marginalisation. Here it is Félix, the white working-class Jew, who lives in the *cité*; whereas Jamal, the educated son of a diplomat, frequents the more affluent quarters of Paris. *Métisse* also warns us against buying into the careless homogenising of essentialised postcolonial and racial identities. When Jamal tries to win

Lola over by remarking that they are both descended from colonial slavery, Lola retorts 'tes grands-parents étaient diplomates'.[7] The supposed certainties of a fixed cultural identity or shared historical past are thus explicitly thrown into question in *Métisse*. Identity is seen instead as a fluid and ongoing process of 'becoming'.

The emerging postcolonial society of *Métisse* is defined by the mix of black, white, Creole, Jewish and Arab faces which populate the cafés, nightclubs, basketball courts, lecture halls, apartments and *cités* of the film. The image of a multicultural Paris found in *Métisse* reflects the cosmopolitan urban environment in which Kassovitz himself was raised – many of the extras featured in the film were in fact friends of the director. Moreover, Kassovitz's decision to direct a feature film requiring the presence of a young desirable black French actor (Hubert Koundé) in a starring role at a time when black actors were largely consigned to secondary or stereotyped roles in French cinema (especially comedy), is a further indication of Kassovitz's political commitment and the way *Métisse* reflects the realities of a contemporary, postcolonial French society.

Unlike other white-authored postcolonial comedies from the early 1990s, Kassovitz does not present us with the image of 'a relatively unproblematic multicultural French society [that] is now able to integrate the socially mobile ethnic minority Other into the new extended family' (Tarr 1997: 72). Prejudices relating to difference emerge from all sides. Characters whom we might expect to display a heightened sensibility towards issues of ethnicity and difference are equally prone to discriminating along such lines. Lola, for example, confides to her grandmother that she feels Jamal is 'trop noir'[8] for her to be dating him. In contrast, Jamal's affluent white girlfriend – the character we would expect to be the most susceptible to racial stereotyping – is surprisingly unable to 'see' his blackness as a defining character of his identity when pressed to do so by her boyfriend.

Such prejudices are not solely confined to issues of ethnicity but also relate to class. Jamal questions Félix's ability as a fast-food delivery boy from a working-class estate to provide for Lola and the baby. Later, when both men are arrested following a brawl in the street and the police side with Jamal as the son of a diplomat, Félix complains 'il vaut mieux être riche et noir que blanc et pauvre – les traditions se

7 'your grandparents were diplomats'.
8 'too black'.

perdent'.[9] This sense of conflict between Félix and Jamal is reinforced by framing within the *mise en scène*, with Kassovitz frequently placing the two protagonists in medium close-up as they square up to one another from opposite sides of the screen. Youth, so often portrayed in mainstream comedy and popular film (including Beur cinema of the 1980s and 1990s) as the site of multiethnic alliance is shown in *Métisse* to be as susceptible to prejudice and ignorance as any other group within society.

Supposed certainties relating to ethnicity and identity therefore emerge in *Métisse* as unstable truths; preconceptions which Kassovitz invites both the audience and his protagonists to challenge. In this context, the question offered by Félix's grandmother to Jamal when he visits the family home for a meal on the Sabbath as to whether or not he is Jewish, is not as ridiculous as it first seems. After all, as she reminds us, 'En Éthiopie il y a des Juifs noirs'.[10] Moreover, by highlighting Félix's Jewish-immigrant origins as much as Jamal's black African identity, Kassovitz reminds us that ethnicity is not solely a 'black' issue.[11] Markers of Jewish ethnicity – the family meal celebrating the Sabbath; the kosher take-away restaurant where Félix works; Max's star of David tattoo which he displays in the boxing gym and on the basketball court – are arguably more prominent in the film than those of Jamal's black African and Muslim origins. Similarly, Félix's grandfather's thick Eastern European accent and occasional lapses into Yiddish – subtitled for a French-speaking audience – are clear indications of difference that contrast directly with Jamal's articulate and perfectly spoken French.

And yet these markers of ethnic and religious difference, so prominent within the working-class Jewish family home in *Métisse*, are less in evidence when Félix mixes in the clubs and streets of his local neighbourhood, where his identity is more visibly defined by his affiliation to hip-hop and urban youth culture. Kassovitz thus uses these shifts within the locale of the *mise en scène* to emphasise a more

9 'it's better to be rich and black than white and poor – we're losing the old traditions'.

10 'There are black Jews in Ethiopia'.

11 More problematic, though, is the marginalisation of the woman's perspective within the narrative. Though initially presented as a strong, independent woman, by the end Lola is ultimately shown to depend on her men, and for much of the narrative is sidelined by the dilemma facing Jamal and Félix, despite the fact that she is the one having the baby.

subtle point about identity. While our sense of self is informed, to different extents, by a number of 'collective constants' (history, ethnic and religious difference) identity is also shaped by our relationship to the changing socio-economic and cultural contexts in which we live. In a similar way, *Métisse* shows us that our sense of self is also determined by the degree to which we choose to invest in ethnic origins or difference as part of our identity. Interestingly, of all the characters in the film it is Lola (of mixed race) who seems to invest least in these cultural, linguistic or material signifiers of ethnicity. Her studio flat appears devoid of any symbolic objects or images linking her to her French-Caribbean origins; unlike the prominently positioned ornaments and map of Africa found in Jamal's apartment. Her sense of self is thus informed to a greater extent by gender difference. Lola is presented, and sees herself, as a strong, independent (western) woman who maintains her right to choose in relation to the pregnancy and refuses to give up either Félix or Jamal. *Métisse* acknowledges, therefore, that cultural identity is determined by a complex network of positionings of which ethnicity or 'race' and class are but two components (gender, sexuality and age being some of the others).

The film ends with Félix and Jamal having apparently learned to tolerate one another's difference, forming a new, if unconventional, family unit with Lola and the baby. This recourse to a safe narrative resolution based around the newly created pluri-ethnic family as metaphor for the tolerant multicultural nation is somewhat surprising given the other differences already noted between *Métisse* and other white-authored postcolonial popular French comedies of the 1980s and early 1990s. Largely as a result of this ending, *Métisse* was criticised by Rozenberg (1993) for presenting a naive exposition of race relations in France. And yet, even in this apparently 'conventional' happy ending, Kassovitz adds one final twist that will undercut any sense of multiethnic utopia. As the two 'fathers' argue over possible names for their son – Félix offers David and Jacob, while Jamal proposes El Kebir or Mohammed – Lola reveals that she prefers Clothère. This suggestion is greeted with cries of amazement by both partners, since the deliberate choice of this somewhat antiquated French name leaves open the possibility that another 'French' lover may in fact be the father of Lola's baby.[12]

12 The possibility of just such a scenario is set up earlier in the film, in the scene where Félix and Jamal drive home from the airport, discussing the holidays they

Unlike the multicultural utopia found in the other contemporary postcolonial French comedies mentioned earlier, *Métisse*'s narrative resolution does not entirely elide the challenges and tensions to the postcolonial family/nation that persist behind the comic film's utopian façade. As Lola's final remark suggests, the potential for prejudice (and the conflict it brings in its wake) to resurface remains. By choosing to end *Métisse* in this way, Kassovitz's film (and by extension its audience) is not distanced from the often problematic realities of 'race', ethnicity and cultural difference in the same way as other white-authored postcolonial French comedies of the 1980s and early 1990s. A popular comedy with hip-hop attitude, *Métisse* therefore illustrates Hall's notion of the popular as a site of struggle; an arena of contestation in which dominant stereotypes surrounding 'race' and ethnicity are certainly produced and promoted, but where they can equally be challenged and subverted by a popular audience.

Métisse emerged, moreover, at a crucial moment in relation to wider socio-political debates on immigration, integration and national identity taking place in France during the 1990s. At the time of the film's release, France had seen the return of the right to power, with the incumbent interior minister Charles Pasqua introducing a series of reforms toughening legislation concerning immigration, revoking the automatic right of citizenship for the descendants of immigrants born in France and increasing police powers to stop and detain any individual suspected of residing illegally in France. This more uncompromising stance by the centre-right had, in part, been influenced by the continued electoral popularity of the extreme right National Front party, which, under the leadership of the openly racist Jean-Marie Le Pen, had secured considerable gains in municipal and European elections in the early 1990s by employing political rhetoric that was openly hostile towards France's immigrant and ethnic minorities. In this context, *Métisse* – a film that presents an essentially positive endorsement of a multicultural France, without denying the potential tensions and confrontations that the realities of living with difference can produce – offers a direct challenge to the xenophobic discourse of the far right and the centre-right in France during the early 1990s.

---

have taken with Lola. Here it emerges that on some of these trips neither Jamal nor Félix accompanied Lola – the implication being that she had taken the trip with a third lover.

La Haine: the *banlieue* as emblematic site of exclusion

For the second instalment of his *fracture sociale* trilogy, *La Haine*, Kassovitz built on the momentum that had been established by *Métisse*. Though his debut feature had attracted a relatively small audience (89,000 spectators) during its short run in France, it had nonetheless identified Kassovitz as a filmmaker to watch. Popular French film magazine *Studio* (Klifa and d'Yvoire 1993: 108–12) featured him in a round table style interview along with three other first-time directors (Pascale Bailly, Laurence Ferreira-Barbosa and Alexandre Jardin); while his performance in *Métisse* earned Kassovitz a nomination for most promising young actor at the 1994 Césars.

In developing the project that would eventually become *La Haine* – provisionally entitled *Droit de cité* – Kassovitz continued to work with Lazennec and producer Christophe Rossignon, who raised a budget of approximately FF 22 million[13] for the film: considerably larger than for *Métisse*, and above the average for a French film in that year, which stood at FF 18 million.[14] Beyond the deferrals, loans and automatic aid secured by Lazennec (totalling FF 7 million), most of the capital raised came from television companies; principally the advanced purchase of screening rights by La Sept (Arte) (FF 4.5 million) and Canal Plus (FF 6 million). A further FF 4 million was offered by Studio Canal (the production branch of Canal Plus) via the Sofica system, which allows tax-sheltered investment in French film production. Though investment by television in French film production is now commonplace – and, indeed, a legal requirement for nearly all French broadcasters – at almost half of the total budget, the proportion of capital provided by the small screen for *La Haine* is significant. Presumably, the television companies (and above all Canal Plus) were attracted by the proposed film's appeal to a youth audience, resulting both from its explosive subject matter (tensions between police and *banlieue* youth) and the fact that Kassovitz was a young director, in tune with the urban hip-hop culture that by this time formed a key reference point in French youth culture. In contrast, the CNC was less enthusiastic about the proposed film. Kassovitz was once again

13 All figures for *La Haine*'s budget are taken from Dale (1997: 247). Original figures quoted by Dale appear in US dollars and so have been converted at the rate of FF 6.7/$1 in order to give an approximation of the budget.
14 Source: *CNC Info* (1996) 'Bilan 1995', no. 261, 9.

denied selective aid, since changes were demanded to the final script that the director was not prepared to make – a further indication of the distance between Kassovitz's own brand of youth-orientated popular cinema, and the type of French films sanctioned in the early 1990s by the funding policies of the CNC.

As with *Métisse*, Kassovitz wrote the screenplay for *La Haine*. This time, however, he resisted the temptation to place himself in the role of the young white Jewish *banlieusard* – preferring to cast the up-and-coming actor and close friend Vincent Cassel. The two remaining lead roles were also taken by young, relatively unknowns: Hubert Koundé who had starred alongside Kassovitz in *Métisse*, and Saïd Taghmaoui – a friend of Koundé's who had been discovered at casting auditions for the film. In *Métisse* Kassovitz had only briefly alluded to the socio-cultural space of the working-class *banlieue*, through fleeting glances of the *cité* in St Denis, home to Félix and his family. The presence of the extended working-class Jewish family in the narrative is indeed testament to the fact that the *banlieue* is not (as many in the main-stream French media would have us believe) the exclusive domain of a criminalised and alienated, predominantly black and Arab, under-class. Nevertheless, in the film the realities of crime and delinquency are not entirely glossed over by Kassovitz; for example, we learn that Félix's brother is known in the local community as a petty hood and drug dealer. On the whole, however, in *Métisse* Kassovitz does not con-cern himself with a detailed exploration of *fracture sociale* within the *banlieue*. Instead, the working-class estates of St Denis function as a means of emphasising the class differences between the two central male protagonists – such as the scene in which Jamel and Lola come to visit Félix's family for dinner and Félix mocks Jamal's concerns that his car will be stolen if left unattended on the 'dangerous' and suppos-edly crime-ridden estate.

In *La Haine*, however, the *banlieue* is identified as the highly charged site of *fracture sociale*. The film recounts a day in the life of Vinz, Saïd and Hubert; three unemployed youths from a deprived housing estate on the north-western periphery of the Paris region. *La Haine*'s narra-tive begins the morning after rioting on the fictional (and ironically named) Les Muguets estate[15] that has been provoked by a police *bavure*

15 Muguet means lily of the valley in French – a soft and sweet-sounding name that bears no relation to the harsh realities of life on the housing estate. The real-life location where *La Haine* was shot is the La Noë estate in Chanteloup-les-Vignes, a suburb to the north-west of Paris.

('blunder'); the shooting of Abdel, a local French youth of Maghrebi origin, who now lies in a critical condition in hospital. In the confusion of the previous night's rioting, Vinz has acquired a policeman's gun; which he claims he will use to kill a cop, should Abdel die from his injuries. A day that begins much like any other for the jobless trio ends with an explosion of violence as Vinz (and possibly Hubert) are shot dead by the police.

Alongside *La Haine*'s highly charged narrative conclusion, the film thus bears witness to the mundane realities of life in the *cité*. Vinz, Saïd and Hubert kill time by swapping jokes and tall stories; running shopping errands for Vinz's mother; congregating in the largely territorialised public spaces of the estate – rooftops, courtyards, a children's playground, the burnt-out shell of the local gym, a vandalised train station – and meeting with contacts from Hubert's small-time drug dealing. (With no real prospect of securing a conventional job, and in order to support his immediate family, Hubert enters into one of the alternative economies operating in the *cité*.) Kassovitz maintains the approach established in *Métisse*, whereby the social issues are explored through the experiences of multiethnic French youth, filtered through references to hip-hop and street culture. To some extent, the narrative also continues the exploration of violence and racism initiated in his second short film, *Cauchemar blanc*, but shifts more noticeably from the anti-Arab violence perpetrated by a group of far-right thugs in his earlier short film to the potentially explosive tension between the police and multiethnic *banlieue* youth.

According to Kassovitz (Bourguignon and Yann 1995: 9) the initial inspiration for *La Haine* came from demonstrations he attended in Paris in 1993 against the death in police custody of Makomé M'Bowole, a French youth of Zairean origin who was killed while being held at a police station in the eighteenth arrondissement. The decision by Kassovitz to relocate events in the narrative of *La Haine* from a district in the historical centre of Paris more readily associated with picture-postcard images of Monmartre and the Sacré-Cœur than police violence to a working-class estate on the very edge of the French capital was, of course, quite deliberate. By the mid-1990s, the increasingly run-down estates of the *banlieue* had become synonymous with exclusion, violence and 'social fracture'.[16]

16 For a detailed history of the post-war French urban periphery and emergence of the working-class estates of the *banlieue* as emblematic sites of marginality,

It had not always been this way. Originally built in the 1950s and 1960s in response to the rural exodus towards France's major cities prompted by post-war modernisation and unprecedented economic growth, these new estates were intended to offer a clean modern living space for French workers and their families. However, the initial zeal of urban planners, architects and politicians for these gigantic housing projects soon faded as the *cités* rapidly revealed their mediocrity in both architectural and structural terms. When amplified to the scale of constructions such as the 4,000 de la Courneuve (originally designed to accommodate 20,000 inhabitants) the uniformity of the tower blocks and banks of low-rise housing fostered a profound sense of alienation amongst residents. Subsequent attempts in the 1970s to reduce the *cité* to a more human scale (smaller buildings grouped around a central courtyard, such as the La Noë estate featured in *La Haine*) fared little better since developers were forced to build on cheaper land at the very extremities of the city, merely reinforcing the identity of these estates as spaces of exclusion. This marginalisation was compounded by economic downturn in France during the mid-1970s and the de-industrialisation of the urban periphery, which led to a concentration of unemployment, social deprivation and criminality in certain areas of the working-class *banlieue*.

Those with the means to do so – notably, the French white-collar families for whom, originally, the estates had largely been constructed – moved away from the *cités* replaced by poorer (mostly non-European) immigrant workers and their families, who, until the mid-1970s had been largely excluded from housing in the working-class banlieue.[17] In a period of economic stagnation and rising unemployment some (not all) of the white, working-class residents who remained on the deprived estates alongside these immigrant families became increasingly susceptible to the inflammatory racist rhetoric of the National

criminality and violence, see: Begag and Rossini (1999); Dubet and Lapeyronnie (1992); Jazouli (1992); and Rey (1996).

17 Until the mid-1970s, most immigrant workers (particularly those from France's former North African colonies) had been accommodated in insalubrious *bidonvilles* (shanty towns) on wasteland at the very extremes of the urban periphery. With the halt to official immigration in 1973 and the introduction of a policy of *regroupement familial* a year later, politicians and local government officials were forced to provide housing for the newly arrived families of immigrant workers. The increasingly dilapidated *cités* provided the obvious solution to this housing problem.

Front that targeted North African immigrants and their descendants as scapegoats for the nation's social ills. This perception of the urban periphery as a site of tension and social disintegration was heightened by localised rioting (*rodéos*) in a number of *cités* around Paris and Lyon in 1981 – sparked by incidents of perceived police brutality against young ethnic minority residents but also a more general expression of anger and frustration at the profound levels of social deprivation experienced on these estates. As the cycle of youth riots continued in the early 1990s, the *cités* of the urban periphery were foregrounded in both media and political rhetoric as the emblematic site of *fracture sociale*; 'no-go' areas of criminality and violence, inhabited by multi-ethnic gangs of disenfranchised, delinquent male youths.

This construction in the French social imaginary of the *banlieue* as a space of marginality, violence and alterity had, by the mid-1990s, also permeated the creative consciousness of French cinema. The release of a cluster of five independently produced features over a period of six months in 1995 – *La Haine*; *Douce France* (Chibane, 1995); *État des lieux* (Richet, 1995); *Krim* (Bouchaala, 1995) and *Raï* (Gilou, 1995) – all focusing on the urban periphery as a site of social exclusion and ethnic difference, led critics (Jousse 1995, Tobin 1995, Reynaud 1996) to speak of the emergence of a new category of film that, for the first time since the western, was primarily defined by its geographical location: the *banlieue* film. And yet, French cinema's interest in the urban periphery, as both a real space of social exclusion and metaphorical site of marginality or otherness, did not suddenly appear in the mid-1990s. Directors had in fact been mapping the socio-cultural terrain of the *banlieue* since at least the 1960s through films such as *Terrain Vague* (Carné, 1960), *Deux ou trois choses que je sais d'elle* (Godard, 1967), *Le Thé au harem d'archimède* (Charef, 1985); *Laisse béton* (Le Péron, 1984) and *De bruit et de fureur* (Brisseau, 1988).

Kassovitz's decision to locate a social drama dealing primarily with the violent tensions between police and an alienated youth underclass (but one that also addresses exclusion, racism and delinquency) on a run-down estate in the Parisian urban periphery was not, therefore, highly original. What was exceptional, however, was *La Haine*'s success (both commercial and critical) and the media interest generated by a medium-budget independent feature directed by a young, relatively unknown filmmaker. Attracting almost two million spectators in France (the third most popular French film of the year); winning the prestigious Palme d'Or at Cannes for best direction; and with Kassovitz being forced into hiding as a result of the intense media attention received by the film for its controversial representation of highly sensitive, topical socio-political subject matter, *La Haine* was the film event of 1995. Though Kassovitz would enjoy even greater box-office success with his police thriller *Les Rivières pourpres* (2000) none of his work before or since has received such extensive media coverage, or such positive critical attention. For this reason *La Haine* represents arguably Kassovitz's most successful attempt at placing the social at the heart of popular French cinema.

What factors might explain *La Haine*'s incredible impact? Certainly the timing of the film's release, only a matter of weeks after a French presidential campaign in which the domestic agenda had been dominated by the issue of *fracture sociale*, was important. Moreover, as Reader perceptively notes (1995: 14) the election of Chirac, an established, highly conservative member of the political establishment to the French presidency was symptomatic of the ideological and political exhaustion felt in France after the false dawn of the Mitterrand years drew to a close. Thus, as one journalist writing for *Libération* suggested, *La Haine* 'hits the right spot in a country still groggy after the coronation of Jacques Chirac' (*ibid.*). And yet, the timing of *La Haine*'s release and its focus on the socio-cultural space of the *banlieue* is not enough alone to explain why the film went on to be such a commercial success, when the other *banlieue* films of the same year attracted only modest audiences.[18] Nor can it sufficiently account for the reasons why *La Haine* became a social phenomenon; provoking such a storm of media interest that the discussion of the film framed debates around *fracture sociale* and the 'crisis' of the *banlieue* in the months following its release – even resulting in an alleged private screening of the film for the incumbent right-wing cabinet, in order that ministers might better understand the 'malaise' of the *banlieue* (Harris 2004: 212). Whether or not this screening actually took place is, in many ways, irrelevant: the fact that such reports may have circulated at all is evidence of the *La Haine*'s profound socio-cultural impact in France following its initial release.

In this context, the underlying reasons for *La Haine*'s success are more usefully understood by the way in which Kassovitz combines a

18 *La Haine* attracted more spectators than the combined audience totals of the other four *banlieue* films released in 1995.

genuine concern for contemporary socio-political realities in France with an explosive narrative and highly stylised representation of *fracture sociale* that appeals above all to a popular youth audience (both in France and abroad). Inevitably, this conscious mixing of the commercial and political; the marginal with the mainstream; militant or civic cinema with the aesthetic of Hollywood or the *cinéma du look*, brought with it a whole series of problems. Indeed, for all the media storm that surrounded *La Haine* as an anti-police film and a 'wake-up-call' to the government regarding the effects of social fracture in the urban periphery, the film was to prove at least as controversial for the way in which Kassovitz chose to represent, stylistically speaking, the socio-cultural space of the *banlieue*.

Popular spectacle and politicised aestheticism in *La Haine*

We have established, then, that *La Haine* shares *Métisse*'s concern to engage a cross-over (popular) audience with key socio-political debates facing contemporary France. But whereas Kassovitz's debut feature essentially employs a largely consensual form of genre cinema – popular French comedy – to enter into a debate with the spectator about racism and the need for tolerance in a multicultural, post-colonial French society, *La Haine* adopts a much more confrontational stance towards its mainstream audience in its exploration of *fracture sociale*. The film thus begins in combative mode with the grainy black and white news footage of a solitary male issuing a defiant verbal challenge to the massed ranks of CRS (riot police) facing him. These images are followed by a short statement, presented in simple white typeface against a black background, that reads: 'ce film est dédié à ceux disparus pendant sa fabrication ... ';[19] presumably a reference to Makomé and others killed in police *bavures* in the mid-1990s. Next we hear Hubert's 'jusqu'ici tout va bien'[20] monologue, accompanied by the image of a Molotov cocktail exploding on a globe which gives way to *La Haine*'s opening credits, superimposed over a montage of TV footage: CRS guards preparing their armoured vans; demonstrations against the murder of Makomé; student riots in the centre of Paris in the mid-1980s as well as more recent social disturbances that

19 'This film is dedicated to those who have disappeared during its production ...'
20 'until now, everything is okay'.

have taken place in the *banlieue*. The montage is cut to the soundtrack of Bob Marley's 'Burnin and Lootin', a song originally written in response to the state-sanctioned police brutality in the shanty towns of Kingston, Jamaica during the 1970s.

The opening sequence of *La Haine* therefore functions as a preface to the action that will follow by establishing the violent tension between *banlieue* youth and the forces of law and order underpinning the film's narrative. It also serves to identify the matrix of local, national and global (diasporic) positionings that inform not only the multiethnic youth culture of the *banlieue* but also, more generally, contemporary youth culture in France. Thus, by combining images of social unrest in the *cité* with footage of student riots in central Paris, Kassovitz deliberately aligns the localised struggles taking place in the *banlieue* with wider social protest movements involving French youth – eliciting a sense of solidarity between the film's mainstream youth audience and its marginalised protagonists. In a similar way, the choice of Marley's defiant reggae anthem to accompany the riot montage of the title sequence, establishes a connection between the *banlieue* and the 'ghetto' culture of the black diaspora (as a globally recognised signifier of resistance against racism and state oppression), a link that is further enhanced later in *La Haine* through the use of hip-hop iconography.

Though the look and feel of *La Haine*'s opening sequence may suggest militant cinema, this more oppositional filmmaking is soon replaced (in stylistic terms at least) by an altogether more polished and seductive visual spectacle. The grainy footage and shaky hand-held images of the riot montage give way to richly rendered monochrome photography and smooth, controlled camera movements. The first scene from the housing estate – in which the camera dollies over Saïd's head to confront the CRS officers guarding the local police station and then cuts to a carefully executed tracking shot that moves along the line of officers – exemplifies this shift. This decision to portray the La Noë/Les Muguets estate in stylish monochrome and with expansive, elaborate camerawork, places *La Haine* in direct contrast with the sombre realism and naturalistic *mise en scène* of other *banlieue* films such as *Hexagone* (Chibane, 1994) and *Raï* (Gilou, 1995) or the grainy black and white, pseudo-documentary images of *État des lieux* (Richet, 1995). As Vincendeau suggests (2000: 316) the use of black and white cinematography functions in *La Haine* as a 'badge of aestheticism', distancing the film somewhat from the 'normal' (colour) documentary.

However, more than being simply a stylistic trait, Kassovitz (Levieux 1995: 20) has argued that the choice of black and white in fact heightens the film's realism, since by presenting 'reality' in a different way – particularly in relation to reports on the *banlieue* shown in colour on French television news – it forces the spectators to question more deeply the 'truth' behind the images they see on screen.[21] In the case of *La Haine*, these truths are the socio-political realities of exclusion, violence and *fracture sociale* faced by male youth in the disadvantaged urban periphery, and the contrast between the real(lived) experience of Saïd, Vinz and Hubert, on the one hand, and the image of the *banlieue* constructed by the dominant societal norm (largely through the mainstream media) on the other.

Kassovitz's conscious aestheticism won praise from most critics (including, for the first and only time in his career to date, the more high-brow cinema journals such as *Cahiers* and *Positif*), while his representation of *fracture sociale* through modish black and white photography and hip-hop iconography appealed instantly to a youth audience. There were, however, a limited number of dissenting voices. Writing for *Les Inrockuptibles* – a respected French weekly popular culture review – Samuel Blumenfeld (1995: 27) contrasted *La Haine* with *État des Lieux* – released only weeks later in France and directed by Jean-François Richet, a committed Marxist filmmaker originating from a working-class estate in the north-west suburbs of Paris. Whereas Blumenfeld praised *État des lieux* for its authentic, politically conscious portrayal of working-class revolt in the disadvantaged urban periphery, he considered the representation of socio-political realities of the *banlieue* offered by *La Haine* to be compromised by 'la volonté de se plier à la règle de l'entertainment'[22] in an attempt to seduce the audience. Richet also entered the debate, apparently dismissing *La Haine* as a work of 'science fiction' (Kassovitz 1998) and as lacking in any grounding in the realities of life in the *cité* (Kaganski and Blumenfeld 1995: 24–5). Further criticism came from a review of the film by

21 'Le noir et blanc a toujours un côté assez exceptionnel parce qu'il fait voir les choses comme on ne les voit pas et c'est pourquoi il draine plus de réalisme.' / 'Black and white is quite exceptional because it makes us look at things in a way we don't normally do, and that's why it brings with it a greater sense of realism.'
22 'the desire to give oneself over to the rules of entertainment'.

Serge Rémy (1995: 20) for the French communist daily, *L'Humanité*, in which the journalist expressed concern that Kassovitz's designer vision of *fracture sociale* – complete with modish soundtrack and high-quality cinematography – risked identifying the director as a young 'demagogue' whose film was more concerned with appealing to a youth audience and the attendant media than addressing the serious socio-political crisis affecting the working-class *banlieue* in France.

Such criticism of *La Haine* appears to be as much concerned with issues of 'authenticity' as it is with the alleged de-politicisation of the social subject matter that arises from Kassovitz's stylised *mise en scène*. In fact, interviews given by Kassovitz at the time of *La Haine*'s release show him to have been keenly aware of such pitfalls in his representation of the *banlieue*:

> Je ne voulais pas faire un film sur la cité. Moi je ne viens pas des cités, il n'est donc pas question que je fasse un film entièrement là-dessus. C'était intéressant de montrer que les problèmes sont aussi sur Paris ... Le but était de rendre la cité belle, avec le côté souple, fluide. J'avais l'argent nécessaire. Il y a des moments où c'est même un peu trop, limite putassier, vidéoclip, quand les idées de mise en scène sont mauvais! C'est le danger: quand on a les moyens on est tenté de tout utiliser. (Bourguignon and Tobin 1995: 10–11)[23]

What is also apparent from the above quote is how conscious Kassovitz was of his position as an outsider in the *cité*. It was for this reason that the director lived on the La Noë estate for almost three months prior to shooting in order to gain an insight into everyday life in the *cité*, but also to build up trust and reassure local residents as to his intentions for making the film (Remy, V. 1995: 44). Similarly, Kassovitz organised a special screening of the film for 250 young people from La Noë to thank them for their cooperation during the filming of *La Haine* (Celmar and Dufrense 1995). The event also included a question and answer with the director and lead actors – giving young

---

23 'I didn't want to make a film just about a working-class housing estate. I don't come from that environment, so there's no way I can make a film exclusively set there. It was interesting to show that the problems [found in the *cités*] also affect Paris ... The aim was to make the housing estate look beautiful, with this supple, fluid aspect. I had enough money to do this. There are moments when it's all too much; a bit of a come on, like a videoclip, when the ideas for the *mise en scène* are poor. That's the danger when you have the money – the temptation is to use everything you have.'

residents from the estate an opportunity to debate the merits of the film and its representation of the *cité* face to face with Kassovitz.

In numerous press interviews following the release of *La Haine* (see for example: Boulay and Colmant 1995, Ferenezi 1995, Remy, V. 1995) Kassovitz defended the film against charges of an inauthentic fictionalising of the *banlieue* by a privileged outsider, claiming that he did not intend to speak 'for' *banlieue* youth through his film. He went on to insist that approval from the critics was welcome, but not essential. Of far greater importance to the director was that the inhabitants of estates such as La Noë did not feel 'trahis' ('betrayed') by the representation of the *banlieue* offered in *La Haine*. Anecdotal press reports from screenings (Celmar and Dufrence 1995, Rouchy 1995) suggest that, on the whole, young people from the *banlieue* responded well to the film. If they had concerns, they were less to do with the film's conscious stylisation and more about the extent to which *La Haine*'s vision of the *banlieue* was articulated almost extensively through the perspective of disenfranchised male youths from the *cité*. The effect of this rather distorted vision of these working-class estates is to belie the complexity of the 'real' *banlieue* as a space inhabited by alienated delinquent youth and the victims of social exclusion, as well as honest, decent working-class families. In this context, the absence of any female protagonists beyond the rather clichéd portrayals of mothers and sisters glimpsed in the domestic sphere in *La Haine* has been identified as problematic (Vincendeau 2000, Tarr 1999).

Despite the claims made by reviewers such as Blumenfeld and Rémy, the aestheticism of *La Haine* has both ideological and political implications, in particular through the ways in which Kassovitz employs *mise en scène* and soundtrack as a means of emphasising the real and imagined divide that exists in contemporary French culture and society between the estate and the more affluent parts of the capital. 'Real' in relation to the social inequalities that deny many of the inhabitants of the disadvantaged urban periphery access to employment, education, wealth creation and political representation. 'Imagined' in the sense that, as emblematic spaces of marginality and *fracture sociale* the run down *cités* of the working-class *banlieue* are, through their representation in the mainstream media and other socio-political discourse as the exclusive site of criminality, unemployment, delinquency and violence, entirely removed from the rest of society.

Although the *cité* is identified as the centre of Vinz, Saïd and Hubert's universe, narrative space and time in *La Haine* are, symbolically, divided almost exactly between the day spent on the estate and the latter part of the day and night in the centre of Paris. The trio journey from the *banlieue* to the centre on the RER train (the Parisian transport system that links the poorer areas of the urban periphery with the more affluent centre). However, the ease with which the RER allows the *banlieusards* to travel to the centre is deceptive. Upon arriving in Paris, the trio are repeatedly shown as redundant, inept, incapable and unqualified; as, for example in the scene where they successfully hotwire a car only to find that none of them know how to drive, or, again, at the art gallery, where they totally misread the socially 'acceptable' rules of behaviour.

Circulating in central Paris, Vinz, Saïd and Hubert are exposed for what they are; inept city bodies which, to the rest of society at least, do not matter. The ability to enter the hegemonic space of the centre by riding in on the RER does not, therefore, foster a greater sense of social integration for the trio. Rather, as François Maspero reminds us in *Les Passagers du Roissy Express* (1990), it merely serves to emphasise the vast distance (as much cultural as socio-economic) that separates the inhabitants of the *cité* and the more affluent areas of Paris, despite their geographical proximity.

The *mise en scène* of *La Haine* explicitly foregrounds this real and imagined city–*cité* binary. Scenes from the La Noë estate were shot in deep focus, relying heavily on (often elaborate) long takes. Through a combination of Steadicam and tracking shots, the camera accompanies the three central protagonists as they wander through the public spaces of the estate. Camera movement is also noticeably more expressive and expansive in the *cité* than Paris, as, for example, in the 180°-pan in the police station; the under-cranked[24] tracking shot in the underground lock-up that mimics the flight of a bullet towards a close-up of Vinz holding the stolen gun; and the celebrated helicopter shot that sends the camera floating above the housing estate, accompanied by the rap music emanating from the DJ's sound system. Finally, the soundtrack from the *cité*, which uses ambient sound rather than incidental or non-diegetic music to accompany Saïd and

24 Under-cranking means running the camera slower than the standard speed when shooting to give the impression of accelerated motion when action is projected on screen.

Vinz's incessant, energetic *tchatche*, was mixed in stereo; adding to this sense of the spectator being immersed both visually and aurally within the La Noë estate.[25]

For the scenes shot in the centre of Paris that make up the second half of the film, Kassovitz deliberately chose to operate with a smaller technical crew, eschewing the more elaborately choreographed, long, single takes employed in the *cité*. In general, scenes located in the centre of Paris were also shot using far greater focal length (so that characters are in sharp focus while the background is blurred). To comply with the director's intention that the contrast between Paris and the estate in *La Haine* should be aural as well as visual, the soundtrack for scenes in the capital was mixed in mono rather than stereo. Kassovitz had originally wanted to push this contrast between the *cité* and city even further, intending for the scenes from the centre of Paris to remain largely untreated in colour, and quite distinct from the stylish monochrome of the La Noë estate (Bourguignon and Tobin 1995: 10).[26] These differences are rendered explicit from the moment the young *banlieusards* arrive in the city. As Vinz, Saïd and Hubert stand motionless against the backdrop of a busy Parisian street, they are captured on screen in a tracking shot with zoom, so that the trio remain in sharp focus while the city behind them is reduced, literally, to a blur. The switch from stereo to mono that occurs at the beginning of this scene compounds this visual effect, creating the impression of an indistinct 'wall' of sound emanating from the city that confronts rather than envelopes the spectator (as it had done in the *cité*).

Kassovitz thus employs an effective combination of *mise en scène* and sound to emphasise the sense of profound dislocation, powerlessness and alienation felt by *banlieue* youth upon arriving in the centre of Paris. This also has the secondary effect of de-familiarising Paris to a cinema audience accustomed to images of the city's monuments, cafés and elegant apartment buildings. Even when the more familiar landmarks of the historic centre are placed on screen in the

25 A good example of this 'immersion' in the soundscape of the *cité* comes thirteen minutes into the film, where Vinz, Saïd and Hubert stop in a courtyard and argue over who owns the moped they can hear speeding round the estate. The sound of the moped moves from left to right, overlapping with the dialogue of the central protagonists as well as the sound of shouts and cries from elsewhere in the estate.

26 For this reason, *La Haine* was, in fact, shot on colour film stock and rendered into black and white during post-production.

second half of *La Haine* they are in some way distorted or obscured:
from the rooftop where Vinz rolls his joint in extreme close-up, the
Eiffel Tower thus appears as a blurred illumination in the far distance.
In effect, we begin to see the capital through the eyes of the young
banlieusards; as an unreadable (because blurred) alien space. To spectator and protagonist alike, then, the *cité* is rendered a more attractive
and inviting space than the centre of Paris – challenging contemporary media discourses that painted the deprived housing estates of
the Parisian urban periphery such as La Noë as a hellish, 'non-place'
of delinquency, violence and otherness.[27] As such, the *mise en scène*
employed by Kassovitz moves beyond superficial street chic and is
inherently political.

The *cité* as point of cultural intersection: the global and the local

Although it may address similar issues of *fracture sociale*, the highly
stylised cine-spatial representation of the *banlieue* in *La Haine* is,
nonetheless, at odds with the sociological approach common to most
other *banlieue* films from the 1980s and 1990s. And yet Kassovitz's
film also sits uncomfortably alongside the 'aesthetic'[28] treatment of
the *banlieue* found in works such as *Deux ou trois choses que je sais d'elle*
or *De bruit et de fureur*. This is because, unlike the more modernist
or avant-garde traditions that inform such *auteur* films, *La Haine*'s
stylised take on the *banlieue* is firmly located within the representational framework of popular youth culture. As was argued in the previous chapter, Kassovitz's cinema is representative of a cultural shift
that has taken place in the past twenty years whereby the popular has
been aligned with increasingly commercialised mass cultural forms
(television, pop music, film) that are experienced through a network
of local, global and (crucially) diasporic positionings. This youth-orientated popular culture is highly receptive to new technologies and
Americanised popular culture. It is also marked by an engagement
with marginality and difference – with all the problems that the

27 For a detailed study of media construction of the banlieue, see Hargreaves
(1996) and Wieviorka (1999).
28 The aesthetic and the sociological are terms used by Vincendeau (2000: 312–13)
to describe the two main approaches that French cinema has taken to the *banlieue* since the 1960s.

incorporation of minority or (sub)cultural forms into the mainstream entails.

La Haine therefore mediates its representation of social fracture through Hollywood, hip-hop and the street culture of *banlieue* youth. Though the film also contains some references to French cinema – the trio's unsuccessful attempts to turn off the lights on the Eiffel Tower by clicking their fingers ('like in the movies'), for example, parodies a similar scene from *Un monde sans pitié* (Rochant, 1990); while Vinz seeking refuge from the police in a cinema could be seen as (a somewhat unexpected) homage to Godard's *À bout de souffle* (1959) – the majority of intertextual references found in *La Haine* are to American cinema. In particular, Kassovitz alludes to the early films of Martin Scorsese (*Mean Streets* (1973); *Raging Bull* (1980) and *Taxi Driver* (1976)). The influence of Spike Lee was also seen to loom large in the film; just as *Métisse* can be interpreted as French reworking of *She's Gotta Have it*, so *La Haine* was deemed by many (Reader 1995: 13) to be heavily influenced by *Do the Right Thing* (Lee, 1989) – a claim that is not entirely justified.[29] Nevertheless, as Kassovitz himself acknowledged, not all of these allusions to Hollywood are intended for – nor, indeed, would they all be identified by – a youth audience:

> il y a beaucoup de références dans le film. *Scarface* de Hawks avec l'affiche 'Le monde est à vous'; je l'ai mis car dans les cités, ils connaissent par cœur le *Scarface* de DePalma. Vous leur parlez de cinéma et ils vous disent: 'Ah ouais! Comme Scarface!' et ils ne connaissent pas l'original, bien sûr. (Bourguignon and Tobin 1995: 8)[30]

For a contemporary French youth audience, then, the most immediate cultural connection comes not through references to Hollywood, but rather from the way *La Haine* aligns itself with a multiethnic youth culture whose influences are as much global as they are local. This identification is primarily articulated through the film's investment in hip-hop; a cultural form incorporating music, dancing, graffiti and, crucially, dress codes and language. Thus the branded sportswear worn by Vinz, Hubert and Saïd immediately identifies them

29 This dialogue in Kassovitz's cinema with Hollywood and American independent cinema will be fully discussed in Chapter 4.

30 'there are lots of references in the film. Hawks's *Scarface* with the poster "The world is yours"; I put that in because in the *cités* they all know DePalma's [remake of] *Scarface*. You speak to them about cinema and they tell you: "Yeah! Like *Scarface*!" and they don't know the original, of course.'

with hip-hop's urban style – originally imported from the African-American ghettos of the USA but now adopted by both young *banlieusards* and French youth beyond the *banlieue* (including Kassovitz himself, who is frequently photographed for interviews wearing the T-shirts, designer trainers and baseball caps that form the constituent elements of this look).

This mix of 'old skool' American hip-hip style: with French designer labels such as Lacoste and Yves Saint Laurent and French street fashion is reflected above all in Hubert's costume. On the one hand, the T-shirt he wears in *La Haine* is emblazoned with the 'Everlast' US sportswear logo that includes, significantly, a reference to 'Bronx NYC' in its design. On the other, his camouflage combat trousers are reminiscent not only of the outfits associated with members of the militant American rap group Public Enemy, but also of those worn a year earlier by French rapper MC Solaar on the cover of *Prose Combat* – the album that confirmed Solaar's success with a cross-over youth audience as France's premier rap superstar.

Though Vinz, Saïd and Hubert's dress may reflect a style adapted from the African-American hip-hop culture, their use of language – in particular inverted slang (*verlan*) – locates the film in a specific local and national context. Local, since *verlan*, a form of nineteenth-century French slang, revived in the mid-1970s, was initially more closely associated with the multiethnic working-class estates of the Parisian *banlieue* than those of the other major French cities such as Lyon and Marseilles.[31] National, because, by the mid-1990s, *verlan* had become embedded in the vernacular of French youth across the country. Despite the fact that *verlan* is now associated with a socio-cultural milieu way beyond the *cité*, the extent to which the trio employ the inverted back slang serves to 'designate their language as *banlieue* speak' (Vincendeau 2000: 315). In so doing it also authenticates their status as members of a specifically French disenfranchised youth class. Unlike, the youthful protagonists of *cinéma du look* films such as *Subway* (Besson, 1985), the trio from *La Haine* do not, therefore, attempt to incorporate American words or phrases into their speech but instead converse in the vernacular of the *cité*. Even

31 A single example will suffice. When in the early 1980s the nomenclature 'beur' (*verlan* for Arab and indicating the French descendant of North African immigrants) appeared it was rejected by many Maghrebi-French youth from Lyon and Marseilles who claimed it was 'Parisian' slang (Durmelat 1998: 201).

in the bathroom scene, where Vinz rehearses Travis Bickle/De Niro's famous 'you talking to me?' speech from *Taxi Driver*, he does not choose to adopt an American accent, but instead delivers the lines in rather crude French. Saïd's incessant *tchatche* and Vinz's aggressive verbal delivery thus play a crucial role in establishing not only the authenticity (as both French and of the *banlieue*) but also the dynamism of the central protagonists' performances. Indeed, when the underlying tension and aggression running through the narrative of *La Haine* does explode to the surface it is articulated as much through language as it is physical violence. In this respect, Kassovitz's use of language in the film presents a further link to hip-hop culture since the trio's verbal sparring and quick-fire delivery echoes the macho postulating and verbal dexterity found in rap music.

Hip-hop iconography: resisting through (sub)cultural style

Interestingly, for a film so immersed in hip-hop culture, rap music does not dominate the soundtrack of *La Haine*, which is a mixture of American soul, funk and electro (early hip-hop dance music) and reggae.[32] In fact only one rap song features directly in the film, and it is French. Significantly, the hardcore beats and explicit lyrics of Expression Direkt's 'Mon esprit part en couilles' are heard not in the *cité*, but on the car stereo as Vinz travels through the centre of Paris (a possible metaphor for the way in which French rap has crossed over from the marginal spaces of the urban periphery into the mainstream of French popular culture). This conscious effort to limit the amount of rap music used in the film, could be read as part of a more general attempt by Kassovitz to incorporate hip-hop culture into the film without falling into stereotypical associations made between rap and the *banlieue*: 'Je voulais que le sujet soit pris au sérieux, que le spectateur sente qu'il n'a pas affaire à des rigolos qui mettent leur casquette de travers et qui font "yo-yo"' (Remy, V. 1995: 44).[33] Hip-hop style nonetheless forms a structuring iconography in *La Haine*. Whereas references to hip-hop culture appear 'naturally' in *Métisse*

32 See the section on French rap in Chapter 1, pp. 30–4, for more details.
33 'I wanted the subject matter of the film to be taken seriously. I didn't want the spectator to feel that they were dealing with a bunch of jokers who were wearing their baseball caps crooked and going "yo-yo".'

– primarily as a reflection of Félix/Kassovitz's personal tastes in music and fashion – in *La Haine* they are deliberately foregrounded through three performance elements: graffiti (or tagging) DJ-ing and break dancing. Three scenes in particular are central to establishing hip-hop iconography as integral to the film's *mise en scène*: Saïd's tagging of the CRS van; the montage of break dancers performing in the entrance to the train station; and DJ Cut Killer's performance from the window of his apartment in the estate. These scenes would undoubtedly have struck a chord with a contemporary French youth audience for whom hip-hop by this point formed a key cultural reference. However, the reasons for including them in the film go beyond the desire to appeal to the modish tastes of youthful spectators – or even as homage to the underground French hip-hop scene of Kassovitz's youth. Instead, the scenes ought to be read as examples of resistance or revolt through (sub)cultural style.[34]

In this context, the graffiti-ed message: 'baise la police' (literally meaning 'fuck the police') left by Saïd on the back of the police van represents a defiant challenge to the forces of law and order and a conscious attempt by Maghrebi-French/*banlieue* youth to resist through hip-hop style. Moreover, by tagging his name on the back of the police van, Saïd is symbolically reclaiming control of a public space that the police have 'invaded'.[35] In another of these keys scenes – the break-dancing show that takes place in the RER station – this notion of resisting through style is, perhaps, less obvious. The visual and aural pleasure derived by the spectator during this scene is undeniable: the stylish black and white cinematography, pulsating funk soundtrack, selective use of slow motion and choice of a fixed-camera position, all serve to foreground the athleticism of the dancers' captivating performance as spectacle. For these same reasons, however, the scene is also in danger of appearing as a superficial interlude in the narrative – more evocative of a pop video than committed social cinema. And yet, by staging their impromptu show in the station, the dancers are (like Saïd) defiantly reclaiming a public space from the police, resisting with the only means at their disposal: their bodies.

34 An idea first formulated by Hebdige (1979).
35 The act of tagging (marking of an initial or pseudonym on a building, vehicle or object in a public space) is most frequently used by the graffiti artist as a means of identifying ownership or territorial control of a given space. That Saïd should choose to place his name on the police van is an act of resistance charged with significance.

This notion of resistance or revolt is further heightened by the narrative context in which the scene appears. The break-dancing is directly followed by a violent confrontation elsewhere on the estate between police and *banlieue* youth, provoked by a gun attack on local officers carried out by the brother of Abdel in revenge for the police *bavure* that has left his sibling critically ill in hospital. It is no coincidence that the crowd involved in the ensuing fracas with the police is made up largely of those who were watching the break-dancers performance in the station (including Vinz, Saïd and Hubert). By juxtaposing the two events in this way Kassovitz therefore proposes a link between the 'cultural' resistance of the break-dancers and the more immediate challenge to the forces of law and order offered by *banlieue* youth (with performance acting as the catalyst for direct action). The seemingly superficial hip-hop iconography of *La Haine* is thus charged with a more militant, political significance.

Kassovitz's use of hip-hop style as both seductive spectacle and a structuring iconography of resistance signals an awareness of the unstable boundaries between youth in its commercial and political guises – or what Hebdige (1988: 19) has termed 'the politics of pleasure' of youth (sub)cultures. For Karen Alexander (1995: 46), however, *La Haine*'s foregrounding of hip-hop is highly problematic:

> [We find in *La Haine*] endless references to and mimicry of African-American culture. This speaks volumes for satellite TV and the globalisation of images of oppression, as a 'style thang', with its Hood street chic, break dancing and hip-hop ... But this is Paris, not New York or Los Angeles; this difference should come into play somewhere ... to filter his narrative through a transatlantic superstructure is to lose a specifically European 'otherness' ... the problem comes when the cinema, music, TV and youth magazines stand in for people's lived experience of the world. (Alexander 1995: 46)

What Alexander's wholly negative critique of *La Haine* fails to acknowledge is that the references to African-American culture (specifically hip-hop) that appear in the film are not a substitute for lived experience, nor are they an attempt to replace the cultural, historical and socio-political specificities of the working-class *banlieue* with an Americanised 'hood street chic'. In an age of global communications technology that has greatly facilitated the transnational exchange of both mainstream and marginal cultural forms (such as hip-hop and reggae) it is hardly surprising that postcolonial youth from within the disadvantaged *banlieue* might identify with and appropriate the styles and sensibilities contained within the urban music and culture of the African diasporas. Nevertheless, this is not a question of superficial cultural imitation. Instead these transatlantic and diasporic influences form one point of reference amongst a network of identity positionings (both local and global) that constitute the multiethnic youth culture of the *banlieue* – which, in turn, inform popular youth culture more generally in France. The hip-hop style employed by Kassovitz in *La Haine* is therefore identifiably 'French' – or, more accurately, a reflection the multiethnic postcolonial culture that now exists in France – as the example of the DJ performance in the *cité* well illustrates.

DJ Cut Killer – one of France's most respected hip-hop DJs and producers – makes his cameo appearance in *La Haine* in the now celebrated scene where break beats, rap and *chanson française* accompany the camera as it rises above the courtyard and floats over the estate – looking towards Paris and beyond. As with the break-dancing analysed earlier, Kassovitz employs a highly stylised *mise en scène* to emphasise this notion of hip-hop performance as resistance. The camera follows Cut Killer's almost ritualistic preparation of the turntables and sound system, building audience anticipation of the performance that ends on a medium-long shot of the DJ as he prepares to send his musical message to the residents gathered in the courtyard below. As the beats kick in this fetishisation of the young DJ's performance is further enhanced by extreme close-ups of Cut Killer's hands on the vinyl and cross-fader as he deftly mixes legendary African American rapper KRS-one's 'Sound of the Police' and 'Nique la police' ('Fuck the police') by Parisian rap crew NTM, with Piaf's 'Je ne regrette rien'. Given the events that have taken place on the estate the previous night, the defiant message contained within the samples and beats emerge as a rallying cry for resistance against police brutality.

Cut Killer's performance in *La Haine* is a further example of the way in which the multiethnic youth culture associated with the *banlieue* offers a point of intersection between local, global and diasporic culture. It also identifies French hip-hop as both a quintessentially postmodern and postcolonial cultural form. By mixing the sounds of French and African-American hip-hop with 'Je ne regrette rien' the DJ transforms a standard from the canon of popular French music, making it at once familiar but also defiantly alien to a Francophone audience. Piaf's song is thus transposed into a format that the French multiethnic youth audience which forms hip-hop's core constituency can relate to. Moreover, with the knowledge that 'Je ne regrette rien' was adopted by French paratroopers fighting in Algeria during the war for independence (Vincendeau 2000: 314) and that Cut Killer (whose real name is Hajoui Anouar) is French of Maghrebi origin, this form of cultural appropriation can also be interpreted as an act of postcolonial resistance.

One further way in which difference comes into play in *La Haine*, distinguishing it from African-American models of both music and cinema, is through its insistence on the *banlieue* as a multiethnic space. In contrast, American hip-hop and so-called 'Hood films' of the 1990s (such as *Juice* (Dickerson, 1992); *Boyz 'n the Hood* (Singleton, 1991) and *Menace II Society* (Hughes Brothers, 1993) define inner-city ghettos almost exclusively along racial lines. French hip-hop has, in fact, always maintained this position as a multiethnic cultural form (in relation to both artists and audience), emphasising tolerance of difference. As well as reflecting the ethnically inclusive ethos of French hip-hop, *La Haine*'s positioning of the black-*blanc*-beur trio at the centre of its narrative is also an intentionally *symbolic* representation of the multiethnic make-up found in the French working-class *banlieue*. In response to those who saw the film's multiethnic trio as a concession to political correctness (Remy, V. 1995: 42), Kassovitz claimed that he had not wanted *La Haine* to become 'une histoire de clans'[36] (*L'Express* 1995: 141) – in other words, portraying the *banlieue* as synonymous with the racially segregated ghettos of urban America – and that he had chosen the multiethnic trio to emphasise the fact that it was not a question of 'Arabs' or 'blacks' against the police, but rather a collective opposition of marginalised youth from within the *cité* (Remy, V. 1995: 42).

Elsewhere, Tarr (1997: 78) views *La Haine*'s black-*blanc*-beur alliance as problematic, in that ethnic difference is largely subordinated *within* the trio in relation to their position as a collectively excluded underclass (particularly the difference of Saïd, the Maghrebi-French youth, who, unlike the other two characters, is never shown to us in the socio-cultural context of the Arab-immigrant family). The on-screen presence of Hubert and Saïd thus bears witness to the reality of postcolonial French society, but the film fails to consider

36 'a tale of clans'.

adequately how their ethnic and cultural difference, linked as it is to France's colonial past, might, in fact, compound the socio-economic exclusion they experience in the *banlieue*. Instead *La Haine* locates multiethnic *banlieue* youth in a transnational context as representative of the oppressed immigrant diasporas that can be found on the margins of all large western cities. This global significance appears to be reinforced by the decision to identify the white member of the trio as Jewish.[37] Kassovitz has offered the fact of his own ethnicity (claiming that the white character could equally have been Portuguese, if the director himself had been of Portuguese-immigrant origins), and a desire to please his own Jewish grandmother, as the relatively straightforward explanation for this choice (Remy, V. 1995: 42). However, the inclusion of the 'Grunwalski story' – in which an old Jewish man the trio meet by chance recounts a surreal tale of his deportation to the Soviet labour camps – serves as a signifier of 'racial' discrimination, violence and diaspora that relates to Vinz's collective Jewish history but also, more generally, to that of Saïd and Hubert as postcolonial bodies; reminding the spectator that the presence of Vinz, Saïd and Hubert in the *banlieue* results from 'specific historical disruptions' (Reynaud 1996: 57).

These more general references to oppressed immigrant diasporas from different times and places in history do not mean that the specificities (and consequences) of ethnic difference as they relate to the trio of *banlieue* youth in the context of contemporary French society are entirely elided from the diegesis of *La Haine*. Indeed, beyond the friendship of the interethnic group, and, above all, in their dealings with the police, 'race' matters. This point is perhaps best illustrated when the trio exit Astérix's apartment block in the centre of Paris and the police apprehend only Hubert and Saïd; Vinz's white face allowing him just enough time to stall the officers (with the excuse of having come to visit his aunt) and make good his escape. As the white member of the gang (and irrespective of his Jewish ethnicity) Vinz is in the privileged position of choosing when to identify himself as part of the alienated multiethnic youth class of the *banlieue*, and when to exploit the fact of his whiteness to evade arrest, and thus avoid the humiliating interrogation which Saïd and Hubert endure at the police station.

37 For an original and illuminating discussion of the post-Holocaust Jew in *La Haine*, see Loshitzky (2005).

The symbolic alliance of the multiethnic trio in *La Haine* is not, therefore, as solid nor as egalitarian as we might have expected. In this respect, though racism, ethnicity and difference do not form the main focus of *La Haine*, the film nevertheless echoes *Métisse*'s more nuanced take on postcolonial race relations amongst French youth.

Similarly, the apparent racism of the two police officers in the interrogation sequence is further complicated because one of them is of Arab origin. Although this fact is not explicitly referred to in the scene – and, in many ways, this distinction is more difficult to ascertain *precisely* because the film is shot in black and white – in the director's commentary for the French DVD release of *La Haine*, Kassovitz refers to this character (played by Zinedine Soualem) as the 'policier rebeu' ('beur cop'). When the scene is (re)viewed by a spectator armed with this crucial information, it transforms a supposedly 'straightforward' representation of institutionalised racism into something far more complex. The beur cop's brutality either suggests that here 'race' is not the issue – in other words that Saïd is brutalised because of his status as a marginal delinquent from the *banlieue*, rather than as a French youth of Algerian origin – or else it indicates that a much more complex series of postcolonial power relations are at work: the beur cop adopts the schizophrenic position of the white racist/colonial oppressor, and attacks the 'Arab' youth in order to negate or repress the powerlessness associated with his own Maghrebi origins beyond the interrogation room.

'*On n'est pas à Thoiry ici*': exposing media stereotypes of *banlieue* youth

Though it would be entirely disingenuous to argue that *La Haine* is not concerned with issues of *fracture sociale* as they affect the deprived estates of the French urban periphery, Kassovitz has insisted (Remy, V. 1995: 42) that the main focus of his film was not the *banlieue* itself but rather the subject of police violence. More specifically, the film is concerned with the growing tension between the police and an increasingly alienated youth underclass (often, but not always, of immigrant origin) that appears to manifest itself most readily on the working-class estates of the *banlieue*, but which is not limited exclusively to the deprived urban periphery. Many media commentators were quick to pick up on Kassovitz's apparent description of the film as 'anti-police' (Boulay and Colmant 1995), a confrontational stance that was further fuelled by press reports of police guards in attendance at the Cannes screening of *La Haine* walking out of the film in protest at its depiction of fellow officers (Vincendeau 2000: 310). In subsequent interviews, Kassovitz nuanced his earlier remarks, claiming that the film was not 'anti-flic' ('anti-police') but rather 'anti-système policier' (Levieux 1995: 20) – critical of a police system that sent armed officers into potentially explosive confrontations with groups of youths from the *banlieue* which they were often ill-equipped to deal with, and of a justice system that failed to deal with the problem of police *bavures*.

La Haine also addresses the violence that emerges from the anger, frustration and overall sense of powerlessness felt by young people in the disadvantaged areas of the *banlieue*. The film takes place in the aftermath of rioting on the housing estate – a destructive form of violent protest, inflicted on the community by its own members, that can be seen as an attempt by the young inhabitants of the *cité* to acquire a semblance of power and autonomy over their lives. In this context – and as more recent disturbances in the *banlieue* of Paris and other large French cities during November 2005 have once again shown – delinquency and rioting become virtually the only way for the alienated youth underclass of the *banlieue* to bring themselves to the attention of the media, politicians and a society that so often overlooks (or chooses to ignore) them (Jazouli 1992: 159).

Such violence is, typically, also directed towards the police as the embodiment of the state 'oppression' that disenfranchised *banlieue* youth come into contact with most directly. This point is well illus-trated by Vinz's repeated threats that he will kill a policeman with the gun found during the previous night's rioting if Abdel should die in hospital. The obvious significance of the gun as a phallic symbol need hardly be explained here, though in *La Haine* it takes on an added dimension in relation to the crisis of masculinity experience by the young male inhabitants of the *cité*. Vinz, Hubert and Saïd are all at different times, and to different degrees, feminised by their socio-economic status as *banlieusards*; a position that is highlighted by their joblessness, lack of money and (despite Saïd's bragging) non-existent sex lives. From the rooftop party to the trendy city art gallery, and the more sinister interrogation in the police station, the trio are, more-over, repeatedly rejected, ejected and detained, treated as passive, controlled (and thus feminised) objects by nearly all those with whom they come into contact.

This feminisation of Vinz, Hubert and Saïd is particularly pronounced upon their arrival in the city (Paris). During the demeaning interrogation that follows their arrest outside Astérix's apartment, Hubert and Saïd are subjected to physical and verbal abuse from the police officers, who apply an explicitly (hetero)sexual connotation to their 'domination' of the two youths: the interrogation takes place in a room where the walls are decorated with photos of topless female models, while the officers address Saïd and Hubert with abusive, sexualized threats and taunts.[38] Hubert and Saïd are thus objectified, denied their sexual identity and humiliated as 'weak' males in this scene. Moreover, in the context of the excessively masculine world of the *cité* presented to us by Kassovitz in *La Haine*, this feminisation of *banlieue* youth at the hands of the police in the centre of Paris is directly equated with a more general sense of humiliation and powerlessness felt not only by Saïd and Hubert, but also Vinz (even though, as we have already noted, Vinz's marginalisation in the centre of Paris is lessened as a result of his whiteness). Vinz's decision to carry the gun with him – which, tellingly, he keeps tucked in his trousers – his willingness to 'display' the weapon to those around him, along with his empty but persistent threats to avenge the death of Abdel, can thus be read as a desperate attempt to reassert his masculinity through the threat and symbols of violence.

Kassovitz explores the effect of these various displays of violence on the disenfranchised male youths of the estate through a discourse that runs alongside the main narrative, concerning the role of the media in perpetuating the negative hegemonic representations of the *banlieue*. In the opening sequence of the film, the spectator is, in fact, introduced to the *banlieue* and its inhabitants through the media: on the one hand through documentary footage of demonstrations against police brutality in central Paris and the *banlieue* and, on the other, via the newsreader's account of the previous night's rioting in the *cité*. Throughout the film, the media only appear to show an interest in Vinz, Saïd and Hubert when their behaviour is consistent with the

38 The officers mockingly suggest that Hubert looks like a girl from behind ('on dirait une gonzesse, de dos') while referring repeatedly to the two youths as 'petites suceuses' ('little cocksuckers') an insult that is deliberately qualified in the feminine form in French.

negative stereotypes assigned to them as the violent disenfranchised male youth of the *cité*. Photographers are on hand to capture the trio's fracas with the attending police officers at the hospital when they are denied access to visit Abdel. The television crew who want to record Vinz, Saïd and Hubert's reaction to the previous night's rioting are (presumably) too afraid to leave their vehicle, the reporter requesting an interview with the engine still running. Hubert's telling remark that 'On n'est pas à Thoiry ici' ('this isn't Thoiry') – referring to a safari theme park just outside Paris – displays an understanding of the extent to which the *banlieue* has become a mediatised theme park of *fracture sociale* for the media and French society at large (Vincendeau 2000: 318). However, following this shrewd evaluation of the media's presence in the *cité*, the trio appear to revert to type: hurling stones and insults at the car, they conform to their expected role as the hostile and aggressive yobs for whom the TV reporters have come looking.

Moreover, it is not only those from the dominant societal norm that appear to collude with media stereotypes of *banlieue* youth as violent delinquents, but also older residents from the estate. When Saïd calls up to the window of Vinz's apartment early in the film, his cries are met by those of an elderly black resident, angrily accusing him of participating in the previous night's rioting. Similarly, during the following scene in the family apartment, Vinz protests his innocence when accused by his grandmother of being involved in burning down the local school. Though both Saïd and Vinz have, to some extent, been involved in the disturbances on the estate, the important point to note here is that they are automatically presumed guilty by their elders, simply because they are young males from the *cité* and, by association, must therefore have been involved in the rioting and looting of the previous night

The pattern of behaviour displayed in the *cité* by Vinz, Saïd and Hubert is repeated in the second half of *La Haine*, when the trio journey into the centre of Paris. Having gate-crashed a private viewing at a gallery, they turn their attention to a couple of the female guests. Initially receptive to Hubert's introductions on behalf of the supposedly 'timid' Saïd, the pair immediately reject what they see as the Maghrebi-French youth's 'aggressive' sexual advances. Betrayed as outsiders by their dress and language – with Saïd still carrying the bruises on his face from the earlier police interrogation – the trio are ejected from the gallery by the proprietor. Their removal from this ostensibly bourgeois, 'cultured' space is accompanied by a hail of obscenities from Vinz, that ends with an uncharacteristic outburst of uncontrolled aggression from Hubert, who overturns a table as he exits.

As with the earlier confrontation in the hospital, Vinz, Hubert and Saïd effectively reinforce the prejudice against them from the bourgeois public in the gallery through their aggressive posturing and the shower of insults aimed at the assembled guests as they are ejected from the private viewing. Yet it is almost as if the trio see no other alternative to this 'expected' behaviour; as if the only way they can be acknowledged outside of the *cité* is by performing to type. Kassovitz is thus questioning the effect of media stereotypes, not only on our broader perception of the *banlieue*, but also on shaping the identity and behaviour of the male youths who inhabit these excluded spaces within society.

As Shohat and Stam have argued (2000: 390) virtually all sociopolitical struggles now take place on the 'symbolic battleground of the mass media'. In France the most obvious example in recent years has been that of the *sans papiers*: 'undocumented' immigrants living in France who are threatened (many unjustly) with deportation and who have brought their struggle to the attention of a wider French public partly as a result of the occupation of churches and public buildings – events that have gained their cause a high media profile. *La Haine* also acknowledges the importance of mainstream media perceptions of the *banlieue*. The disenfranchised male youth of the estate are keenly aware of the extent to which media images construct the wider public perception of the *banlieue* as the emblematic site of marginality and criminality. This recognition is apparent in Hubert's comments to the female journalist, discussed earlier. It also emerges during the altercation with local police on the roof of one of the apartment blocks earlier in the film. Amid the crowd, one of the youths from the estate confronts the officers by pointing a camcorder at them – a symbolic attempt to document an alternative record of events to those provided by police reports and images from the mainstream media.

And yet, as with so much else in the film, the youths from the estate are shown to be virtually powerless in their attempts to combat such negative media stereotypes of *banlieue* youth. As we have already seen, when provoked, Vinz, Saïd and Hubert appear unable to prevent themselves from conforming to type as the aggressive and hostile *banlieusard*. The trio also share with the rest of society a fascination for the spectacle of violence in the *banlieue* presented by the mainstream media – seen principally through Vinz's interest in the footage of the rioting on the estate that appears on the television in Darty's apartment. *La Haine* thus considers how the disenfranchised male youth of the *cité* are constructed by the media as totemic figures of the criminality, delinquency and violence affecting French society as a whole that are to be feared and thus controlled. Just as importantly, the film questions how the proliferation and apparent immutability of such negative media stereotypes leads to them being internalised and acted out by nihilistic *banlieue* youth . Kassovitz shows us, then, that while the mass media may well be the 'symbolic battle ground' on which socio-political struggles take place, considerable inequalities exist in this struggle in relation to power and access to the means of production.

The underlying discourse in *La Haine* on the demonisation of *banlieue* youth by the dominant societal norm offers a clear example of how the dominant societal norm attempts to control and subordinate minority social groups through their representation in the mass media and popular culture. The risk is, of course, that by exploring the socio-political realities of the *banlieue* through the experiences of the disenfranchised male youth of the urban periphery, Kassovitz's film ends up perpetuating precisely the types of stereotypes (of the disadvantaged urban periphery as a space of violence and exclusion occupied almost exclusively by male delinquents) that he intends to challenge. There are two possible responses here in defence of the film. Firstly, that the crisis facing the disenfranchised male youth of the banlieue is so acute that this uneven focus on the young male *banlieuesard* is a strategic, even political, choice by the director (a similar argument has been put forward in America for the foregrounding of African-American male subjectivities in 'hood' movies of the 1990s). Second is that Kassovitz engages with these stereotypes not to endorse but precisely to dispel the myths that surround them and to expose the ways in which the mainstream media constructs a distorted representation of *banlieue* youth that is colluded with by the dominant societal norm. The central trio of *La Haine* are therefore portrayed as complex and at times contradictory characters, challenging their devaluation as one-dimensional delinquents: Hubert deals drugs, but

largely to support his immediate family; Saïd is far from the aggressive sexual predator imagined by the young women in the Parisian art
gallery; while Vinz's aggressive macho postulating and threat to kill
a policeman should Abdel die actually masks a considerable vulnerability – one that is exposed when the opportunity arises to shoot even
a 'worthless' skinhead.

Conclusion

By challenging the impact and effect of negative stereotypes on both
wider society and *banlieue* youth themselves in *La Haine*, Kassovitz
not only addresses broader concerns with the ways in which social
and political power are mobilised through cultural discourse but also
questions how images of the marginal are circulated, received and
consumed on a local, national and global level. *La Haine*'s explosive
finale draws precisely on this series of local and global (diasporic)
references as a means of interpreting the exclusion of male youth
from the disadvantaged estates of the Parisian urban periphery. By
placing Hubert in a 'Mexican standoff'[39] with Notre Dame (a plain-
clothes officer) in the film's final scene, Kassovitz brings the conflict
between police and *banlieue* youth underpinning the narrative to an
explosive conclusion by employing a dramatic technique originally
found in Peckinpah's 1960s westerns and more recently revived by
Hong Kong action-*auteur* John Woo (and, of course, Tarantino). And
yet Kassovitz does not allow this spectacular display of male violence
to detract from the film's exploration of social exclusion as experienced by alienated male *banlieue* youth. As the shot(s) ring out, the
screen is plunged into darkness and, just as importantly, silence. The
credits that follow the final scene appear against a black screen, again,
without sound. We do not, therefore, know the outcome of the armed
stand-off between Hubert and the policeman – was there one shot, or
two? Were the guns in fact fired into the air? But we are left to imagine
the likely outcome – another pointless death in the *banlieue* – and
thus forced to reflect on the circumstances that have brought events
to their violent conclusion.

Of course, Kassovitz is running a risk with this strategy of placing

39 The term refers to a violent dramatic device whereby two protagonists involved
   in an armed face-off are left with each holding a gun to the other's head.

social struggles in the popular sphere. Popular culture is after all the site of commodification – the place where culture enters into circuits of power, capital, technology and desire. The danger in *Métisse* and *La Haine* then is that, as Hall (1996: 468) puts it: 'there is always a price of incorporation to be paid when the cutting edge of difference and transgression is blunted into spectacularization'. However, as Kassovitz has shown with his use of street culture and hip-hop iconography in these two films, the line between the commercial and the political; between selling out to the mainstream and 'keeping it real' for the underground is never that clearly defined.

In the context of *Métisse*, the incorporation that Hall speaks of comes from working within the framework of popular French comedy – traditionally a space in which difference can be foregrounded, provided that, in the end, the contradictions or tensions engendered by such difference are in some way resolved in relation to the dominant societal norm. And yet, Kassovitz uses this quintessentially popular French genre as, precisely, the space in which to challenge rather than assuage mainstream attitudes and anxieties concerning issues of cultural or ethnic difference and the 'certainties' of national identity in a postcolonial French society. Thus, as the possibility of a third potential father of the baby is introduced by Lola in the final gag of the film, tensions or contradictions within the newly formed postcolonial family remain unresolved.

In *La Haine*, the spectacularisation of difference and transgression proved much more controversial, leading Kassovitz to be accused of producing 'designer' visions of exclusion. Nevertheless, as has been argued earlier in this chapter, Kassovitz does not provide a film that is all style and no substance. Instead he resists through subcultural style, while using the heavily stylised and visually seductive *mise en scène* to enhance (not detract from) the film's social-political 'message'. Moreover – and as Vincendeau (2000: 319) has identified in relation to *La Haine*'s 'spectacular male violence' – such an approach is entirely necessary if Kassovitz is to reach and inform the cross-over mainstream, national (and, indeed, international) audience he desires for his particular brand of social cinema.

References

Alexander, Karen (1995), 'La Haine', Vertigo, 5 (autumn/winter), 45–6

Begag, Azouz and Rossini, Reynald (1999), Du bon usage de la distance chez les sauvageons, Paris: Seuil

Boulay, Anne and Colmant, Marie (1995), '"La Haine ne nous appartient plus"' (interview with Kassovitz), Libération, (31 May)

Bourguignon, Thomas and Tobin, Yann (1995) 'Entretien avec Mathieu Kassovitz: les cinq dernières secondes', Positif, June, 8–13

Bosséno, Christian (1992), 'Immigrant cinema: national cinema. The case of Beur cinema', in Richard Dyer and Ginette Vincendeau (eds) Popular European Cinema, London: Routledge, 47–57

Blumenfeld, Samuel (1995), 'On a raison de se révolter' (review of Etat des Lieux (Richet, 1995)), Les Inrockuptibles, (14 June), 27

Celmar, Rep and Dufrense, David (1995), 'De la croisette à la villette', Libération, (5 June)

Dale, Martin (1997), The Movie Game: The Film Business in Britain, Europe and America, London: Cassell

Dubet, François and Lapeyronnie, Didier (1992), Les quartiers d'exil, Paris: Seuil

Durmelat, Sylvie (1998), 'Petite histoire du mot beur: ou comment prendre la parole quand on vous le prête', French Cultural Studies, 9 ii (26), 191–208

Ferenezi, Aurélien (1995), 'Je ne veux pas qu'on trouve mon film sympa' (interview with Kassovitz), Infomatin, (31 May)

Hall, Stuart (1981), 'Notes on deconstructing the popular', People's History and Socialist Theory, in Raphael Samuel (ed.), People's History and socialist theory London: Routledge, 227–40

—— (1996), 'What is this "black" in black popular culture?' in Morley, David and Kuan-Hsing, Chen (eds), Stuart Hall: Critical Dialogues in Cultural Studies, London and New York, Routledge

Harris, Sue (2004), 'New direction in French cinema: introduction', French Cultural Studies, 15 (3), October, 211–17

Hargreaves, Alec G. (1996), 'A deviant construction: the French media and the banlieues', New Community, 22 (4), 607–18

Hebdige, Dick (1979), Subculture: The Meaning of Style, London/New York: Methuen

—— (1981), Hiding in the Light, London: Routledge

—— (1988), Hiding in the Light, London and New York: Routledge.

Jazouli, Adil (1992), Les Années Banlieues, Paris: Seuil

Jousse, Thierry (1995), 'Le banlieue-film existe-t-il ?', Cahiers du cinéma, 492, 37–9

Kaganski, Serge and Blumenfeld Samuel (1995), 'Contrebande', Les Inrockuptibles, (14 June), 24–7

Kassovitz (1998),'Les aventures de Mathieu Kassovitz' interview in Steadycam, consulted at www.mathieukassovitz.com/itw/steadycam.htm (site last accessed 19/7/05)

Klifa, Thierry and d'Yvoire, Christophe (1993), 'Metteurs en scène: premiers pas', Studio, December, 108–12

Levieux, Michèle (1995), 'Le noir et blanc draine plus de réalisme' (interview with Kassovitz), *L'Humainté*, (29 May), 20

Loshitzky, Yosefa (2005), 'The post-Holocaust Jew in the age of postcolonialism: *La Haine* revisited', *Studies in French Cinema*, 5 (2), 137–47

Maspero, François (1990), *Les passagers du Roissy Express*, Paris: Seuil

Morley, David and Kuan-Hsing, Chen (eds) (1996), *Stuart Hall: Critical Dialogues in Cultural Studies*, London/New York, Routledge

Reader, Keith (1995), 'After the riot', *Sight & Sound*, November, 12–14

Rémy, Serge (1995), 'Banlieue haute tension', *L'Humainté*, (29 May), 20

Remy, Vincent (1995), 'Entretien avec Mathieu Kassovitz: "C'est pas interdit de parler aux mecs des banlieues"', *Télérama*, 2368, (31 May), pp. 42–6

Rey, Henri (1996), *La Peur des banlieues*, Paris: Presses de la Fondation Nationale des Sciences Politiques

Reynaud, Bérénice (1996), 'Le'hood: *Hate* and its neighbors', *Film Comment*, 32 (2), March/April, 54–8

Rouchy, Marie Elisabeth (1995), *Télérama*, 2372, (28 June)

Rozenberg, G. (1993), 'Lola un peu autrement', *Le Quotidien de Paris*, (18 August).

Shohat, Elia Habiba and Stam, Robert (2000), 'Film theory and spectatorship in the age of the posts' in *Reinventing Film Studies*, Christine Gledhill and Linda Williams, London: Routledge, 381–401

Tarr, Carrie (1997), 'French cinema and postcolonial minorities', in Alec Hargreaves and Mark McKinney (eds) *Postcolonial Cultures in France*, London, Routledge

—— (1999), 'Ethnicity and identity in the *cinéma de banlieue*', in Phil Powrie (ed) *French Cinema in the 1990s: continuity and difference*, Oxford: Oxford University Press, 172–84

Tobin, Yann (1995), 'État des (ban)lieues', *Positif*, 415, 28–30

Vincendeau, Ginette (2000), 'Designs on the banlieue: Mathieu Kassovitz's *La Haine* (1995)', in Susan Hayward and Ginette Vincendeau (eds), *French Film: Texts and Contexts*, London, Routledge

Vincendeau, Ginette (2001), 'Café Society', *Sight & Sound*, 11/8, 22–5

Wieviora, M. (1999), *Violence in France*, Paris: Seuil

3

Postmodern social fables

As has already been suggested in the previous chapter, there are compelling arguments for viewing Kassovitz's first three feature films as constituting a *'fracture sociale* trilogy'. This is not to say, however, that alongside the continuities there are not also differences between the three films. If *La Haine* had already marked a shift from the lighter comic tone of *Métisse* towards a more combative sense of resistance through hip-hop style and an impending sense of social crisis, then in *Assassin(s)* (1997), the final part of the trilogy, Kassovitz was to move towards an altogether bleaker, increasingly nihilistic vision of contemporary French society. Although *La Haine* takes place in the aftermath of rioting provoked by a police *bavure* and ends with the shooting of Vinz (and possibly Hubert), the explosive violence that threatens to break through in the various confrontations between *banlieue* youth and the police is, for the most part, contained until the final moments of the film. In *Assassin(s)*, this violence, its affects and consequences are played out from the start and in far more explicit and controversial fashion. Consequently, whereas Kassovitz's previous two features attempted essentially to engage (socio-politically speaking) with their popular audience at the same time as entertaining them, *Assassin(s)*'s polemical approach aims to confront, enrage and disgust its spectator into responding to the social issues of violence and youth alienation played out on screen.

Assassin(s) tells the story of Max Pujol; an aimless 20-something, who having lost his father as a child, lives alone with his unsympathetic mother in the Paris suburbs. With limited aspirations, and few future prospects beyond the short-term vocational training course on which he is enrolled, Max engages in acts of petty crime along with Mehdi, a teenager from the run-down estate adjacent to Max's home, who is obsessed with money, cars, television and video games. Having broken into a local supermarket one night, Max stumbles on the bodies of the store manager and a female employee who have been murdered. This gruesome discovery leads Max to Wagner, an ageing professional killer who inducts him into his world of violence and murder. Following a botched assassination – undertaken while his mentor is in hospital – Max is shot dead by Wagner for having enlisted the help of Mehdi. The killing results in an armed stand-off between Wagner and Mehdi, with the former reluctantly accepting to train the latter – his only remaining accomplice. In the final third of the film, Wagner decides to quit his 'trade' due to deteriorating physical and mental health, and orders Mehdi to return to school. After performing a mock execution on Wagner as he lies in his bed, Mehdi leaves to carry out a previously agreed contract killing on an affluent middle-aged woman as she sleeps in her home. The next morning, Mehdi arrives at the gates of his school where he is refused entry by a security guard. The film ends with a television newsroom report that shows CCTV footage of Mehdi carrying out the random assassination of students and teachers at his former school before eventually taking his own life.

Strictly speaking, *Assassin(s)* was inspired by the director's early short film of the same name. Kassovitz became interested in developing the characters and germ of a storyline – the violent initiation of a young man into the world of a hired killer – contained within the 10 minute short. From here, emerged the idea for the two-hour feature film. Despite its links to the original short film, in many ways *Assassin(s)* could not have been made without *La Haine*. Firstly, because the critical and commercial success of *La Haine* meant Kassovitz was able to secure a sizeable budget of FF 40 million for his next feature – twice that of *La Haine* – along with the promise of considerable artistic freedom to develop the project in the way that he saw fit. The director also benefited from the continuity provided by producer Christophe Rossignon who had worked with him since his first short, *Fierrot le pou*. Secondly, *Assassin(s)* could not have been made by Kassovitz without the experience of *La Haine* in the sense that the open hostility towards the mass media (and above all television) contained within the narrative of *Assassin(s)* was largely borne out of Kassovitz's own negative dealings with the French media following the release of his second feature (Kassovitz 1998).

Finally, *Assassin(s)* is linked to *La Haine* in the sense that it develops a discourse established in the earlier film concerning the role of the media in perpetuating stereotypes of a disenfranchised youth class as violent, nihilistic and out of control – and the extent to which such media stereotypes are internalised and acted out by *banlieue* youth. An indication of the way in which Kassovitz would expand this socio-political subject matter in *Assassin(s)* can be found in the montage sequence from *La Haine* where Vinz hides from the police in a cinema in central Paris. As he switches from screen to screen in the cinema, he watches a series of violent American films that the spectator of *La Haine* hears, but does not see, such as *Dirty Harry* (Siegel, 1971) and *Predator* (McTiernan, 1987). Vinz is then shown sitting alongside a mother and her son watching an animated movie, making the shape of a gun with his hands and firing imaginary bullets at the screen – a gesture that is copied by the young boy. By alluding to the negative effect on youth of violence disseminated by mass media, but also the way in which an acceptance of such violence is passed on from one generation to another, this scene from *La Haine* prefigures the key themes and preoccupations of *Assassin(s)*.

One further consequence of *La Haine*'s success for *Assassin(s)* was that it brought Kassovitz to the attention of the highly respected, veteran French screen actor Michel Serrault. Despite harbouring certain reservations about the film, Serrault, who had also been impressed by Kassovitz's performance in *Regarde les hommes tomber* (Audiard, 1994), accepted to play the ageing assassin Wagner on condition that Kassovitz acted alongside him in the role of Max. Though wary of the additional pressures this would place on him during the shoot, Kassovitz was adamant that the film could not be made without Serrault and so agreed to the actor's demands. This included bringing filming forward six months to fit in with Serrault's other professional commitments, despite the fact that the script (co-authored by Kassovitz and director Nicolas Boukhrief) was not yet finished.

The resultant shoot was a demanding and tense affair, especially for Kassovitz who was working on both sides of the camera, while also completing nightly revisions to the script for the next day's scenes (Les Frères K 1997: 54). Due to Serrault's limited availability, Kassovitz was forced to work intensively for one month with the veteran actor, and then one month on the remaining scenes with the debutant Mehdi Benoufa, who had been cast in the role of the delinquent youth, Mehdi.[1] Additional pressure was added to an already demanding shoot in that the film had to be completed in time for screening at Cannes in May 1997, where it would be opening the festival. Complications arose between the director and his technical crew – many of whom had worked on Kassovitz's two previous films – who were unhappy with the constant changes being made to the shooting script; or, in Kassovitz's opinion (1998) had become complacent since the success of *La Haine*. The professional and personal tensions on set combined with the film's nihilistic narrative, bleak subject matter and graphic portrayal of violence, pushed Kassovitz to the edge of physical, creative and emotional exhaustion – according to Serrault (*Nouvel Observateur* 1997) there were some days where filming would be abandoned altogether because Kassovitz was unhappy or unsure of the direction the film was taking.

'A film made to be hated'

Once finished, Kassovitz's own doubts about the film that had surfaced during shooting were compounded by an excessively hostile response from the French press at Cannes – a situation that was, it must be said, exacerbated by the director's behaviour (at turns provocative and uncooperative) during press conferences at the festival. Amid a torrent of bad reviews, one critic from *Figaro* (Baignères 1997) famously dubbed *Assassin(s)*: 'Le film le plus nul depuis l'invention du cinéma'.[2] Although Kassovitz claimed (1998) to have been expecting a backlash against his first film post-*La Haine*, even he must have been surprised by the vitriolic attacks directed at both director and film by French reviewers. He did point out, however (*ibid.*), that, while the press screening of the film had been a disaster, *Assassin(s)* was much better received by the public at Cannes; thus maintaining a position (one shared with Luc Besson) in which the general audience response is valorised far in excess of the critics' opinions.[3]

1 Interestingly, in the original screenplay for *Assassin(s)* the character of Mehdi had been called Félix – a reference to *Métisse* and further evidence of the interconnectedness of the three films as a trilogy.
2 'the most worthless film since the invention of cinema'.
3 'Par contre, à la grande projection, il y a eu plus d'applaudissements que de sifflets. Mais ça, les journalistes n'en ont pas parlé'. / 'Whereas at the gala screening there was more applause than whistling. But the journalists didn't talk about that'.

Elsewhere, Kassovitz's response in the face of such extreme criticism of the film has been inconsistent. On the one hand, he has offered a (typically) robust and outspoken defence of his work: describing *Assassin(s)* (ibid.) as a 'testament' to the socio-political realities of its time, and the film of which he is most proud. On the other, in an extended interview with *Première* (Les Frères K 1997: 50–4) Kassovitz effectively dismissed his attempts at a serious exploration of violence in *Assassin(s)* in favour of the superficial and highly stylised violence of Jan Kounen's *Dobermann* (1997) – a film that was released in the same month as *Assassin(s)*.

The schizoid attitude displayed by the director to his own film (both during and after production) is, perhaps unsurprisingly, reflected in the filmic text itself. With its relatively large budget, high-profile release at the Cannes festival and casting of Serrault in the starring role, *Assassin(s)* appeared to signal Kassovitz's arrival in mainstream French cinema following the cross-over success of *La Haine*. The film essentially reworks popular American genre cinema (the violent neo-*noir* thriller) using the established trope of the *tueur à gages* or hired killer, most memorably employed in French cinema by Jean-Pierre Melville in *Le Samouraï* (1967) – a director much admired by Kassovitz, who shared the young filmmaker's passion for American film culture. *Assassin(s)* employs the high production values typically associated with mainstream cinema in both France and Hollywood that Kassovitz has always aspired to in his work but which, for financial reasons, had been far more of a struggle to reproduce in his earlier films, in particular *Métisse*. *Assassin(s)* thus contains subtle special effects; expansive camera work; precise, stylised lighting in certain scenes (in keeping with contemporary American neo-*noir* thrillers *The Usual Suspects* (Singer, 1995) and *Se7en* (Fincher, 1995));[4] as well as a mix of studio-bound interiors and elaborate location shoots – such as the car chase through Paris. The choice of Carter Burwell's understated, but conventional, orchestral score to heighten atmosphere and audience reaction in particular scenes is further evidence of *Assassin(s)*' more mainstream production values. It also marks a distinct change from the soundtrack found in Kassovitz's previous

4 The sequence in which Max and Wagner murder Mr Vidal is exemplary in this regard, although elsewhere – for example at the racecourse or during the car chase – the chiaroscuro lighting is rejected by Kassovitz and his director of photography, Pierre Aïm, in favour of more naturalistic 'flat' lighting.

films which tend to rely exclusively on ambient, diegetic sound or else employ modern pop/rap music to establish tone or mood.

And yet, unlike Kassovitz's previous 'social' films, *Assassin(s)* also contains elements that consciously subvert or deny the mainstream pleasures found in the film – and not only because of its explicit representation of violence. The final edit is over two hours long, whereas both *La Haine* and *Métisse* run for almost exactly ninety minutes – the preferred length of mainstream distributors and exhibitors. Narrative structure is also more fragmented and less dynamic than in Kassovitz's previous feature films. *Métisse* is driven by the antagonistic relationship between Félix and Jamal that emerges as a result of the enigma surrounding Lola's pregnancy (who is the father of the baby?). In *La Haine*, despite the occasional surreal tangents taken by the film – for example the Grunwalski interlude, or Vinz's daydreams (the cow on the estate; the killing of the policeman in Les Halles) – the narrative is arguably even more tightly structured with the day carefully divided into chronological segments and between socio-geographic spaces (Paris and the estate). Moreover, the threat of confrontation between police and *banlieue* youth in *La Haine* simmers beneath the surface – all of which leads, seemingly inexorably, to the film's explosive finale. In contrast, *Assassin(s)*'s narrative develops unevenly and does not follow the conventional cause-and-effect logic preferred by mainstream narrative cinema, where characters' psychological motivation for the acts they commit are clearly mapped out for the spectator. The behaviour of the protagonists in *Assassin(s)* is, instead, largely contingent, and, at times, their actions go unexplained. We understand little of the psychology of either Mehdi or Wagner; whereas Max, the character with whom the audience are most encouraged to develop a sense of empathy, is unexpectedly killed off a little over half way through the film.

Kassovitz has claimed (Tirard 2000) that *Assassin(s)* was the first film in which he took himself seriously as an 'artist'. Despite its mainstream production values, the film displays a willingness to experiment in order to disconcert its audience; an approach that is more commonly associated with art cinema. It is worth noting here that Kassovitz had not previously been prepared to adopt this more experimental approach in either the consensual comedy of *Métisse* or the seductive spectacle of *La Haine*. The personal worldview expressed in *Assassin(s)* and use of form and style to frame socio-political debates therefore brings the film closer to more traditional notions of the *auteur* in post-war French cinema from which Kassovitz has consistently attempted to distance himself.

While the looser narrative structure, repeated last-minute revisions to the script and the inclusion of contingent, undefined characters in *Assassin(s)*, undoubtedly reflect a desire on the part of the director for greater experimentation, they also emerged as a result of the constraints placed on the film at all stages of production. As already mentioned, development of the screenplay for *Assassin(s)* was curtailed by nearly six months due to Serrault's other professional commitments, leading to an unfinished script being constantly revised onset. Comparing the published version of the original screenplay (Kassovitz and Boukhrief 1997) with the film itself, there are a number of significant revisions – the majority of which appear to have been introduced as a result of Serrault's absence during the second half of filming. The most obvious of these is a greater emphasis on the insertion of TV images and the film's 'zapping' aesthetic associated with Max and Mehdi. There is also a lack of scenes contextualising Wagner's past, or helping to explain Mehdi's own motivations. Similarly, a number of scenes which gave further substance to the relationship between Max and Wagner have been omitted from the film, as well as a meeting with a character named Léon – whose inclusion was presumably intended, in part, as a reference (or homage) to the eponymous hero of Luc Besson's *Léon* (1994).

In addition to the highly pressured development of the script, leading to a somewhat extemporaneous, experimental shoot, the deadline for screening at the Cannes festival in May 1997 greatly accelerated the editing process. Kassovitz has suggested (1998) that the final cut of *Assassin(s)* screened at the festival and then immediately placed on general release would have benefited from a greater cohesion – in practical terms, the removal of scenes totalling at least ten minutes' worth of film. And yet, the tensions and conflicts – stylistic, thematic, ideological – found within *Assassin(s)* that make it a more demanding and, at times, contradictory film, also deliberately function to foreground the controversial issues Kassovitz wishes to address, propelling the peripatetic and sometimes faltering narrative to its bleak conclusion.

Generational conflict: *film noir* versus the TV aesthetic

The most obvious of the thematic tensions running through the narrative is that of generational conflict. Kassovitz places an antagonistic cross-generational trio at the centre of *Assassin(s)*. In his mid-sixties, Wagner represents the past: an older generation that retains some semblance of control, but which is ailing and whose time will soon be at an end. Mehdi, the teenage delinquent from the run-down housing estate is the future: a nightmarish vision of an anomic and nihilistic youth class who appear entirely disconnected from any sense of community or civic responsibility. Finally, Max, in his late twenties, occupies a mediatory position between Wagner and Mehdi (the old and young). He also embodies the present – Kassovitz's generation – those born in the 1960s and 1970s who have grown up to find the supposed ideological certainties and economic assurances of their parents' era replaced by a distinct sense of uncertainty, precariousness and social dislocation. In broader, more allegorical terms, this generational conflict can be read in two ways. First, as a confrontation between France's ageing, reactionary political class and an alienated youth class: Wagner is, significantly, approximately the same age as Chirac – a politician whose election to the Elysée palace in 1995 was according to Reader (1995: 14) 'symptomatic of ideological and political exhaustion and the sense of powerlessness it brings in its train'. There is also the suggestion – contained in the old photo album discovered by Mehdi – that Wagner, like Chirac, (and indeed Le Pen)[5] may have served in the Algeria war; further aligning the ageing assassin with this older generation of ideologically compromised politicians who appear largely out of touch with the realities of everyday life for an alienated multiethnic youth underclass. More specifically, in the context of contemporary French cinema, this generational conflict might equally be read as one between a younger generation of *jeunes cinéastes énervés* such as those outlined at the end of Chapter 1 (Kassovitz, Gans, Kounen, *et al.*) and the more embedded practices of an artisanal, *auteur*-led French cinema.

Wagner is thus the dysfunctional patriarch, imparting the secrets

5   Wagner's blatant homophobic and racist outbursts at dinner with Max's mother as well as his dismissive attitude towards the 'liberal' approach of the arresting officers in the police station could equally associate him with the leader of the French National Front.

of his deadly trade to Max (the proto-son), who in turn attempts to pass these onto Mehdi. The first direct evidence of this generational conflict that runs through the narrative comes when Wagner shoots at Max for having entered his apartment without permission. Wagner's benevolent act at the police station – agreeing not to press charges – is, we later discover, only motivated by a desire to initiate Max into the world of the hired killer. During the meal at the Pujol home that follows, the palpable sense of a divisive ideological and cultural gap between the generations is complimented by the *mise en scène*. Visibly uncomfortable with the racist and homophobic jokes being traded over the dining table, Max sits on the sofa with his back to Wagner and his mother. He is placed at the front of the frame; bathed in a cold blue light from the television, while Mme Pujol and Wagner, who are deliberately filmed slightly out of focus during the first part of the scene, sit in the brightly lit background.

Elsewhere in *Assassin(s)*, this spatially coded generational conflict within the *mise en scène* threatens to explode into violence in the Mexican stand-off that takes place between Mehdi and Wagner following the death of Max. Significantly, Max is killed by Wagner precisely at the time when he is developing a greater rapport with his proto-father; as if Kassovitz's intention is to refuse any sense of intergenerational harmony within the narrative. Relations between Wagner and Mehdi are, if anything, even more strained. Wagner is unable to understand the teenager's fascination with television and violent video games; while, for his part, Mehdi refuses to submit to the law of the (proto-) father, disobeying Wagner's 'order' for him to leave the apartment and return to school. The only common ground shared by the two protagonists, then, is an impulse towards violence.

The purpose of placing this intergenerational trio at the centre of *Assassin(s)* is, presumably, to avoid associating the problems of violence found in contemporary French society solely with youth. More specifically, Kassovitz holds the older generations (including his own) responsible for the violent example – disseminated through the media and perpetrated in real life – that has been passed on to an alienated youth underclass:

> Au bout d'un moment, à un certain niveau de merdier, dans les quartiers, dans les cités, les gens les plus violents, ceux qui font peur, sont ceux qui ont 15 ans parce qu'ils n'en ont plus rien à foutre. Et

c'est à cause de l'éducation qu'on leur a donnée et surtout de l'exemple qu'on leur a montré. (Kassovitz 1997)[6]

This notion of collective responsibility was emphasised by the posters used to promote the release of *Assassin(s)* – also placed on the cover of the video and DVD – in which Wagner seems to be offering a gun to the spectator, with the caption below reading 'Toute société a les crimes qu'elle mérite'.[7]

In a similar way – and perhaps mindful of the criticisms levelled against *La Haine* – Kassovitz elected in *Assassin(s)* to move beyond the *cité* as the exclusive and emblematic site of social crisis. Though Mehdi fits the somewhat predictable type of delinquent Maghrebi-French youth from a deprived housing estate, Wagner lives in a 'traditional' working-class district of Paris, while Max has been brought up in a nondescript working-class *pavillon* (suburban house). The *pavillon* is nonetheless qualified in *Assassin(s)* as a space of marginality both by virtue of its proximity to the run-down estate, and the fact that it is bordered by a motorway flyover – presumably the *périphérique* ring road that encircles Paris – and railway bridge; identifying it as a type of 'non-place' or geo-social space of exclusion similar to the Les Muguets estate in *La Haine*, easily bypassed or overlooked by the rest of society.

Foregrounding the trio of Wagner, Max and Mehdi as in some way 'representative' of French society is, of course, problematic. Not least because – as had happened previously in *La Haine* – by focusing exclusively on male subjectivity Kassovitz effectively excludes female experience from the social. This position appears to be confirmed by the characterisation of Max's mother in the film (played by Danièle Lebrun). The only female protagonist of any substance to appear briefly in *Assassin(s)*, she is placed exclusively in the domestic sphere – thus denying her any wider socio-political relevance in the narrative. She is, moreover, portrayed as a 'bad' matriarch: exasperated by Max's delinquent activities, she either berates her son, or else infantilises him by addressing him using the childish nickname of 'Pitoune'.

The conflict between an ailing, established order and a nihilistic

6 'In the neighbourhoods and on the housing estates, there comes a point when things are so messed up that those who arouse the most fear are 15-year-old kids who no longer give a damn. And this is down to the education they've been given and, above all, the example we have shown them.'

7 'Every society has the crimes that it deserves'.

youth class is, equally, played out through stylistic tensions in *Assassin(s)*. The characteristic elements of Kassovitz's visual style established in his earlier films – a carefully controlled *mise en scène* that combines mobile camerawork with precisely executed long takes and elaborate composition – remain, but are placed alongside two competing styles: the 'zapping' aesthetic associated with Mehdi and Max, and classical references to *noir* cinema, linked predominantly (though not exclusively) to Wagner.

Stylistically, the neo-*noir* influence in *Assassin(s)* is most apparent in the use of contrastive (chiaroscuro) lighting, a composite visual element of *film noir* that alludes to both the characters disturbed psychology and their moral ambiguity. The chiaroscuro style is associated with the violence we see on screen and is deliberately applied in certain key sequences – such as the murder of Mr Vidal, and Mehdi's first solo contract killing – as well as to specific locations; most notably the interior of Wagner's flat. It is, moreover, combined with the cold blue light emitted from the various television screens we encounter in the diegesis and a muted palette of greens, browns and greys found in the décor and clothing of these key scenes.

Before the first murder, Max and Wagner – in classic *noir* fashion – move in and out of the shadows as they pass under the streetlamps outside Mr Vidal's home. When they force their way into the house, the glow emitted from the television in the living room adds to the effect of the contrastive lighting employed in the room. Following the murder, Max remains motionless in the street outside, still unable to come to terms with the act he has just committed, looking on as Wagner disappears once more into the shadows beneath the railway bridge. This use of *noir*-style lighting in *Assassin(s)* is not constant, however. In other scenes – for example at the racecourse, the police station and outside Mehdi's school – Kassovitz and his director of photography Pierre Aïm opt for 'flatter', more naturalistic lighting. The effect of these aesthetic decisions is, therefore, to create a conflict within the *mise en scène* that reflects the broader tensions running through the film.

References to American *noir* and neo-*noir* in Kassovitz's film are not only stylistic. The urban setting of *Assassin(s)*, its emphasis on violence and alienation, as well as its focus on three generations of masculinity in crisis binds the film closely to many of the classic conventions and atmosphere of *film noir*. In particular, it evokes

Scorsese's *Taxi Driver* (1976) – one of the most violent American neo-*noirs* ever to reach a mainstream audience. Indeed, Kassovitz 'borrows' certain visual techniques from *Taxi Driver*, notably the slow overhead tracking shot as a means of contemplating the result of the violence that has just been played out on screen. The overhead shot that moves from the Mexican stand-off between Wagner and Mehdi to Max's corpse – repeated in Wagner's flat after Mehdi returns from his first solo contract killing – evokes the penultimate scene from *Taxi Driver* where the camera surveys from above the bloody aftermath of Travis's attempt to rescue Iris from her pimp. *Assassin(s)* also contains further intertextual references to Scorsese's film, such as the extreme close-up of an aspirin dissolving in a glass of water shot from the point of view of Max/Travis, as well as, more generally, the restless panning and tracking of the camera synonymous with the visual style of *Taxi Driver*.[8]

If Wagner is naturally associated with the more classical *noir* elements that surface intermittently in *Assassin(s)*, then Mehdi and Max are more closely aligned with the postmodern 'zapping aesthetic' employed in the film. This term refers to the viewing practices of contemporary (youth) television spectators who switch (zap) randomly from one channel to another, creating a fragmented viewing experience that is primarily characterised by its discontinuity. In *Assassin(s)* the 'real' world of the diegesis – that is to say, the one inhabited by Max, Mehdi and Wagner – is thus interspersed and juxtaposed with images and excerpts from television: variety shows, wildlife documentaries, news reports, commercials and a violent parody of the inane teen-sitcom *Hélène et les garçons*. The extent to which these TV images intrude into the filmic world of *Assassin(s)* varies. Sometimes, as with Max's opening monologue, the Nike advert or the parody of *Hélène*, the TV image occupies the entire screen, displacing the diegetic world inhabited by Max, Mehdi and Wagner. (In this context, the 'colonisation' of the cinema screen by the TV image is a telling metaphor for the extent to which, since the early 1990s, French film production has become increasingly dependent on investment from the small screen.) More often, though, these TV inserts are contained within the diegesis – integrated into the décor by their appearance on the screens of sets being watched by the protagonists. Dialogue between Max and Mehdi frequently takes place in front of the TV,

8 For a detailed analysis of *Taxi Driver* as *film noir*, see Kolker (2000: 217–22).

with the camera positioned as if offering a point-of-view shot from the television itself and the youthful protagonists bathed in the light emanating from the small screen.

Although not dominating the film to the extent found in *Merci la vie* (Blier, 1991) – where colour, spatial and temporal dislocation and multiple narrative strands are highlighted to a much greater degree – Kassovitz's use of the zapping aesthetic in *Assassin(s)* nonetheless has a destabilising effect on both narrative and *mise en scène*. The director's intention was to leave the cinema audience with the impression that they were indeed flicking through channels on a television set: 'je voulais qu'un petit gosse regarde la télé, qu'il tombe sur le film *Assassin(s)* et au milieu du film il zappe parce que le film était trop long' (Les Frères K 1997: 54).[9] Even in their more 'contained' mode, the presence of these images on TV screens in *Assassin(s)* goes beyond mere decoration to constitute an active element within the *mise en scène*. One such example comes during the murder of Mr Vidal, where the 'natural' violence presented in the wildlife documentary is juxtaposed with Max's initiation into the world of the hired killer. The small screen also bears witness to the violent acts committed within the diegesis: Max views the stolen surveillance videotape of Wagner murdering the supermarket boss and one of the cashiers on a television set in his bedroom, while the CCTV images of Mehdi killing teachers and classmates that appear on the TV news are passively viewed by Wagner from the residential home to which he has been admitted.[10] Television can therefore be said to constitute a fourth protagonist in *Assassin(s)*; one that replays, accompanies (and is thus implicated in) the violence committed by all three central protagonists.

Most contemporary reviewers criticised the insertion of these televisual fragments into the narrative of *Assassin(s)*, claiming either that the link between violent images from the small screen and the violent acts committed was too simplistic (Murat 1997: 42 and Lefort 1997) or else that the TV images inserted were simply too random – signifying little or nothing in relation to the film's narrative (Jeancolas 1997a: 120). Such a response reflects the extent to which (and not for the first

9 'I wanted it to be like a little kid watching the TV who chances on *Assassin(s)* and in the middle of the film switches over because it's too long.'

10 In the same shot an apparition of the dead Max, seated out of focus behind Wagner, can also be made out by the attentive viewer.

time) Kassovitz's intentions for his film have been misunderstood by French critics. In fact, the arbitrary nature and sense of discontinuity engendered by the TV images inserted into *Assassin(s)* is precisely the point – the images are not all supposed to make sense, nor necessarily be of direct relevance to the action that takes place. For Max, zapping even becomes a means of evading reality. When forced by Wagner to assume responsibility for the killing of Mr Vidal he temporarily 'switches over'; retreating into the 'safety' of the inane variety programme playing on the television in the background. Max's intention is, precisely, to watch something that has no relevance to the ugly reality of the violence that surrounds him – placing himself in front of the small screen in an attempt to block out the desperate cries for mercy coming from his beaten and bloodied victim.

For Mehdi, however, television does not offer a means of retreating from reality. Instead it emphasises how the line between lived experience and mediatised reality for the teenager has been blurred. In a scene from *Assassin(s)* that was criticised for supposedly oversimplifying the link between television and violence, Mehdi murders a rich woman as she sleeps in her bed. Having casually flicked through the channels on the TV set in the room, he returns to the body to discharge the remaining bullets from his gun. The scene in question undoubtedly works in a none too subtle way to reinforce the position maintained throughout the film by Kassovitz regarding the harmful effect of television violence on its audience. For his part, the director claimed that this direct and polemical approach was deliberate, intended to provoke a reaction: 'Faut enfoncer le clou. Faut être vulgaire. La sophistication je la laisse à B.H-L'[11] (Murat 1997: 42). And yet, Mehdi is not merely presented as a 'natural-born killer' whose violent predisposition is instantly awoken by the small screen. Indeed, we should note that he commits the initial violent act (firing the bullet that kills his victim) before sitting down to watch the television. The fact that he returns to the body after zapping through the programmes on offer is, therefore, more usefully read as an indication of the teenager's inability to distinguish between fantasy and the horrific reality of his actions.

What is more, the images consumed by Mehdi in *Assassin(s)* do not constitute a constant diet of hard-core violence and murder. Instead,

11 'You have to make your point forcefully. You have to be crass. I'll leave sophistication to B. H-L [writer-philosopher Bernard Henri-Lévy]'.

it is a mixture of the shockingly violent and the insipid or banal that emerges from the small screen as the teenager casually flicks through the channels on offer. For Mehdi, then, violence is subsumed into a mixture of game-shows, documentaries, commercials and sitcoms, until it becomes just one more element of the programming/reality on offer. The vapid French teen-sitcom *Hélène et les garçons* is thus transformed on the small-screen of *Assassin(s)* into a disturbing parade of rape and extreme violence, accompanied by canned laughter, that is consumed indifferently by its youth audience. In the same way, when Wagner takes Max to a crowded fast-food restaurant, the two men munch on burgers and fries while they discuss the most suitable weapon for killing the customers that surround them. The distinction between the real world and the mediatised 'reality' emanating from the small screen becomes increasingly hard to determine for *both* spectator and protagonist. In this respect, the zapping aesthetic employed in *Assassin(s)* accurately reflects the blurring of boundaries between the real world and the mediatised reality of the violent acts perpetuated in the film. It is, moreover, entirely appropriate that Mehdi and Max should engage with a mode of reception that is essentially fragmented and decentred – reflecting, as it does, their own alienated position outside of the societal norm.

Media, violence and nihilistic youth

Kassovitz (1998) described *Assassin(s)* as 'un film fait pour être détesté':[12] not only because it anticipated the critical backlash against his work post-*La Haine*, but also due to the film's extreme and uncompromising portrayal of violence. Put another way, *Assassin(s)* functions on the premise that it is not possible to make a 'pleasant' film denouncing violence:

> L'ambition d'*Assassin(s)* c'était de mettre quelqu'un devant un écran de télé et de le laisser les yeux ouverts, comme dans *Orange Mécanique*. Le but du film, c'était: vous avez payé pour voir le film, vous ne pouvez pas sortir sinon vous allez perdre votre argent et, maintenant, vous allez subir le film. (*ibid.*)[13]

12 'A film made to be hated'.
13 ' The intention with *Assassin(s)* was to put someone in front of a TV screen and to leave them with eyes wide open, like in *A Clockwork Orange*. The aim of the

The film is therefore far removed from the ironic, postmodern violence employed by Tarantino, the explosive, fetishistic *mise en scène* of male violence found in the Hollywood action movies, or, in the French context, the cartoonish violence of Jan Kounen's *Dobermann*. It is particularly revealing to compare the representation of violence found in *Assassin(s)* to that of Kounen's film since both are French features, initially released within one month of each other and directed by young, male directors who look to Hollywood as much as to French cinema for their inspiration.

In *Dobermann* Kounen combines ultra-violence with a BD aesthetic to present larger than life protagonists who roam the streets of Paris killing almost compulsively and without consequence. The extreme violence perpetrated by the film's eponymous 'hero' (played by Vincent Cassel) and his misfit gang of criminals – killing a policeman by throwing a grenade into the motorbike helmet he is wearing and closing the lid; 'Dob' eliminating his rival, the corrupt and equally violent detective Cristini, by forcing his head from a speeding car into the path of an oncoming vehicle – are grotesque and excruciating acts intended to shock and (perversely) amuse the spectator, void of any truly subversive political or artistic intention. *Dobermann*'s ultra-violence is thus presented as a highly stylised, but ultimately meaningless spectacle. A fetishistic emphasis is placed on the weapons used and destruction that results from over-the-top shoot outs, such as the nightclub scene towards the end of the film, where Kounen oscillates between extreme close-ups of weaponry and frenetic editing of the gunfight, on the one hand, and death and destruction shot in slow motion and from multiple angles, on the other. Violence is also (predictably) eroticised, presumably to appeal to the film's target audience of young heterosexual males. Dob follows his assault on a security van by 'making out' with his accomplice/girlfriend Nat (Monica Bellucci) in the car as they speed away from the robbery, while Nat, dressed in a short leather skirt, later blows up the entrance to a bank with an oversized (and obviously phallic) rocket-launcher.

More worrying, is that this ecstasy of violence in *Dobermann* is entirely de-contextualised. Its perpetrators are divested of any responsibility for the consequences of their actions: as if in a video

---

film was [to say to the spectator]: "you've paid to see this film, you can't leave without losing your money and so now you're going to be subjected to what the film has to offer".'

game, Dob and his gang merely reload and move onto the next target. This approach is, presumably, intended to provide its director with an alibi against a critique of the film that reproaches *Dobermann* for its representation of violence (not to mention casual sexism and homophobia). How, runs the argument, can Kounen be held to account for the extreme portrayal of violence in a film that is not meant to be taken seriously and is a work of cartoonish fiction rather than reality?

The representation of violence, its affects and consequences found in *Assassin(s)* is in direct contrast to that of *Dobermann* – a fact that makes Kassovitz's aforementioned preference for Kounen's film (Les Frères K 1997: 50–4) in favour of his own all the more perplexing. As spectators in *Assassin(s)*, we are forced to suffer with Max as he commits his first murder under Wagner's tutelage. The killing of Vidal is thus edited into a 12-minute sequence that appears to unravel in real time. Max does not simply appear, blow his elderly victim away and then move on to his next target – the *modus operandi* employed in *Dobermann* – but rather suffers, and is forced to confront, along with the spectator, the 'reality' and consequences of the violent act for both victim and assassin. Vidal is viciously beaten, dragged and bound by his assailants, before Wagner bullies his young protégé into shooting the elderly man with his own hunting rifle. As Max weeps, struggling to keep the weapon trained on his victim, the camera cuts to Vidal's bloodied face, filmed from the point of view of the young assassin. When the shot that kills Vidal is eventually fired, Kassovitz simultaneously cuts from the rapidly edited close-ups that bring the sequence to its climax to a long shot in which the camera surveys the whole room, with Max standing over the dead body of his victim as the television continues to blare out in the background. Tellingly, in a sequence which is on the whole typical of the stylised *mise en scène* associated with Kassovitz's filmmaking, this final moment is resolutely, unsparingly naturalistic – the director urging us to contemplate the consequences of the violence on screen. Here then is the power and conviction of *Assassin(s)* which has been doubted by most French critics – the director forces us to see just how ugly and unacceptable such violence is, rather than simply dismissing it as Kounen does.

Many contemporary French critics who reviewed *Assassin(s)* – particularly those who were at the press screening in Cannes, where the film was unceremoniously booed and whistled – found it hard to accept Kassovitz's perfectly serious intentions for *Assassin(s)* to engage in a wider debate about the media's portrayal of violence, its debilitating effect on contemporary French society and particularly on a disenfranchised youth class. While Kassovitz had professed (1998) to expecting a critique of film style from journalists, a number turned supposed reviews of the film into altogether more personal attacks on the young filmmaker for producing what they saw as a self-righteous, naive and ultimately hypocritical tract on violence, the media and youth.

Writing for *Libération*, Gérard Lefort (1997) labelled the film patronising, and 'enfantin' ('childish') in its denunciation of the harmful effects of television on young people, comparing Kassovitz to an amiable if embarrassing drunk venting his spleen at a party: 'on a envie de lui dire, d'une part que c'est ni l'heure ni l'endroit, et d'autre part qu'on l'aime bien quand même et qu'on est d'accord sur tout avec lui, histoire de s'en débarrasser'.[14] In his review of *Assassin(s)* for *L'Humanité*, Jean-Pierre Léonardini (1997) was far more acerbic; dismissing Kassovitz as 'un enfant gâté prenant la pose du moraliste à la petite semaine...'[15] and attacking the film as 'fake' for giving the appearance of tackling tough social issues while in fact presenting an ideologically suspect discourse surrounding themes of insecurity and violence as they relate to contemporary France: '*Assassin(s)* ... travaille sur l'équivoque monocorde et la confusion, sur l'inflation des signes de crise, sur un maximalisme dégueulasse apte à filer la frousse, suivant les critères idéologiques d'un esprit au fond pas très net'.[16]

In a more measured critical appraisal of *Assassin(s)* written some weeks after the Cannes première, Jean-Pierre Jeancolas (1997: 119–20) observed how the vitriolic (and largely derivative) press attacks on *Assassin(s)* emanating from the festival had made it almost impossible for public and critics alike to respond objectively to the film upon its initial release. Despite prefacing his review with the above caveat, Jeancolas nonetheless went on to post his own misgivings about the film. On the one hand, he found it hard to accept *Assassin(s)* as social

14 'on the one hand, we want to tell him that it is not the time or the place [for this discussion] and, on the other, that we like him all the same and are in complete agreement; just to get him to leave'.
15 'a spoilt brat posing as a moralist with quick-fix solutions.'
16 '*Assassin(s)* employs a one-dimensional ambiguity and works on confusion, on inflating signs of crisis, through a repellent maximalism capable of inciting fear, following the ideological framework of a mind that deep down is rather confused.'

cinema, given what he saw as the absence on screen of the society in question. For Jeancolas, the film's protagonists may well be seen to inhabit the landscape of contemporary France, but their characters are given little in the way of socio-cultural or historical background that might locate them *within* the context of this society. The characters of Wagner and above all Mehdi are thus, according to Jeancolas, little more than 'abstractions' – existing in a parallel universe where they are able to transgress the laws of a society that has no hold on them. On the other hand, he judged the violence in *Assassin(s)* to have been filmed with such a degree of 'efficiency' that the crimes appear 'indulgent' – an argument that is hard to accept, given the earlier analysis of Kassovitz's portrayal of violence in *Assassin(s)* in comparison to *Dobermann*. Finally, Jeancolas cast doubt on the sincerity of Kassovitz's intentions to denounce the harmful effects television on contemporary society, given that the film was co-produced by TF1. In Kassovitz's defence, we might argue that, rather than displaying complicity, the very fact the director took money from France's richest commercial station precisely to launch an attack on the harmful effect of television on society indicates the subversive intent behind the film. Moreover, the very nature of *Assassin(s)'* production history, with constant revisions and additions to the original screenplay during shooting, further supports this idea that TF1 did not truly understand what they were financing, and were effectively investing in the film based on Kassovitz's success with *La Haine*.

Possibly the most serious allegation levelled against *Assassin(s)* by the critics, however, was that Kassovitz had directed a film that was, at best, naive, and, at worst, hypocritical and ideologically suspect – distanced in various ways from the social realities it attempted to engage with. And yet, the social *is* foregrounded in *Assassin(s)*. The difference is, however, that Kassovitz shifts the focus away from the usual preoccupations of French social cinema with verisimilitude, authenticity and faithfulness of record to what we might describe as 'postmodern realism'; whereby actual social tensions are enacted through the fragmented narrative, abstract characterisation and conflict between stylisation and naturalism in the *mise en scène*. Thus Kassovitz's use of the zapping aesthetic points not to some abstract or ironic postmodern style, but rather to the actual blurring of boundaries between real-life and mediatised reality (particularly as it relates to violence) in contemporary western audiovisual culture.

The most extreme and disturbing example of this media phenomenon to appear in recent years on French screens was arguably that
of the televised police shooting of Khaled Kelkal.[17] A disaffected
Maghrebi-French youth from the *banlieue* of Lyon with links to
Islamist extremists, Kelkal was the prime suspect for a series of terrorist bomb attacks in French cities in the summer of 1995. Following
a massive police manhunt that was accorded extensive media coverage in France, Kelkal was eventually shot dead by police marksmen
– with the events screened on prime-time television only minutes
after they occurred. M6, the channel with the most complete footage
of the shooting, crucially chose to edit out the call from a police officer
to 'finish off' the wounded suspect only moments before his death.
The television station defended its on-the-spot editorial decision as an
attempt to avoid sensationalising the killing – though just what could
be more sensational than virtually live images of a police marksman
shooting a suspected terrorist is hard to imagine. Nevertheless, M6's
attempts to tamper with footage that was ostensibly being broadcast
as 'live and direct' only added to the suspicion surrounding police
claims that they were acting in self-defence by 'finishing off' Kelkal.
As if the diffusion of images on prime-time television of an individual
being shot dead, regardless of his or her status as a terrorist suspect,
was not offensive enough – and further evidence to support the
claims made in *Assassin(s)* about the extent to which programmers
consider contemporary television audiences are now largely desensi-
tised to images of violence – the editorial decisions made during the
coverage of Khaled Kelkal's killing also raise serious questions about
the media's ability to distort (for whatever political, editorial, financial or ideological reasons) the representation of violence and reality
presented on screen.

Beyond the wilfully polemical discourse concerning television's
representation of violence, there are other (very real) social tensions
embedded within the narrative of *Assassin(s)* that offer an explanation
for the violent behaviour of disenfranchised youth in the film. Even
the most casual observer of French politics and society over the past
decade could not have failed to notice the extent to which the fear
of escalating levels of violence and, in particular, juvenile violence –
often addressed under the umbrella term of *insécurité* – has emerged

17 The following summary of events is taken from Hargreaves (1997: 88–9). See
also Jauffret (1995).

as a key socio–political concern.[18] In the 2002 French presidential campaign, the extreme-right candidate Jean-Marie Le Pen played on this fear of *insécurité* as a means of justifying his racist anti-immigrant stance to the electorate, and securing his passage to the second round of the elections.

In *Assassin(s)* Kassovitz does not, however, exploit the fears over violence and delinquency (so clearly present in French society during the late 1990s) as the earlier quote from Lombardi suggests. Rather, the film legitimately relates these social problems to the precarious economic situation faced by France's alienated youth. While unemployment remained a key socio-political concern throughout France in the 1990s, for young people the situation was particularly acute: according to INSEE statistics, in 1997 – the year *Assassin(s)* was released – unemployment levels for 16 to 25-year-olds stood at 29 per cent.[19] Max's position as a temporary employee in a welding-shop thus reflects the depressing employment prospects faced by almost a third of young people in France during the late 1990s. In effect, his 'apprenticeship' with Wagner is the best job opportunity Max is ever likely to be offered: a point that is reinforced during his initiation where, in an attempt to coax the youth to pull the trigger and murder his elderly neighbour, Wagner describes the hired killer as a 'craftsman', practising one of the few remaining true professions available to an unqualified, working-class youth such as Max.

This fear of failing, of remaining marginalised, overlooked by society, is what motivates Max's actions in the film far more than any imitation of the violence disseminated through the media. Competing with this desire for social acceptance, however, is a fatalism regarding the apparent immutability of his status as marginal. Consider the opening lines of the film, spoken by Max in voice-over:

Putain. Ça ne pourrait que se terminer comme ça. Il parait qu'avant de mourir on voit sa vie passer devant ses yeux. Moi avec la vie de merde que j'ai eue, je me demande ce que je vais voir ... Pour moi, tout a commencé quand le vieux a dit 'tu me déçois ... beaucoup'. Mes profs disaient que j'étais bon à rien. Ma mère elle disait que j'étais mauvais en tout ... moi je pense que j'étais comme tout le monde, ni bon, ni mauvais, juste influençable. [20]

18 See, for example, Wieviorka (1999) and Samet (2001).
19 Statistics consulted on: wwww.insee.fr (site last accessed 27/1/05).
20 "Fuck. It couldn't end up any other way. It seems that, before dying, you see

Although it is precisely this 'fear of failing' – exposed by Wagner's calculated put-down ('tu me déçois ... beaucoup') – that pushes Max to assume responsibility for the murder of Mr Vidal, the intense pessimism contained within his opening monologue also suggests that he is resigned to the fate determined for him by teachers, parents and society in general. This seemingly hopeless struggle against failure and exclusion (one to which, as the youth unemployment figures quoted above attest, many young people in France growing up in the harsh economic climate of the 1990s could undoubtedly have related) manifests itself through increasingly desperate acts of violence. Thus, when mocked by Mehdi for parading around the *cité* in a BMW with a loaded gun, but lacking the 'couilles' ('balls') to actually kill someone, Max turns the gun on himself and invites the teenager to pull the trigger.

Both Mehdi and Max respond to their alienation with the same self-destructive impulse; condemning themselves to a position of marginality and, ultimately, death. In contrast to Max's fragility, however, Mehdi is anomic and nihilistic. Beyond the violent acts he commits, the only thing that seems to engage the teenager is a pursuit of the material possessions promoted and vicariously consumed through television. This synthesis of violence and consumerism, which in fact acts as yet another form of alienation, is most obviously highlighted by the insertion into the narrative of *Assassin(s)* of an actual television advertisement for global sportswear giants Nike in which international soccer icons battle with devilish monsters on a football pitch in a Roman amphitheatre – ending with Eric Cantona blowing a hole in the opposition goalkeeper. It is also well illustrated in the scene where Max and Mehdi dispose of the stolen BMW in order to destroy any links to the murder victim. Rather than simply abandoning the vehicle, the youths fire rounds into the BMW until it explodes – the spectacle of gratuitous violence emphasised by Kassovitz's rendering of the destruction in slow motion. In response to Mehdi's regret for having destroyed 'un BM tout neuf' Max asks 'contre quarante ans de carrière tu choisis quoi?', to which the teenager replies without

---

your whole life pass before your eyes. With the shitty life I've had, I wonder what I'll see ... For me it all began when the old man told me "you disappoint me ... immensely". My teachers told me that I was good for nothing. My mother said that I was bad at everything. I reckon I was just like anyone else: neither good nor bad, just easily influenced.'

hesitation 'le BM'.[21] Instant material and consumer gratification as the only logical antidote to exclusion is thus given primacy over longevity or any socio-ethical accountability for the acts of violence being committed. (Similarly, when he first learns of Max's 'apprenticeship' with Wagner as an assassin, Mehdi's response is shockingly prosaic: he merely enquires whether or not the job 'pays well'.)

In marked contrast to the constant verbal flow in *La Haine* which offers Vinz, Saïd and Hubert an outlet for expression (both anguished and comical) as well as the opportunity to resist the status imposed on them as marginalised other, Max and Mehdi are, for the most part, unable to verbalise their feelings of alienation and despair. Violence therefore becomes the sole means of externalising such feelings. The ending of *Assassin(s)* is indicative of the prevailing sense of self-destructive fatalism displayed by the film's youthful protagonists. Recorded images from French television news show Mehdi caught on CCTV carrying out the random assassination of students and teachers at his former school before eventually taking his own life. Significantly, we never see the events as they occur in 'real' time within the diegesis. Instead, the final sequence of *Assassin(s)* shows repeated TV images of the massacre, interspersed with comment and analysis from a televised news report (fronted by TF1's instantly recognisable presenter Patrick Poivre d'Arvor). Mehdi's own suicide – crucially, absent from the screen – is relayed to us by another television journalist, broadcasting from the school where the killings took place.

These final moments of the film thus serve to reinforce the commentary running through *Assassin(s)* on media (television) representation and violence. On the one hand, the TV reports of the school killings reproduce precisely the sort of saturation coverage of murder and violent crime that, through their seemingly endless repetition of events and recycling of images, has the effect of potentially desensitising spectators to the gravity and true impact of the violence that has occurred. On the other, the final scene of *Assassin(s)*, which segues from the fictional narrative to what appears to be footage from an actual news debate on delinquency and violence chaired by a real TV presenter (Patrick Poivre d'Arvor), returns us to one of the film's key themes: the extent to which the distinction

21 'Against a career of forty years, what would you choose?' ... 'the brand new BMW'.

between real life and mediatised reality has become increasingly ambiguous in contemporary western audiovisual culture.

The synopsis of *Assassin(s)* with its focus on marginalised youth, dysfunctional or absent families, and an anomic society dominated by violence, brings to mind the cinema of Luc Besson, in particular *Nikita* (1990) and *Léon*. However, in contrast to *Nikita* (where the youthful female assassin works for the secret service), and *Léon* (where Besson's theme of pure love permits an ultimately optimistic ending), *Assassin(s)* locates itself in the 'everyday' surroundings of a contemporary French society in moral decay, with little chance of redemption. *Assassin(s)*'s increasingly bleak worldview contains none of the underlying optimism for social cohesion found in *Métisse*, nor the occasional moments of relief from the building tension in *La Haine* (such as DJ Cut Killer's performance, Vinz's comical attempts to cut Saïd's hair, or the drunk who dances manically on the bonnet of a patrol car to help the trio evade the police). Instead, *Assassin(s)* relentlessly follows on from where the sombre and violent finale of *La Haine* left off. The film's desolate social landscape not only sounds a bleak warning for the future of an increasingly alienated youth underclass, it also reflects the work of a director exasperated by the fact that, in socio-political terms, nothing had changed since *La Haine*.

Attracting 446,548 spectators during a fourteen-week run,[22] *Assassin(s)* produced respectable results at the box office but fell far short of the expectation surrounding both director and film following the phenomenal success of *La Haine*. In many ways the more modest audience figures achieved by the film can be explained by the fact that *Assassin(s)* falls between two groups of spectators – Kassovitz's core youth audience and that of a more mature, 'discerning' art house or *auteur* cinema – mirroring the generational conflict running through the film itself. This is not to say, however, that we should identify the bridging position occupied by *Assassin(s)* as a failing of the film. Instead, *Assassin(s)* ought to be read as a legitimate attempt by Kassovitz to combine these two apparently antithetical approaches (popular genre cinema and the art film) as a means of re-establishing the link between the *auteur* and popular cinema that has been largely absent in France since the 1960s, largely as a result of New Wave's legacy. Moreover, as was argued earlier in the chapter, the stylistic and generic

22 Figures from *Le Film français*, 'Classement films: 1997', no. 2703, 23 January 1998.

tensions that arise within *Assassin(s)* in fact serve to foreground the controversial social themes that the film addresses.

Assassin(s) is undoubtedly a problematic film, in some instances wilfully so; explicitly polemical in its attack on the harmful influence of television and structured around conflict and ambiguity. And, for these reasons, it is also arguably Kassovitz's most complex and intellectually stimulating film to date. The expectation amongst critics and audiences prior to *Assassin(s)* had been for Kassovitz to repeat the formula so successfully established in *La Haine* of dealing with social issues via controversial, but essentially accessible, youth-orientated cinema ('Tout le monde pensait que ça allait être un film de gangsters' the director laconically stated in one interview (Kassovitz 1998).[23] Instead, *Assassin(s)* deliberately attempts to incorporate elements more commonly associated with art cinema – fragmented narrative; explicit, uncompromising representations of transgression or taboo (often sex; in this case violence); ambiguous characterisation of protagonists – into his own brand of popular social cinema. Ironically, Kassovitz's own performance three years earlier as a fragile disaffected youth turned hired killer in Audiard's outstanding debut *Regarde les hommes tomber* – a film whose explanation of the violence committed by its protagonists is at least as oblique as that found in *Assassin(s)* – was lauded by the same reviewers (presumably approving of Audiard's *auteurist* credentials) who now derided *Assassin(s)* as naive and confused. This apparent refusal by many critics to take Kassovitz seriously in *Assassin(s)* points as much to the continued (and, on this evidence, seemingly unbridgeable) divide in French cinema culture between the popular mainstream and the 'artisanal', *auteur*-led independent sector as it does to any shortcomings (real or imagined) in the film itself.

Postmodern social fables

As a director whose first three features are firmly anchored in contemporary socio-political subject matter, Kassovitz's *fracture sociale* trilogy contributes to a long tradition of the director as social commentator in French cinema that includes Renoir, Carné, Varda, Boisset, Charef, Guédiguian and Tavernier (to name but a few). Kassovitz's commit-

23 'Everyone thought it was going to be a gangster film'.

ment to the social issues and marginal protagonists found in his *fracture sociale* trilogy is clear, despite what certain detractors may suggest. Further evidence of the socio-political awareness underpinning Kassovitz's first three films comes from the fact that the young filmmaker was one of the original signatories of the call to civil disobedience published in *Le Monde* and *Libération* on 12 February 1997 by fifty-nine French filmmakers in protest against the proposals for a tightening of the already oppressive immigration laws by the incumbent right-wing government.

Given the aims, intentions and representational strategies of the *fracture sociale* trilogy, Kassovitz's particular brand of social cinema can be compared with the spectacularisation of politics found in French civic cinema of the 1970s, employed by directors such as Costa-Gavras (with whom Kassovitz has recently worked) and Yves Boisset. Certainly Kassovitz would have been familiar with the work of these directors, if only due to the fact that such filmmakers moved within similar social, artistic and political circles to his parents in the 1960s and 1970s. Political thrillers such as *Z* (Costa-Gavras, 1969) and *L'Attentat* (Boisset, 1972) used the drama and topicality of contemporary socio-political events – political intrigue, corruption and state-sponsored assassination – in order to attract audiences, and were thus attacked by contemporary critics for depoliticising the subject matter of their films. Similar criticism has been levelled against Kassovitz in the 1990s for *La Haine*'s apparent glamorisation of exclusion.

However, there are clear differences between the approach to socio-political subject matter employed in civic cinema of the 1970s and Kassovitz's 1990s *fracture sociale* trilogy. Firstly the political thrillers of the 1970s, such as those of Boisset and Costa-Gavras, tended to focus on high-profile (often international) political events: the assassination of a Greek minister (*Z*), the Ben Barka affair (*L'Attentat*) or the assassination of a judge investing political links to organised crime (*Le Juge Fayard, dit 'le Shérif'* Boisset, 1976). In contrast, Kassovitz's trilogy highlights youthful protagonists who, for the most part, find themselves entirely excluded from such spheres of political or financial influence. Secondly, though Kassovitz's films may share with civic cinema the suspicion or mistrust of state institutions (police, politicians and the justice system) as they relate to the individual citizen, they have moved beyond what Hayward (1993: 243) describes as the 'politics of paranoia' found in French cinema of the 1970s. In

Kassovitz's trilogy, the threat does not come from shadowy figures or unidentified powers within governmental or institutional forces. Instead, the dangers of racism, joblessness, exclusion and violence faced by the youthful protagonists are quite clearly out in the open. Finally, the ideological 'weight' found in civic cinema and the political thrillers of the 1970s – whereby many films articulated a clearly identifiable commitment to left-wing/Marxist political agenda – is largely absent from Kassovitz's trilogy. In this respect, his work is consistent with the more dispersed, fragmented and ambiguous political commitment displayed by other young French directors during the 1990s (O'Shaughnessey 2003: 195–9).

Kassovitz's *fracture sociale* trilogy therefore contributes to a resurgence of social cinema in France in the 1990s. This 'new realism' as it has been termed refers less to a defined movement in French cinema that has emerged sharing a clear political agenda, and more to a diverse group of filmmakers who have effected a 'raw' and 'immediate' re-engagement with socio-political subject matter.[24] Aesthetically, these films tend to be characterised by a naturalistic *mise en scène*, combining a documentary-style approach with intimate (often handheld) camera work that suggests empathy for the characters. The films are 'political' not by virtue of any particular militant or ideological position they espouse, but rather by the social realities they choose to represent on screen and their depiction of alienated protagonists with whom directors and spectators can relate (Jeancolas 1997b: 58).

While *Métisse*, *La Haine* and *Assassin(s)* quite clearly fit with the thematic concerns of new realism – namely its approach to the 'political' and sympathetic focus on marginalised youth – stylistically, they are quite distinct from the naturalistic, pseudo-documentary aesthetic that dominates this new wave of social cinema from the 1990s. Visually, Kassovitz draws on a stunning, seductive and carefully composed *mise en scène*, closer to that of Scorsese or Luc Besson than the more 'conventional' social realism of directors such as Guédiguian, Dridi, Zonca or Masson who are firmly located in the realm of the *auteur* and more traditional French social realism. Not only is Kassovitz more inclined to the visual pleasures and productions values of mainstream popular cinema than other contemporary French directors of 'social' cinema, he is also keen to use subcultural youth style (above

24 See Powrie (1999); O'Shaughnessey (2003); Jeancolas (1997b) and Higbee (2005) for more details.

all hip-hop) as a means of articulating the socio-political struggle taking place in his films.

If critics have taken issue with Kassovitz's particular brand of social cinema, it is arguably because they have misunderstood its intentions. As Jeancolas suggests (1997a: 119) Kassovitz's aim is not to hold a mirror up to society and offer a representation bound by the conventions of French social realist cinema (verisimilitude and social 'truth' achieved primarily through a naturalistic, pseudo documentary style). Instead, he attempts to address contemporary socio-political issues hrough fictional narrative with a message and a seductive, often stylised, *mise en scène* intended for a popular audience.

What Kassovitz offers us then is not social realism, but rather what might be termed 'postmodern social fables'. Thinking of these films as social fables seems particularly appropriate for a number of reasons.[25] The fable finds it origins in oral (folk) culture and is therefore essentially a means of storytelling for a popular audience. In a similar way, Kassovitz has intended for his social films to reach the mainstream as well as his core youth audience. Secondly, the fable's clear identification as a tale of fiction relieves the artist or fabulist from the burden of authenticity and verisimilitude. In the same way, while *La Haine* and *Assassin(s)* clearly address urgent social problems facing France's alienated youth underclass, Kassovitz had not intended either film to speak for these young people, nor to document their social environment (above all the working-class *banlieue*). Approaching *Assassin(s)* in this way allows for a much more balanced and constructive re-reading of the film than has appeared to date and understanding of its potential as 'social cinema' to provoke and engage debate around key socio-political issues facing France in the 1990s.

Finally, the notion of the fable as a popular fictional tale with a social message is echoed in all three films. In *Métisse* Kassovitz selects a familiar trope from popular comedy (the *ménage à trois*) to relay a message of tolerance within a multicultural, postcolonial society – while *Assassin(s)* foregrounds a moral dimension to the narrative with allusions to Wagner as the devil (not least through the momentary glimpse of a reptilian tale sticking out of the back of his coat as he disappears into the night following the murder of Vidal). *La Haine*'s

25 This description of *Métisse* as a social fable was first suggested by producer Christophe Rossignon. Jeancolas (1997) later applied the same term to Kassovitz's social cinema in his review of *Assassin(s)*.

narrative includes a number of anecdotes and stories – such as the Grunwalski narrative told by the old man in the café toilets. Principal amongst these is Hubert's tale, which frames the opening and ending of the film:

> C'est l'histoire d'un mec qui tombe d'un immeuble de cinquante étages ... au fur et à mesure de sa chute il se répète pour se rassurer: jusqu'ici tout va bien, jusqu'ici tout va bien, jusqu'ici tout va bien ... l'importance c'est pas la chute, c'est l'atterrisage ... [26]

Indeed, when repeated over the final images of *La Haine*, Hubert emphasises the social dimension of his tale (and by extension that of the film) by replacing 'mec' (bloke) for 'société' (society).

Why then insist on the idea of these films as 'postmodern' social fables? Traditionally the fable was seen as a form of moral instruction, with the fabulist adopting the position of the teacher or corrector of morals. In contrast, suggests Lyotard (1997: 101), the postmodern fable offers no remedy; asking 'not that it be believed but only that we reflect on it'. Similarly, Kassovitz does not prescribe solutions or dictate a response from a position of moral authority in his *fracture sociale* trilogy – though his forceful polemic in *Assassin(s)* was interpreted as moralising by some critics. If anything, he is a storyteller who encourages dialogue with his audience – presenting us with the problems, and allowing us as spectators to consider their complexities without necessarily offering a definitive solution.

In this respect, Kassovitz's social fables are resolutely postmodern. They also go further. One of the true strengths of 'critical' postmodernism is the way in which it grapples with the problems of defining a world in which 'meaning is in rout, media has become a substitute for experience and what constitutes understanding is grounded in a decentred world of difference, displacement and exchanges' (Giroux 2002: 59). Kassovitz's social fables show themselves to be engaging with the discourse of critical postmodernism then for the way that they engage politically and culturally with questions of difference,[27]

---

26 'It's the tale of a bloke who falls from a fifty-storey building who, to comfort himself on his way down, repeats: so far so good, so far so good ... it's not the fall that matters, but the landing'.

27 As we have already noted, however, issues of gender and sexuality – with only the partial exception of Lola in *Métisse* – remain entirely absent from Kassovitz's *fracture sociale* trilogy.

marginality and identity, while also questioning how power relations between centre and margin (particularly in relation to a disenfranchised male youth in France) are constructed and perpetuated through the mass media.

Though the natural demographic for Kassovitz's social 'fables' may well be a popular youth audience, the intention is also to challenge a much wider social spectrum with these films. According to Kassovitz (Boulay and Colmant 1995), *La Haine* was not only intended for those from the working-class *banlieue* or even a mainstream youth audience, but also for an older, educated and more affluent generation of *soixante-huitards* (like his parents) 'qui ne sont pas au courant que dans un commissariat on peut se faire tabasser'.[28] Having attracted the attention of his cross-over–mainstream audience, Kassovitz then presents us with films that question – and, in their more extreme moments, issue a direct challenge to – hegemony's understanding of the socio-political realities writ large on screen. As such they can quite clearly be understood in relation to Hall's notion (1981: 239) of the popular as a site of 'constant contestation', one of collusion with but also resistance against the dominant cultural norm. With *La Haine* and *Assassin(s)* Kassovitz even takes this challenge one step further, by providing a discourse on the ways in which the mainstream media chooses to represent these social crises and the marginalised spaces, communities and individuals they directly affect.

The first two instalments of Kassovitz's *fracture sociale* trilogy (*Métisse* and *La Haine*) therefore address socio-political issues facing France in the 1990s – racism, exclusion and violence – but in ways that (stylistically and in terms of narrative and genre), will engage, not exclude, a popular or mainstream audience. This point about engaging a cross-over–mainstream audience is crucial. Surely the reason *Assassin(s)* is deemed to have failed where *La Haine* succeeded so spectacularly is that, with its conscious attempt to disgust and repel through the uncompromising on-screen violence and its combination of mainstream production practices with more experimental arthouse elements (that effectively disengaged much of Kassovitz's core youth audience) it repulsed the very audiences he hope to reach.

28 'who are not aware that in a police station [in France] people still get beaten up'.

References

Baignères, Claude (1997), *'Assassin(s)'* (review), *Figaro*, 17 May

Boulay, Anne and Colmant, Marie (1995), *'"La Haine* ne nous appartient plus"' (interview with Kassovitz), *Libération*, (31 May)

Hall, Stuart (1981), 'Notes on deconstructing the popular', *People's History and Socialist Theory*, in Raphael Samuel (ed.), *People's History and Socialist-Theory* London: Routledge, 227–40

Hargreaves, Alec (1997), 'Gatekeepers and gateways: postcolonial minorities and French television', in Alec Hargreaves and Mark McKinney (eds) *Postcolonial Cultures in France*, London, Routledge, 84–98

Hayward, Susan (1993), *French National Cinema*, London: Routledge

Higbee, Will (2005), 'Towards a multiplicity of voices: French cinema's age of the postmodern, part II – 1992–2004', in Susan Hayward, *French National Cinema* (2nd edition), London: Routledge

Giroux, Henry A. (2002), *Breaking into the Movies: Film and the Culture of Politics*, Oxford: Blackwell

Jauffret, Magali (1995), 'M6 jette le trouble', *L'Humanite*, (4 October), consulted at www.humanite.presse.fr/journal/1995-10-04/1995-10-04-735417 (site last accessed 14/7/05)

Jeancolas, Jean-Pierre (1997a), 'Assassin(s): êtres plats et petits écrans', *Positif*, no. 437/8, 119–20

—— (1997b), 'Une bobine d'avance', *Positif*, 434, 56–8

Les Frères K (1997), 'Kounen et Kasso se lâchent', *Première*, July, 51–4

Kassovitz, Mathieu (1997), Press release for *Assassin(s)* (interview with Kassovitz), consulted at mathieukassovitz.com/assassins/interviews/mathieu1.htm (site last accessed 21/7/05).

—— (1998), 'Les aventures de Mathieu Kassovitz' interview in *Steadycam*, consulted at www.mathieukassovitz.com/itw/steadycam.htm (site last accessed 19/7/05)

—— and Boukhrief, Nicolas (1997), *Assassin(s): scénario et photographies autour du film*, Arles: Actes Sud

Kolker, R. (2000), *A Cinema of Loneliness*, Oxford/New York: Oxford University Press

Lefort, Gérard (1997), 'Assassin(s)' (review), *Libération* (18 May)

Léonardi, Jean Pierre (1997), 'Petite panoplie de zappeur pompier incendiaire', *L'Humanité* (17 May)

Lyotard, Jean-François (1997), *Postmodern fables*, trans. George Van Den Abbeele, Minneapolis: University of Minnesota Press

Murat, Pierre (1997), 'Face à la violence, faut enfoncer le clou' (interview with Mathieu Kassovitz), *Télérama*, 2470, (14 May), 40–2

Nouvel Observateur (1997), (Interview with Michel Serrault), (21 May) BiFi dossier de presse.

O'Shaughnessey, Martin (2003), 'Post-1995 French cinema: return of the social, return of the political?', *Modern & Contemporary France*, 11/2, 189–203

Powrie, Phil (1999), 'Heritage history and New Realism', in Powrie (ed.) *French cinema in the 1990s: Continuity and Difference*, Oxford: Oxford University Press, 1–21

Reader, Keith (1995), 'After the riot', *Sight & Sound*, November, 12–14

Rouchy, Marie Elisabeth (1995), *Télérama*, 2372, (28 June)

Samet, C. (2001), *Violence et délinquance des jeunes*, Paris: Documentation Française

Tirard, Laurent (2000), 'Mathieu Kassovitz: la leçon de cinéma' Studio, no. 160, consulted at www.mathieukassovitz.com/rivieres/interviews/studio. htm (site last accessed 22/7/05)

Vincendeau, Ginette (2000), 'Designs on the *banlieue*: Mathieu Kassovitz's *La Haine* (1995)', in Susan Hayward and Ginette Vincendeau (eds), *French Film: Texts and Contexts*, London, Routledge

Wieviorka, M. (1999), *Violence en France*, Paris: Seuil

4

Interfacing with Hollywood

The release of *Assassin(s)* in France in 1997 was to prove a defining moment in Kassovitz's directorial career. The film's intensely polemical stance, its more experimental approach (in terms of film form and style), combined with a wholly negative worldview and graphic depiction of violence, effected, for the first time, a conscious distancing by Kassovitz from his popular audience. Though it would be incorrect to claim that *Assassin(s)* was an unmitigated commercial failure – it attracted, after all, a respectable 441,157 spectators in France[1] – it was almost inevitable that the film would be viewed in such terms, given the phenomenal success of *La Haine* (over two million spectators in France) two years earlier and the media-crafted persona of Kassovitz as an outspoken, rebellious *auteur* that had emerged as a result. The release of *Assassin(s)* also constituted a pivotal moment for Kassovitz resulting from the intensely hostile response to the film by the French press at its Cannes première. Though he had planned to maintain the focus on the social for his fourth feature film,[2] the apparent refusal of the French critics to take Kassovitz seriously as a socially engaged *auteur* led to a deliberate shift post-*Assassin(s)* away from the more personal, controversial and politicised social cinema of his earlier films – albeit one destined for a popular (youth) audience – towards

1 Source: CNC, quoted in Powrie (1999: 258).
2 'Je vais faire encore un film dans cette lignée et puis après, terminé'/ 'I'll make one more film along these lines and then that's it.' comments made by Kassovitz in the French press release for *Assassin(s)*, available for consultation at www.mathieukassovitz.com/assassins/interviews/mathieu1.htm (site last accessed 21/9/05).

the unashamedly mainstream genre cinema of *Les Rivières pourpres* (2000) and *Gothika* (2003).

The degree of negative and often highly personal criticism directed at *Assassin(s)*, following on from the tense and pressured conditions under which the film had been completed in time for the Cannes festival, led Kassovitz to the verge of depression and nervous exhaustion (Aubel 2003: 20). Having asked the film's producer, Christophe Rossignon, to honour a series of prearranged promotional engagements on his behalf, Kassovitz left France for the relative sanctuary of Los Angeles. Arriving in Hollywood as a virtual unknown, the director embarked on a period of self-imposed exile from the French film industry that would last for approximately two years until his return to begin pre-production on *Les Rivières pourpres* in 1999. Initially, Kassovitz travelled to Los Angeles at the invitation of Jodie Foster who had admired his work since *La Haine*, having used her production company, Egg Pictures, as a distribution outlet for the film in North America. The young French director thus spent his time in Los Angeles learning the 'business' of Hollywood, making contact with studio representatives and independent producers (*ibid.*: 21–4), while continuing to develop future projects – including working on a screenplay for a science-fiction movie with cult American author and screenwriter Earl Mach Rauch (Dupuy and Guillomeau 2000).

The fact that Kassovitz chose to move to Hollywood following the perceived failure of *Assassin(s)*, rather than merely absconding temporarily from Paris (the centre of film production in France) to lie low in the provinces, is a telling indication of his global ambitions as a filmmaker. This desire to attract international audiences for his films, not to mention an eagerness to work in genres such as the action thriller and science fiction that are typically viewed by producers as 'unworkable' in the context of the French film industry, indicates, once again, the influence of Luc Besson on Kassovitz's career trajectory. In fact, Kassovitz's growing reputation in France since the success of *La Haine* allowed him to forge a professional relationship with Besson. The young director was first granted a cameo role as a clueless armed robber in *Le Cinquième élément* (Besson, 1997) appearing (briefly) alongside Bruce Willis, and then assisted Besson in the production of *Jeanne d'arc* (Besson, 1999). In the same year, along with Jan Kounen, the pair founded a Los Angeles-based production company, 1B2K. On the one hand, the creation of 1B2K could be viewed as a positive endorsement by Besson – effectively the sole French exponent until the late 1990s of youth-orientated action cinema – of two talented new directors working within the French industry who shared his desire to compete with Hollywood for popular, youth audiences. On the other hand, some within the industry have suggested that the production company represents little more than a strategic alliance on Besson's part: an attempt to exert a degree of control at the level of production over the young pretenders to his throne.[3]

This more cynical interpretation is supported by the fact that, at the time of writing (July 2005), 1B2K has yet to develop a project for any of its three founders. Besson continues to channel his creative energies through his own production company, Les Films du Dauphin (and now Europa Corp), working increasingly in the capacity of producer and screenwriter; while both Kounen and Kassovitz have elected to develop future projects through their respective production networks (for Kassovitz, Kasso Inc. and MNP Entreprise, a joint venture with long-time associate Christophe Rossignon).

For his part, Kassovitz has jokingly described 1B2K as 'plus une association de malfaiteurs que d'un vrai projet de production' (Conter 2000: 17).[4] While this throwaway remark is typical of the director's interview style, it nevertheless reveals how he sees himself positioned as something of an outsider in both the French industry and Hollywood. Whatever the individual or collective motives behind the creation of 1B2K in the late 1990s, the Hollywood-based production company nonetheless provided Kassovitz with a platform from which to enhance his profile in the United States when he temporarily relocated to Los Angeles.

Although Kassovitz has, in many ways, followed Besson's lead in relation to his career trajectory as a director, there are still clear distinctions between the two filmmakers. First, whereas Besson has remained as far as possible within the French film industry to produce features such as *Le Cinquième élément* – a science-fiction blockbuster that 'beats Hollywood at its own game' by subverting the codes and conventions of American genre cinema (Hayward 1999: 246) – Kassovitz has proved more willing to work *within* the

3 See, for example, Vincent Cassel's comments about the creation of 1B2K and Kassovitz's relationship with Besson in an interview with *Technikart* (February 2004), consulted at www.vincentcassel.com (site last accessed 21/9/05).

4 'more like a criminal conspiracy than a real production company'.

Hollywood system: both in terms of adhering largely to the codes and conventions of American genre cinema, and by physically relocating to North America to work on *Gothika*.[5] Another difference is that, while Besson has maintained extensive authorial control over all his features to date, in directing *Les Rivières pourpres* and *Gothika* Kassovitz has accepted the constraints imposed by both studios and producers. For his part, Kassovitz (quoted in De Bruyn 2004a: 104–5) has explained his decision to direct these mainstream commissioned features as a necessary interim compromise; a way to gain the trust of major producers in France and Hollywood that will enable him to both finance and distribute more personal and ambitious projects to a global audience in the future. However, this shift raises inevitable questions of Kassovitz's status as an *auteur*, given that in his first three films, working with far more personal material, he occupied a central position as scenarist, director, editor and, in *Métisse* and *Assassin(s)*, through his performance as an actor.

A predilection for American-influenced genre cinema combined with a willingness to compromise authorial control in later films has ensured that, even though *Les Rivières pourpres* and *Gothika* employ a largely mainstream aesthetic and are relatively uncontroversial in terms of their subject matter, the polemic surrounding Kassovitz's directorial career remains. Some within the French film industry, such as the president of the National Federation of French cinemas (FNCF), Jean Labé (1999: 14) have welcomed what they see as Kassovitz's attempts to win back popular audiences by competing directly with Hollywood in genres such as the action film that have typically been deemed beyond the capabilities or budgets of French cinema. Other, more critical voices (Bonnaud 2000; Blumenfeld 2000; *L'Humanité* 2004), have suggested that what Kassovitz offers in these later films is little more than a poor imitation of Hollywood. Furthermore, Kassovitz's eagerness to embrace American influences and production practices in his films is seen by these same critics to signal an assimilation into a type of filmmaking traditionally demonised in contemporary French cultural and political discourses as a threat to the diversity and vitality of French national cinema.

5 Funded by Warner Brothers Studios and Columbia under the banner of Dark Castle Pictures, *Gothika* was filmed on sound stages and locations in Canada. The film was produced by Robert Zemeckis and Hollywood mogul Joel Silver (producer of blockbusters such as *Leathal Weapon*, *Die Hard* and *The Matrix*).

And yet, no one with even a passing interest in Kassovitz the filmmaker should be surprised either by the choices he has made post-*Assassin(s)* or his clear affinity with Hollywood, given that these influences have been present throughout his directorial career. *Métisse*, his first feature film, was essentially a reworking of Spike Lee's *She's Gotta Have It* (1987). Even his two most militant films to date; the politically conscious *La Haine* and the wilfully polemical *Assassin(s)* – with its stylistic references to neo-*noir* and, more specifically, *Taxi Driver* (Scorsese, 1976) – owe a clear debt to American cinema. Moreover, Kassovitz's keen understanding of the need to entertain and engage his audience, even in his more politicised films, suggests an affinity (albeit at times for different ends) with the principle of entertainment that dominates Hollywood production. Consider, for example, this quote from the director when discussing the 'authenticity' of *La Haine*'s social realism and the film's explosive finale:

> Heureusement *et* malheureuesement, au cinéma, on doit embellir les choses, donner un peu de romance à ce qu'on décrit. Même si on essaie d'être le plus vrai possible, on caricature pour intéresser; et on est obligé de raconter une histoire, même si elle paraît invraisemblable ... Il faut rester vrai tout en étant graphiquement intéressant. (Bourguignon and Yann 1995: 11)[6]

As was noted in Chapter 1, not only did Kassovitz develop a passion for American films as a result of regular family outings to the cinema as a child, he also gained an appreciation, thanks to his parents' expertise as filmmakers, of how these films worked in terms of narrative, structure and *mise en scène* to elicit a particular emotive response from the spectator. Perhaps the visit that most marked Kassovitz came in the mid-1970s when the 10-year-old was taken by his father to the Cinémathèque to see *Duel* (Spielberg, 1971).[7] The young boy

6 'Fortunately and unfortunately in cinema you have to embellish things, give a bit of romance to what you're describing. Even if you try to be as authentic as possible, you simplify to keep things interesting; and you're obliged to tell a story, even if it doesn't seem entirely realistic ... you have to remain true as well as being visually engaging'.

7 *Duel* was originally made for television in the USA. Following its domestic success, an extended version gained a theatrical release in foreign cinemas – including France. The film's largely positive critical reception by more highbrow critics (in contrast to Spielberg's later films) is reflected by the fact that Kassovitz went with his father to see the film at the Paris Cinémathèque: a venue that had gained a reputation as a Mecca for cinephiles due to its patronage

was immediately struck by Spielberg's directorial style – accurately described by Kolker (2000: 257) as a proficient, if ideologically problematic, structuring and control of *mise en scène* that encourages the spectator to 'surrender themselves' to the narrative. Kassovitz claims to have received his greatest lessons concerning *mise en scène* from Spielberg, and has been a passionate defender of his films ever since. It is worth quoting Kassovitz at length here to understand just why it is that he holds Spielberg in such esteem:

> Ma plus grande leçon de *mise en scène*, je l'ai reçue en allant voir les films de Spielberg. C'est là que j'ai compris la différence entre les faiseurs, c'est à dire ceux qui ne se servent de la caméra que pour filmer ce qui se passe devant, et les vrais cinéastes, qui savent exprimer un point de vue à travers leur *mise en scène*. Spielberg a une vraie conscience de la caméra. Chez lui, elle est un acteur à part entière, elle fait partie intégrante du film. Il la fait vivre et elle ne vit jamais gratuitement ... La différence entre cette *mise en scène* et celle d'un faiseur, c'est comme la différence entre un zoom et un travelling. D'un côté, on s'approche optiquement, et de l'autre, on s'approche physiquement. La différence de sensation est énorme. Spielberg m'a appris ce qu'était l'efficacité en matière de *mise en scène*, et je ne parle pas d'efficacité commerciale, ni même d'efficacité visuelle, mais véritablement d'efficacité cinématographique.[8] (Kassovitz quoted in Tirard 2000)

As the above quote makes clear, it is the 'physicality' and 'efficiency' of Spielberg's *mise en scène* that Kassovitz values so highly. By this, he refers not only to the way that Spielberg allows the camera to navigate through the on-screen space inhabited by his characters, but also the effect this has in suturing the spectator into the narrative.

in the 1950s by *Cahiers* critics and luminaries of the French New Wave such as Bazin, Chabrol, Godard and Truffaut.

8 'I received my greatest lesson in *mise en scène* from going to see the films of Spielberg. That was where I understood the difference between the practitioners, by which I mean those who merely use the camera to film what takes place before the lens, and true filmmakers who are able to express a point of view via their *mise en scène*. Spielberg has a real awareness of the camera. In his films the camera is an actor, an integrated part of the diegesis. He makes the camera live and always for a reason ... The difference between his *mise en scène* and that of a practitioner is similar to the difference between a zoom and a tracking shot. With the former, you approach optically, with the latter you approach physically. The difference in the sensations they produce is enormous. Spielberg taught me what efficiency meant in terms of *mise en scène*, and I'm not talking about commercial efficiency, nor even visual efficiency, but actual cinematographic efficiency.'

The 'lessons' that Kassovitz has taken from Spielberg can there-fore be seen in the way the camera accompanies Vinz, Saïd and Hubert around the estate in *La Haine*; encouraging a clear identifica-tion on the part of the spectator with the experiences of the young, marginalised *banlieusards*. His influence is also apparent in the care-fully orchestrated car-chase sequence in *Les Rivières pourpres*, or the camera's restless patrolling of the corridors of the psychiatric prison in *Gothika*. A more specific reference to Spielberg's visual style comes from the repeated use by Kassovitz of the tracking shot with zoom – or track-zoom – a camera movement that gives the impression of the subject in focus moving forward rapidly while the background appears to slip away. Most famously employed by Spielberg in *Jaws* (1975) to express Chief Brody's alarm at witnessing the shark attack on the young boy, Alex Kinter, the track-zoom appears in all of Kassovitz's films to date, to the extent that it can be identified as one of the visual signatures of his *mise en scène*. However, in Kassovitz's films the track-zoom does not function as simply a superfluous intertextual nod to Spielberg. In *La Haine*, as we have already noted (see Chapter 2), the track-zoom marks the transition of the trio from the periphery to the centre and, as such, is invested with a political significance.

Kassovitz's admiration for Spielberg is not without its complica-tions, however. Spielberg's films are highly problematic for the way in which they attempt to suture the spectator into a reactionary ideo-logical position (as it relates to gender, race and sexuality). Of course, in its current theorising around questions of ideology and spectator-ship, Film Studies has moved beyond apparatus theory of the 1970s – which largely dismissed the monolithic spectator as an ideological dupe – to embrace a more open reading of the multiple and contra-dictory positionings of spectatorship that also permits the possibility of resistance within the filmic text to the dominant ideology. However, just because we acknowledge the ability of the spectator to resist or subvert the preferred reading offered by the director, does not mean that Spielberg's attempts to suture his audience into a safe, conser-vative space should go unchallenged.

The deliberate manipulation or ideological suturing of the spec-tator in Spielberg's films is thus effected through a highly controlled *mise en scène*, often linked to or expressed through the perspective of a child, that encourages a sense of nostalgia and heightened sentimen-tality. This strategy is, furthermore, combined with a safe narrative

resolution that offers spectators a comfortable (desirable even) surrogate 'reality', allowing them to escape from the hard truths of an
uncomfortable world (Kolker 2000: 256–7). Spielberg's approach also
functions to obscure or naturalise the more problematic and conser-
vative ideological elements implicit within the narratives of his films.
While the ideological positionings offered by Kassovitz are in no way
as fixed or reactionary as those found in Spielberg's films, his reluctance (or, perhaps inability) to see such problems in the American
director's work has implications for his own cinema, particularly in
relation to Kassovitz's treatment of gender and the virtual absence
until *Gothika* of a female perspective in his films.

If Kassovitz has learned lessons in the effect/affect of form and
style from Spielberg, he could not be further removed from the
American director in terms of the worldview presented in his films.
Whereas Spielberg seems compelled to replace discomfort and misery
with satisfaction and security (in essence, the happy ending), Kassovitz is inclined to expose a society ill at ease with itself. His films thus
foreground tension and conflict, often in an attempt to disconcert his
spectator or provoke a reaction: a mechanism that is pushed to its
limits in *Assassin(s)*. The highly mobile camera employed by Kassovitz in a film such as *La Haine* does not, therefore, merely inhabit
on-screen space in the Spielbergean sense. Rather, the camera's restless energy reflects a sense of discomfort or unease experienced by
the protagonists. Similarly, whereas Spielberg's relentless suturing of
the spectator, 'never permits the viewer reflective space' (*ibid.*: 288)
in Kassovitz's *fracture sociale* trilogy (as was argued in Chapter 2) we
are encouraged, precisely, to (re)view and then reflect; to engage and
then respond.

This desire to disrupt and disconcert his spectator links Kassovitz to another American director of the post-classical Hollywood
era: Martin Scorsese. Kassovitz has claimed Scorsese's *Mean Streets*
(1974) – not *Jaws, Close Encounters of the Third Kind* (Spielberg, 1977)
or *Schindler's List* (Spielberg, 1997) – as his favourite film of all time
(Bourgignon and Tobin 1995: 8). Similarly, allusions to the films of
Scorsese from the 1970s and early 1980s are far more common in
Kassovitz's work than to the films of Spielberg. In particular, Scorsese's influence looms large in *La Haine*: the introduction of the three
central characters by name – Saïd's graffiti tag; Vinz's ring; the poster
announcing Hubert's previous fight – is a clear reference to *Mean*

Streets; the slow motion, black and white images of Hubert boxing evoke *Raging Bull* (Scorsese, 1980); while Vinz's 'C'est à moi que tu parles?'/ 'You talkin' to me?' speech in front of the mirror is directly inspired by *Taxi Driver* – a film which (as discussed in Chapter 3) also forms a key reference point in *Assassin(s)*. This cinephile tendency to borrow or reappropriate characters, moments or themes from other directors is itself a strategy that Kassovitz has largely inherited from Scorsese; an *auteur* who, as Lesley Stern (1995) has so convincingly argued, incorporates into his own films thematic and stylistic influences from classical Hollywood (Ford), British cinema (Powell) and the French New Wave (Godard).

Scorsese's influence on Kassovitz's filmmaking constitutes more than just a series of intertexual references, however. As Susan Morrison (1995, cited in Vincendeau 2000: 322) remarks, elements of the American *auteur*'s early films – the restless, fluid camerawork, 'a reliance on idiosyncratic male actors, use of a pop-score ... and near hysterical tension lying just beneath the surface, ready to erupt at any moment' – are recalled in *La Haine*'s soundtrack and portrayal of spectacular male violence. Therefore, if Kassovitz obtains his technical cues as a *metteur en scène* largely from Spielberg, his concerns as an *auteur* are more closely aligned with Scorsese. Like Scorsese, Kassovitz is concerned with predominantly male protagonists occupying an on-screen space of tension and violence; presenting a pessimistic world-view, verging on the nihilistic, that rejects the security of narrative resolution (the happy ending) employed so obsessively by Spielberg. In common with Scorsese, many of Kassovitz's films are concerned with violence – its representation and affects – and use either the act or (just as importantly) the threat of violence to explore a dysfunctional, fragile masculinity. Similarly, Kassovitz takes his lead from Scorsese in the sense that the violence portrayed in his films may at times be explicit (and thus controversial) but it is never gratuitous. Finally, the two directors foreground marginal, often ambivalent, characters in their films – gangsters, petty crooks, delinquents, assassins – who may disgust us through their actions, but who also have an attraction for the spectator that results more from a sense of fascination or pity than conventional desire.

If Spielberg provides a technical and stylistic reference point for Kassovitz, and Scorsese has influenced the pessimistic worldview found in his films, his approach to the 'business' of selling and promoting his (often) controversial films connects Kassovitz to African-American director Spike Lee. This link between Lee and Kassovitz has as much to do with the personalities of the two directors as any shared formal or stylistic traits that appear in their films. Both are filmmakers who have chosen to address the socio-political realities of violence, racism and exclusion; in Lee's case in relation to the African-American community, and for Kassovitz through the representation of an alienated youth underclass. Both directors have also been criticised for representing controversial social themes and marginalised protagonists in their films from a relatively privileged socio-economic position. Just as Kassovitz was accused in *La Haine* of profiting from the malaise of the *banlieue* (see Chapter 2), so Spike Lee, who is from a liberal, middle-class African-American background – the son of a schoolteacher and a jazz-musician, educated at Morehouse College (a historic black college in Atlanta whose alumni includes Dr Martin Luther King, Jr.) and the NYU film school – has been criticised for his representation of black inner-city communities in films such as *Do the Right Thing* (1989) and *Clockers* (1995).[9] Similarly, both directors have been brought to task for the representation of (or lack of) female protagonists in the largely male-centred narratives of their films.

Lee and Kassovitz are, moreover, outspoken personalities who have railed against conditions within their respective film industries. Despite his commercial success, Spike Lee sits uncomfortably within mainstream American cinema and has spoken out against what he perceives as the 'glass ceiling' against blacks found in Hollywood. For his part, Kassovitz (as already discussed in Chapter 1) has attacked the CNC for its refusal to offer selective financial aid for his particular brand of popular, youth-oriented cinema. Finally, both directors have enjoyed/endured an ambivalent relationship with the media in their respective countries and have been accused of courting controversy with their films partly as a means of attracting a style-conscious youth audience.

Beyond the similarities between Lee and Kassovitz as polemical figures whose rebellious image has, in part, been (self-)constructed with at least one eye on the media and the 'business' of selling their films at the box office, there are also direct comparisons to be made between individual films made by the two directors. *Métisse* was

9 By way of an example and for a summary of the American press's response to *Do the Right Thing*, see Reid (1997: 134–52).

labelled a French remake of Spike Lee's debut feature, *She's Gotta Have It* (1986), released seven years earlier. Like Lee, Kassovitz chose to cast himself in one of the lead roles – both directors play bicycle couriers who compensate for their lack of physical prowess with rapid wit, and an idiosyncratic charm. The two characters – Mars Blackmon (*She's Gotta Have It*) and Félix (*Métisse*) even dress similarly in loose-fitting sportswear and wear distinctive, thick-rimmed glasses. In spite of such obvious similarities, to label *Métisse* a simple 'remake' of *She's Gotta Have It* would not be entirely accurate. Instead, Kassovitz transposes Lee's New York-centred narrative concerning an African-American woman's right to choose between her three black lovers (which itself constitutes a social satire of African-American machismo) into a very French postcolonial comedy, concerned less with the predicament of its female lead than it is with exploring the tensions of difference in a pluri-ethnic contemporary French society. *Métisse* is thus clearly inspired by the scenario and attitude of *She's Gotta Have It*, but displays its difference as French cinema through its Parisian setting, multiethnic cast and grounding in the traditions of popular French comedy.

If *Métisse* was regarded as a French remake of *She's Gotta Have It*, then *La Haine* was seen by a number of French critics as transferring elements from *Do the Right Thing* from New York to the deprived estates of the Parisian *banlieue* (Bourgignon and Tobin 1995; Reader 1995). Both films, moreover, took a real-life episode as the inspiration for the stylised fiction that evolved. The idea for *La Haine* came to Kassovitz following the death in police custody of a French youth of Zairean immigrant origin, while Spike Lee took his narrative inspiration from an incident that occurred in Howard Beach (New York), where a group of white youths attacked and chased three blacks from a pizzeria, causing one to die when he ran into traffic (Reid 1997: 139). Once again, however, such comparisons between the two films need to be nuanced. *La Haine* does indeed borrow from the narrative structure of *Do the Right Thing* – namely, the chronicling of tensions within an ethnic-minority neighbourhood over a twenty-four-hour period that leads, seemingly inexorably, to an explosive and violent climax. However, the film is clearly focused on the multiethnic realities of the French *banlieue*, placing the *blanc*-black-*beur* trio from the Les Muguets estate in confrontation with the police. In *Do the Right Thing*, on the other hand, the tension that emerges does not (initially) result from conflict between the police and gangs of local youths, but, rather, from antagonism between different ethnic groups; principally the predominantly African-American inhabitants of the Bedford Stuyvesant neighbourhood and the Italian-American owners of the local pizzeria. Also, Kassovitz's use of a hip-hop aesthetic as a structuring point of resistance through (sub)cultural style (already discussed in detail in Chapter 2) is more deeply embedded in *La Haine* than it is in *Do the Right Thing*, where jazz is as prominent in the soundtrack as rap music.

Métisse, and to a far lesser degree *La Haine*, are, therefore, not so much remakes as French 'retakes' or reinterpretations of Lee's work. The fact that Kassovitz should choose to reinterpret the themes and narrative elements in these Spike Lee films is significant, given that the remake is largely seen as the property of American cinema; the phenomenon of the Hollywood remake constitutes an integral part of the studios' protectionist strategy against foreign films gaining access to the US box office, as well as providing further evidence of American resistance to the cultural difference of 'other' national cinemas. Kassovitz thus reverses the trend and shows that, in this case, American cinema can provide a valid point of reference and inspiration for French cinema but that it needs to be reworked in order for it to connect more directly with a French audience – proof that French cinema can assimilate American influences without becoming a 'Coca-colonised' version of Hollywood.

While Kassovitz's links to Scorsese (as cinephile, *auteur* and Hollywood maverick) and Spike Lee (as outspoken independent African-American *auteur*) are more easily accepted by French critics from the high-brow cinema journals such as *Cahiers du cinéma* and *Positif*[10] his admiration for Spielberg is altogether more problematic. The director's vocal and apparently unswerving loyalty to Spielberg is viewed disparagingly in certain sectors of the French film industry, where the sentimentality, populism (verging on demagogy) and blatant commercialism of Spielberg's cinema are anathema to the perceived artistic merit and cultural worth of cinema as the 'Seventh Art' in France. Let us not forget that at the height of the culture wars between

10 See, for example (Bourguignon and Tobin 1995: 8–13) in which interviewers from *Positif* are happy discussing the influence of Lee and Scorsese on *La Haine*, though appear more reluctant to engage with Kassovitz's enthusiasm for Spielberg's influence on his filmmaking style.

France and the USA (Hollywood) in the build-up to the GATT nego-tiations in December 1993, it was Spielberg's *Jurassic Park* (1993) that went head to head at the French box office with heritage superproduc-tion *Germinal* (Berri, 1993). Just as Berri's film allegedly reinforced the artistic and cultural merits that marked French cinema's 'difference' to Hollywood, so Spielberg's film represented American cinema's attempts to colonise French screens with crass commercial 'product'. This celluloid 'war' even involved direct intervention from the incum-bent French culture minister, Jacques Toubon, who agreed to pay for additional prints of *Germinal* so that the film was released on roughly the same number of screens as *Jurassic Park* (Grantham 2000: 123).

Despite such barely disguised hostility from the industry, Kasso-vitz has repeatedly affirmed in interviews his admiration for Spielberg as an *auteur* (see for example Aubel (2003) and Tirard (2000)). In an article with *Première* (Les Frères K 1997) to mark the release of *Assassin(s)*, Kassovitz was photographed wearing a T-shirt emblazoned with the logo for *The Lost World* (Spielberg, 1997) the sequel to *Jurassic Park* .[11] More recently, in 2001, the director publicly defended Spielberg against criticism from none other than Jean-Luc Godard, dismissing the iconic *auteur*'s disparaging remarks concerning Spielberg's worth as a filmmaker as 'typical of the insularity and pseudo-intellectualism of French cinema culture' (Jeffries 2001). There is a certain irony to this exchange in that, by valorising a popular Hollywood director over a type of French cinema which he sees as reactionary and out of touch with the realities of modern France, Kassovitz is effectively adopting a position not dissimilar to that taken five decades earlier by the very director he aims to criticise (Godard) along with Truffaut and others in the pages of *Cahiers du cinéma*. More pertinently, however, it points to the seemingly unbridgeable divide for the director in contemporary French cinema culture between the *auteur*-led independent sector and

11 A public service advertisement directed by Kassovitz for the SNCF (shown in French cinemas in the summer of 2004 and available to view on Kassovitz's official website) constituted a virtual homage to Spielberg in as much as it used a computer-generated dinosaur – reminiscent of those in *Jurassic Park* – wreaking havoc on the train and its passengers to warn of the dangers of straying unauthorised onto railway lines. Though the advertisement appeared to be designed to appeal to younger spectators, it was actually commissioned as much to inform an adult audience, following an incident in 2004 when com-muters alighted without permission from a train that had broken down just outside of a Paris station.

mainstream commercial cinema – which, in many respects, was what prevented more high-brow French critics taking Kassovitz seriously as a popular *auteur* in a film such as *Assassin(s)* .

Kassovitz's defence of Spielberg is also significant in that it reveals the extent to which the director emerges from a new generation of French cultural consumers and a growing number of French film-makers for whom Americanised popular culture (and in particular cinema) is not viewed as a foreign influence, or suspect cultural import, but is instead accepted as an integral and established part of contemporary French culture. The idea of Americanised popular culture emerging as a 'natural' element within contemporary popular culture in France is important in relation to Kassovitz's cinema and also the polemical response generated by his films amongst French critics and audiences. It is, therefore, worth pausing for a moment to consider why this change might have come about.

First, Hollywood's growing share of the French box office in the 1980s and 1990s – which, according to CNC figures, rose from 30 per cent of audience share in 1980 to a height of sixty-three per cent in 1998 –[12] has undoubtedly encouraged a greater identification amongst contemporary French audiences with the iconography, stars and genres of American cinema. When statistics referring to the sale of video and DVD titles in France during 2000 are consulted, this preference for American cinema rises further still: 71 per cent for Hollywood and 20 per cent for French films (Montebello 2005: 185). Similarly, though French television stations (in particular Canal Plus) may be legally required to buy and screen a higher proportion of French films, Hollywood blockbusters still tend to dominate the prime-time viewing schedules (Ganne 1998: 15–16).

Further evidence of this affinity with Hollywood can be seen in the results from a survey carried out in 1994 by *Première* to establish a 'best of all time' film list in which thirty-six of the top forty films selected by those questioned were American (Frodon 1995: 693). Admittedly, this survey is somewhat self-selecting, given that the readers of a magazine such as *Première* are mostly young and inclined towards Hollywood and mainstream French cinema. Nevertheless, its findings

12 To give an indication of trends since the mid-1990s, between 1995 and 2004 Hollywood commanded an average of approximately 53 per cent of French cinema audiences, compared to that of 35 per cent for French productions. All figures available online at www.cnc.fr (site last consulted 7/7/05).

support the idea of this shift for many younger spectators towards identifying with American cinema over French films reflected in the other audience figures quoted above.

In contrast to the economic protectionism practised by Hollywood in the American market, in Europe Hollywood studios argue for the withdrawal of quotas and the free circulation of audiovisual products. Hollywood thus employs its superior economic power to aggressively pursue audiences in foreign markets; a situation motivated largely by the fact that, since most Hollywood films recuperate production costs in the North American market, revenues generated from foreign box offices and related products (DVD sales, merchandising, television rights) provide a much higher profit margin. In the mid-1990s, the Hollywood majors thus forged alliances with French distributors and exhibitors, investing considerable sums in marketing and promotion to ensure maximum exposure for their films at the box office. This arrangement has had a particularly damaging effect on smaller, independent French productions, which are denied the opportunity to establish themselves in theatres and build audiences via word of mouth.[13]

Viewing these various developments as a whole, it is therefore possible to argue that, in terms of market share, box-office success and media exposure, American cinema has, since at least the late 1980s, usurped French production for a younger generation as the dominant mainstream cinema in France.

The phenomenal success of Hollywood films with foreign audiences cannot be accounted for by economic power alone. It has also been explained by their ability to seem at once instantly familiar but also specifically 'other'; allowing for the transmission of what appear to be universal values and shared aesthetics, which are then customised and reinterpreted by local audiences (O'Regan 1992: 332–3). Of course, French audiences' fascination with Hollywood is not a new phenomenon, and is almost as old as cinema itself. However, for a

13 In the past, a film such as *Diva* (Beineix, 1981) produced on a relatively modest budget with no recognizable stars and by (a then) unknown director, took more than a year to establish itself in independent French theatres before winning awards at the French Césars and then crossing over to a mainstream audience. This situation would be almost impossible in France today where, with fewer independent and art-house theatres, films are withdrawn from the screens of larger exhibitors if they fail to make a substantial return within the first few weeks.

younger generation of French spectators who have grown up with Hollywood as arguably the dominant cinema in terms of screen exposure (in both cinemas and on television) and market share, American cinema appears less and less as the exotic 'other'. Recent technological advances in global communications (beginning in the 1980s, but which have had a more profound impact since the 1990s) and the increasing prominence of transnational, multimedia corporations, have further eroded the geographical, temporal and cultural markers of national boundaries. They can thus help explain this subtle but significant shift, whereby the ubiquity and immediacy of Hollywood, its films, stars and iconography has made American cinema more familiar than ever before to contemporary French audiovisual consumers. This is not to suggest that French spectators perceive Hollywood stars as any less glamorous or their films as any less spectacular than before; rather that our ability as consumers to access all forms of Hollywood 'product' has rendered them less exotic in terms of their distance from our everyday lives or their cultural difference. Though not a new phenomenon, the dubbing of American films into a foreign language adds to this increased intimacy or familiarisation with Hollywood – the language barrier, the most immediate marker of national or cultural difference is removed, leaving the filmic image to cross borders and boundaries with less resistance from 'local' audiences.

Central to this transformation of Hollywood's place within French audiovisual culture in the 1990s and 2000s, is the fact that technological advances have introduced modes of reception that further familiarise foreign audiences to Hollywood. Until the arrival of home video and the deregulation of French television in the mid-1980s, previous generations of spectators would have viewed Hollywood films exclusively in cinema theatres – a collective, semi-public experience which necessarily removes the individual from the familiar surroundings of their domestic environment and transports them to another (fictional) world on screen. Today, audiences are just as likely to watch/consume Hollywood in the intimate surroundings of their own home, through terrestrial and satellite television, DVD home cinema and even downloaded from the internet. Before, going to see a film was conceived almost exclusively in terms of an excursion or social outing (the audience seeking out Hollywood as the distant and exotic 'other' culture). Now, in addition to the traditional cinema-going experience, Hollywood 'comes to us'; is transmitted directly into our homes, onto laptops and portable DVD players as never before; permeating more deeply the experiences and cultural practices of our everyday lives as a result.

The reality is, then, that these American cultural influences are now, for better or worse, embedded within French national cinema and, more generally, into what Hall (1995: 29) refers to as 'global mass culture'. As Tom O'Regan notes (1992: 336), Hollywood has become less an American property on loan to the rest of the world, than a shared transnational cultural resource that is customised or recoded by local audiences and incorporated into the national cinematic idiom by local filmmakers. The reality of American popular culture as an established presence in contemporary French culture, is readily acknowledged by Kassovitz as both a filmmaker and cultural consumer:

> When you talk about young kids ... American music, American dress, American attitude is really important. More people are going to Euro-Disney than to the Louvre. So American culture is really a part of our culture.[14]

Of course, France's ambivalent relationship with American culture – of which cinema has served as the most prominent example – characterised by fascination and appropriation, on the one hand, and hostility and resistance to the American 'invasion', on the other, has persisted since at least the early twentieth century (Vincendeau 1992: 51–7). However, in a transnational media age where images of Americanised popular culture permeate national cultural borders more easily, carry an increasing weight within popular youth cultures throughout the world and are more accessible than ever before, American popular culture (including cinema), now forms an identifiable part of French popular culture beyond any mere influence or imported trend. Thus in the context of Kassovitz's cinema – and, indeed, for an increasing number of young French directors – to speak of cross-cultural 'exchange' between American and French cinema or an imitation of Hollywood is something of a misnomer. Firstly because, as has already been highlighted, the relationship between French and American cinema is anything but equal. But also because the references to Hollywood and American cinema that appear in the films of directors such as Kassovitz, Gans, Kounen and Pitof are not borrowed or imported as such but rather constitute elements that have been

14 A transcript of the press interview with Kassovitz and Jodie Foster is available on Kassovitz's official website: www.mathieukassovitz.com/haine/interviews/mathieu-jodie.htm (site last accessed 1/8/05).

assimilated for some time and are now embedded in French film culture (it is, after all, hard to 'import' something that to, varying degrees,
you already possess).

One final point to add here is that, despite the inequalities of power
that exist between French cinema and Hollywood, France is, of course,
not powerless to resist. Indeed for many filmmakers of Kassovitz's
generation, such as Erick Zonca and Laetitia Masson, who identify
themselves unambiguously with the *auteur* tradition, French cinema
defines itself precisely *against* the Hollywood 'other' (Ferenczi *et al.*
1999: 18–21). Further resistance to this perceived American colonisation of French national cinema can be seen in the policies of Jack Lang
during the 1980s, who as minister of culture attempted to introduce a
whole raft of reforms relating to production, distribution and exhibition that would allow a clearly identified French national cinema to
compete with Hollywood for popular audiences and thus retain the
dominant share of the domestic box office. The fact that Lang's initiatives largely failed – by the beginning of the 1990s, Hollywood had in
fact increased its share of French audiences, who only returned in the
late 1990s with the arrival of a number of new French youth-orientated blockbusters influenced in no small part by the genres and production practices of Hollywood – is proof that cultural policy cannot
necessarily determine audience tastes, and further evidence of the
affinity amongst a new generation of French cultural consumers and
practitioners with Hollywood. In the context of these cultural debates
and the often ambivalent relationship between French cinema and
Hollywood, let us now consider Kassovitz's two most recent films: *Les
Rivières pourpres* and *Gothika*

Les Rivières pourpres: continuity and difference

In autumn of 1999 Kassovitz returned to France from two years of
self-imposed exile in Los Angeles[15] to direct *Les Rivières pourpres*; a
crime thriller adapted from the bestselling French novel of the same
name by Jean-Christophe Grangé,[16] which the director intended

15 Kassovitz had, in fact, made various trips back to Paris during his time in Los
   Angeles, including to act in *Le Plaisir (et ses petits tracas)* (Boukhrief, 1998) and
   Amélie (Jeunet, 2000).
16 *Les Rivières pourpres* (1998), Paris: Albin Michel.

(Dupy and Guillomeau 2000) to be a French version of contemporary American psychological thrillers such as *Se7en* and *Silence of
the Lambs* (Demme, 1991). The decision to work for the first time on
a commissioned feature adapted from original material by another
author was not the only difference between *Les Rivières pourpres* and
Kassovitz's previous films. The director's nine-year collaboration with
Christophe Rossignon and Lazennec[17] was replaced by the French
'major' Gaumont and mainstream producer Alain Goldman whose
previous credits included *1492* (Ridley Scott, 1992) and *Vatel* (Joffé,
2000). This new alliance with Goldman and Gaumont resulted in a
significant increase in budget from FF 40 million for *Assassin(s)* to
nearly FF 100 million (€15 million) for *Les Rivières pourpres*, as well as
the opportunity to work with Jean Reno, one of French cinema's big-
gest and most exportable stars. When interviewed by Parisian weekly
Le Journal du dimanche (Lacomme 2000), Kassovitz thus spoke of the
film as 'une carte d'entrée dans un nouveau club: celui des productions ambitieuses et chères entre 100 et 200 millions'.[18]

Principal photography for *Les Rivières pourpres* was completed
over a period of three months in early 2000, with extensive location
shooting in the French Alps, including a technically challenging and
perilous sequence filmed entirely on (and inside) a glacier at an altitude of over 3,000 metres. In addition to the film's obvious technical
challenges, *Les Rivières pourpres* gave Kassovitz the opportunity to work
with a whole new group of artists and technicians – including Besson's
regular director of photography since *Nikita* (1990), Thierry Arbogast.
Kassovitz thus parted company with nearly all of the technical crew
who had worked with him on his first three features. Though such
a dramatic replacement of personnel was, almost certainly, imposed
on Kassovitz by Gaumont and Goldman, it also reflected the fact that
tensions between the director and his crew experienced during the
shooting of *Assassin(s)* had not been forgotten.

Finally, *Les Rivières pourpres* represented a new departure for

17 Kassovitz maintains professional links with Rossignon through MNP Entreprise
    – a production company co-founded by the two men. Rossignon also appears
    briefly in *Les Rivières pourpres* (as the policeman who arrives on the bridge after
    the car chase towards the end of the film) thus maintaining the in-joke between
    director and producer, which had seen him appear in cameo roles in *Métisse* and
    La Haine (both times as a taxi driver).
18 'A pass into a new club: that of ambitious and expensive productions between
    FF 100 and FF 200 million'.

Kassovitz in the sense that it was his first *policier* (crime film); along with comedy, the staple genre of popular French cinema post-1945. It was also, significantly, the first film in which Kassovitz and his characters ventured beyond Paris and the *banlieue* – with the action taking place in the French Alps and the fictional Guernon University. At least one constant remained, though, in the form of Vincent Cassel who acted alongside Reno as the ambitious and impetuous young detective Max Kerkerian. (Since his explosive performance as Vinz in *La Haine*, Cassel had rapidly established himself as one of French cinema's most popular young male stars).

Kassovitz began working on the screenplay for *Les Rivières pourpres* with Grangé in the final months of 1999. The adaptation from page to screen was complicated by the fact that, in addition to a dense plot and the two parallel narratives at the centre of the story, the original novel contained numerous secondary characters that were firmly intertwined within the central strands of the narrative. While one reviewer (*Le Monde* 2000) commented that, given the complexity of the novel, any film version of *Les Rivières pourpres* would need to last at least five hours, Kassovitz was obliged to adhere to the exhibitors' preferred length of between 90 and 120 minutes, given the commercial nature of the project (in fact the film runs for 101 minutes).

Such constraints led Kassovitz and Grangé to remove a substantial amount of content found in the novel; not an uncommon practice in film adaptation, but one that led to accusations from certain French reviewers that the characters in the film lacked depth, especially in relation to the exposition of the dubious past of both police detectives found in the book (Goudet 2000: 50). Other critics (Bonnuad 2000) took issue with the way in which Kassovitz combined the discourse surrounding eugenics that underpins the narrative of the original novel with a poorly articulated, slight and simplistic anti-fascist discourse. The screenplay also saw the removal of a number of secondary figures from the novel, including the local police officer who assists superintendent Niémans with his enquiries upon his arrival from Paris – a character that was originally to be played by Kassovitz. In terms of the novel's structure, Kassovitz maintained the use of parallel narratives for the first half of the film, but chose to make two highly significant modifications. Firstly (against the wishes of Goldman) he cut the explosive introduction in which, during rioting following a football match in Paris, Niémans beats a hooligan to the point of death. Secondly, the ending of the film was revised to incorporate a more spectacular digitally enhanced finale in the mountains above the university, complete with computer-generated avalanche.

One of the most curious consequences of the adaptation process, however, relates to the character of the young detective who works alongside Niémans. In the original novel, he is named Karim Abdouf, a young French police officer of Moroccan descent who originates from the deprived housing estates of the Parisian *banlieue*. In the film, Kassovitz and Grangé maintain the character's streetwise edge; he is from Paris and we are first introduced to him sharing a joint with some youths from a local *cité*. However, in order to allow Cassel to play the part credibly, the young detective is now named Max Kerkerian and he is of Eastern European origins. Kassovitz has claimed that it was Cassel who inadvertently convinced him to rewrite the part, when he sought his old friend's advice as to which Maghrebi-French actor he should cast in the role.[19] Nevertheless, the decision to remove a starring role for a young Maghrebi-French actor, which could either have been filled by Sami Naceri (established as a popular star after the success of *Taxi* (Pirés, 1997)) or else by experienced screen actors such as Roschdy Zem or Sami Bouajila, is somewhat surprising given Kassovitz's record for promoting acting talent from ethnic minorities in his previous films. Whether this casting choice is viewed as a missed opportunity or disappointing compromise, it is also suggestive of the extent to which Kassovitz felt under pressure to acquiesce to the demands of Goldman and Gaumont – who would, one imagines, have preferred to see Reno paired on screen with Cassel the up-and-coming, critically acclaimed (white) French star with cross-over box-office appeal.

The version of *Les Rivières pourpres* adapted for the screen by Kassovitz and Grangé focuses squarely on the parallel investigations of two police detectives. Veteran homicide inspector, Pierre Niémans, is called from Paris to the university town of Guernon in the French Alps following the macabre discovery of the mutilated corpse of a student hidden halfway up a rockface – the first victim of a serial killer with an undisclosed motive. Max Kerkerian, a young lieutenant seconded from Paris to the Alpine town of Sarzac investigates a burglary at the local primary school and the desecration of a tomb at a nearby cemetery

19 See the interview with Kassovitz on the UK-released DVD of *Les Rivières pourpres*.

of a young girl killed in a horrific traffic accident. As the two cases converge and more bodies are discovered, Niémans and Kerkerian learn the motive of the serial killer: to expose and exact revenge on the perpetrators of a Nazi-style eugenics programme secretly practised at Guernon University, whereby the healthy babies of local mountain villagers born at the university hospital are swapped with the babies of university employees and later paired off with the sons and daughters of academics to produce a 'super race' of healthy bodies and healthy minds. The identity of the serial killer is finally exposed as Judith, the 'hidden' twin sister of Fanny (both played by Nadia Farès) a glaciologist working at the university. While Fanny was swapped at birth, Judith remained with her biological parents and had been presumed killed in the road accident investigated by Kerkerian – an accident that was, in fact, an attempt by the university elite to murder the twin and thus cover up any evidence of the eugenics programme. The film ends with Niémans and Max confronting the twin sisters at the top of a cable-car station in the mountains where Judith is killed by an avalanche.

The *policier* as generic interface between France and America

As this brief synopsis shows, despite the best attempts of Kassovitz and Grangé, the film narrative of *Les Rivières pourpres* remains complex and rather convoluted. Moreover, its emphasis on serial killers and explosive action sequences is more in keeping with the American thrillers than the traditional conventions and concerns of the French crime film (the *policier* or *polar*).[20] The *policier* has been one of the staple genres of French cinema and generally recognised in France as uniquely placed as a result of it subject matter – which considers criminality, deviance and social taboos as well as the nature of crime and its repression – to articulate socio-political concerns (Powrie 1997: 75). This is not to say, however, that the *policier* should be seen as a genre in which socio-political realities are always objectively observed. For example, in the 1980s, when issues of immigration and national

20 In the 1990s, a number of highly successful serial-killer narratives emerged from Hollywood (*The Silence of the Lambs*; *Se7en*; *Copycat* (Amiel, 1995). Though far less prominent in French cinema, the serial killer has, interestingly, appeared as much in *auteur* films (*J'ai pas sommeil* (Denis, 1993); *Roberto Succo* (Kahn, 2000)) as in mainstream features such as *Les Rivières pourpres*.

identity were at the forefront of socio-political debate in France, the *policier* increasingly offered a stereotypical depiction of the non-European immigrant population as France's criminalised 'other' (see, for example, *La Balance* (Swaim, 1982); *Police* (Pialat, 1985) and later *L.627* (Tavernier, 1992)).

The *policier* has, moreover, always formed the natural point of interface between French and American cinema (Hollywood). This is due in part to the fact that it emerges through a complex series of influences from both French and American popular literature and cinema (Vincendeau 1992: 68–71; Powrie 1997: 76).[21] The French crime film is therefore open to exchange with the Hollywood crime film due to the existing interest in the genre on a domestic level, but also able to dialogue or negotiate with Hollywood from the secure and established position of the genre *within* French popular culture. This hypothesis is supported by the fact that the exchange between the French *policier* and American crime film has been arguably more equal than in other genres. Duvivier's *Pépé le Moko* (1936) can thus be seen as influenced by American gangster films of the early 1930s. However, the French *noir* style contained within this and other popular poetic realist films of the 1930s can, equally, be seen as one of the contributing influences on later US *film noir* of the 1940s and 1950s. In cinematic terms, then, the *policier* emerges as one of the few points of generic interface between American and French cinema:

> 'the French *policier* is thus a rich network of intertextual relations ranging from imitations, reworkings and parodies, to mere allusions and, importantly, autonomous parallel forms. The Americans may have cornered the market in gangsters, they do not have a monopoly on crime and mystery. (Vincendeau 1992: 69)

And yet, the *policier* is also more than a site of stylistic and intertextual exchange between French and American cinema in the crime genre. As Forbes (1992: 74) has pointed out, the clear association of the genre with issues such as the growth of cities, criminality and the means of policing the modern urban environment, make the *policier* the perfect

---

21 On the French side, the *policier* is influenced by gothic and realist novels (Balzac and Hugo), and the *Vidocq* crime series from the nineteenth century; the *romans policiers* of the early twentieth century, the series of *Fantômas* films by Feuillade (1913–14) and the Maigret adaptations of the 1930s and 1940s. From America come the hard-boiled novels of Hammet and Chandler; Hollywood gangster films of the 1930s and *film noir* of the 1940s and 1950s.

arena for exploring anxieties surrounding modernisation, American-isation and the shift towards an urban-based, consumer society in France post-1945. The *policier* thus becomes a vehicle for articulating both France's fascination with American culture and seduction by American-style consumerism, as well as a means of expressing equally strong feelings of hostility and ambivalence towards the increasing influence of American cultural and economic power over contempo-rary French culture and society – another reason that has been used to explain the genre's enduring popularity in French cinema post-1945. In this respect, the *policier* would also appear to be the natural genre for Kassovitz to explore his own fascination with American cinema and American popular culture in general.

Reinventing the French crime film or imitating Hollywood?

However, by 1999, when Kassovitz commenced production on *Les Rivières pourpres*, the *policier* was in decline as a result of changes in audience tastes and production trends in French cinema. Firstly, the *policier*'s function as a means for articulating social concerns was usurped in the 1990s by the more direct engagement with political and social issues found in the work of a disparate wave of indepen-dent filmmakers such as Masson, Zonca, Guédiguian and Kassovitz under the loosely defined rubric of new realism or the *retour du poli-tique*. Many of these directors had also been associated with a resur-gence of *auteur* cinema in the 1990s (in the form of *jeune cinéma*) further detracting from the importance the *policier* had enjoyed in the 1980s, when, as Powrie suggests (1997: 76), in the absence of a readily identifiable *auteur* cinema during this period, the *policier* pro-vided a creative space in which new young directors (potential *auteurs*) could establish a name for themselves. Finally, whereas comedy, the other staple genre of French cinema post-1945, continued to attract French audiences in the 1990s, the *policier* was declining in popu-larity. On one side, a more mature, middle-class French audience was displaying an increasing preference for the heritage film; on the other, younger audiences were opting for the visual pleasures of big-budget, spectacular action films such as the *Taxi* series, *Le Pacte des loups* and *Le Cinquième élément*. This is not to suggest, however, that French audiences had lost their appetite for crime films in the 1990s; rather, as box-office figures show, they were simply more inclined towards the American thriller, which was enjoying a period of renewal in the 1990s with films such as *Silence of the Lambs*; *Se7en* and *The Usual Suspects*.

Les Rivières pourpres needs, therefore, to be understood in the context of the decline in popularity of the *policier* in the 1990s, which inevitably forces the genre in new directions in order to survive. It also needs to be considered in relation to the genre's strategic historical and cultural importance as an interface between French cinema and Hollywood. Kassovitz was astute enough to realise that the *policier* no longer held the same attraction for French audiences; *Les Rivières pourpres* thus distances itself quite clearly from many of the traditional codes and conventions of the French crime film, taking its cue much more directly from American cinema. Most obviously, the film dispenses with the *policier*'s traditional emphasis on the nature of crime and its repression, an approach that attempts a psychological exploration of either the criminal or law enforcer and an emphasis on reflection as much as action.

And yet, initially, *Les Rivières pourpres* appears, paradoxically, to conform to many of the norms of the French *policier*. As already noted, Kassovitz rejected the explosive and violent introduction of Grangé's original novel favoured by producer Alain Goldman, for a far more restrained and reflective opening. The film begins with the camera inspecting in slow, deliberate movements and extreme close-up the mutilated body of the first victim as it lies hidden in a crevice. This sequence is followed shortly after by a post-mortem in which repeated close-ups of Niémans/Reno 'investigating' the corpse suggest an empathy with the victim as well as an attempt to understand the motives of the serial killer. However, this more contemplative approach is soon replaced by an emphasis on action or spectacle: be it Kerkerian's fight with a local gang of skinheads; Niémans' trip to the glacier by helicopter; or the two dramatically choreographed chase sequences that occur towards the end of the film.

When interviewed (Dupy and Guillomeau 2000), Kassovitz has spoken of how this decision to prioritise energy and movement in *Les Rivières pourpres* – not simply in terms of action on screen, but also narrative structure and editing style – was largely dictated by the constraints of the genre; by which he means the American crime thriller rather than the French *policier*. As at least one reviewer (Péron

2000) pointed out, the chase scenes in *Les Rivières pourpres* identify Kassovitz as one of the few contemporary French directors capable of competing with Hollywood in this type of kinetic, action–suspense sequence. Indeed, we could even read the car chase along the narrow winding mountain roads – the BMW of Niémans being aggressively pursued by a large American style jeep – as an intertextual reference to Spielberg's *Duel*, the director whom Kassovitz views as the master of the action–suspense film.

It is no coincidence that this shift towards action in *Les Rivières pourpres* is initiated by Kerkerian's arrival in the narrative. Vincent Cassel's performance style, established in *La Haine*, combines athleticism and physicality with a potentially explosive nervous energy that is expressed verbally as much as physically, and contrasts directly with the more restrained, brooding masculinity of Niémans (another reason, perhaps, why Cassel was cast in the role alongside Jean Reno). With the pairing of Niémans and Kerkerian, Kassovitz draws on the trope of the mismatched cop duo commonly found in American crime films, from the action comedy of the *Lethal Weapon* series (1987–98) to far darker crime thrillers of the 1990s. Indeed this combination of the cerebral, world-weary detective with the aggressive, ambitious young lieutenant in *Les Rivières pourpres* is reminiscent of the pairing of Morgan Freeman and Brad Pitt in *Se7en*; a film repeatedly cited by Kassovitz (*ibid.*) as a key influence on the look and ambience of *Les Rivières pourpres*.

The French connection: *Les Rivières pourpres* and the *cinéma du look*

Despite the seeming abundance of American influences in *Les Rivières pourpres*, which is precisely why a number of critics (Bonnaud 2000; Blumenfeld 2000) dismissed the film as little more than a pale imitation of Hollywood genre cinema, Kassovitz does establish a definite sense of French 'difference' in the film. For the director, *Les Rivières pourpres* was thus: 'un film à l'américaine fabriquée à la française. Parce qu'un film comme ça, aux États-Unis, avec une star comme Jean, ils le font pour le double. Ici, ça reste très artisanal' (Dupy and Guillomeau 2000).[22]

22 '...an American-style production made in the French way. Because in America with a film like that and a star like Jean [Reno] it would cost twice as much to make. Here, it's more artisanal'.

And yet, even if Kassovitz borrows extensively from the American crime thriller in terms of a reliance on the buddy cop duo and a fast-paced, action-led narrative, he nonetheless uses these elements to adapt a bestselling French *roman policier* (crime novel). Elsewhere, the film employed the talents of French special-effects artists Jean-Christophe Spadaccini, Denis Gastou et Pascal Molina to create the highly detailed and immensely lifelike model of the mutilated corpse of the film's first victim. The quality of the life-size sculpture was such that it allowed Kassovitz to explore the surfaces of the model in extreme close-up for the opening scenes of the film; a level of artistry that suggests a further difference from Hollywood, where more traditional special effects are increasingly being replaced by computer-generated visuals.[23]

The geographical location of *Les Rivières pourpres* instantly establishes the film as 'other' to the typical urban locale of the American crime film. Indeed, even for a French crime film, *Les Rivières pourpres* is unusual in that it takes place outside of the city and, in particular, Paris. Kassovitz makes extensive use of the setting in the French Alps as a means of enhancing the dark and sinister atmosphere of the film. Rather than connoting a site of health and vitality, the mountains are an oppressive force: looming menacingly above the university, harbouring the corpses of the serial killer's victims as well as offering the environment in which the ailing children of the local alpine villages are raised. In particular, the film works on the contrast between the vast open spaces of the mountains and the dark, sinister interiors of the town: the university library; Dr Cherneze's clinic; Fanny's home and the convent in Sarzac.

Kassovitz also exploits the French Alps as cinematic spectacle. The sequence in which Niémans and Fanny are taken by helicopter to the glacier in search of clues that will lead them to the next body – the ice placed by the killer in the eye sockets of the first victim could only have come from the mountains, it transpires – was filmed entirely on location at an altitude of more than 3,000 metres. The results of this technically challenging and highly dangerous shoot make for possibly the most visually alluring scenes of the whole film – the natural beauty of the glacier appearing in stark contrast to the computer-generated avalanche created for the overblown final scene of *Les*

23 Digital effects are also, of course, employed in *Les Rivières pourpres*, most obviously in the avalanche sequence at the end of the film.

Rivières pourpres. For some critics, however, this use of the stunning mountain scenery was an unnecessary indulgence that bore little relation to the overall narrative:

> Le récit semble alors passer au second plan, rien de plus qu'un prétexte pour envoyer une équipe dans les Alpes et fixer quelques images d'une grande beauté plastique. Alors que ses personnages s'échinent à rechercher ce qui est caché sous les apparences, Kassovitz n'est jamais meilleur que lorsqu'il filme la surface des choses.[24] (Higuinen 2000: 106)

What is so striking about this review from *Cahiers du cinéma* is that it recreates (whether consciously or not) many of the same criticisms in relation to the primacy of image over narrative, style over substance that were levelled against the 1980s *cinéma du look* and in particular the films of Luc Besson – a comparison that would no doubt have delighted Kassovitz, even if it was intended as something of a critical slight on the film. Indeed, the filming of the Alps in *Les Rivières pourpres* could be compared to that of the natural expanse of the ocean in *Le Grand bleu* (Besson, 1988).

This link to the look cinema of the 1980s, and the foregrounding of spectacle over narrative thus highlights another difference between *Les Rivières pourpres* and American mainstream cinema, in which continuity and cohesion are paramount and where logical progression of the narrative has traditionally been valued above all else. Even though the more recent popularity of American action–spectacle cinema has displaced some of the 'classic' characteristics of Hollywood narrative cinema (Arroyo 2000: vii), such films still maintain a focus on spectacle that is synonymous with action, and one that propels the narrative to its high-octane conclusion.

In contrast (and despite the fact that a similar combination of action–spectacle is quite clearly foregrounded elsewhere in the film) the glacier sequence in *Les Rivières pourpres* places the emphasis firmly on spectacle and action to the detriment of narrative, in a manner that is consistent with the *cinéma du look*. Whereas, the American action/ spectacle film moves us relentlessly from one thrill to the next, in *Les*

---

24 'The narrative seems to fade into the background, being nothing more than a pretext to send a film crew into the Alps to shoot some extremely beautiful images. Whereas his characters wear themselves out by constantly searching for what lies beneath the facade, Kassovitz is never better than when he films the surface of things.'

Rivières pourpres the glacier sequence functions almost as a moment of retreat and reflection. As if to highlight this point, it is the more cerebral and physically unconditioned Niémans who ventures in to the Alps with Fanny, not the young, athletic Cassel (the star body who, more in keeping with Hollywood action heroes such as Tom Cruise and Bruce Willis, would have propelled the narrative forward, as he does elsewhere in the film). Therefore, Kassovitz's use of the spectacular mountain scenery as a means of establishing the foreboding and oppressive mood of the film is, equally, consistent with the classic French *policiers* of the 1950s in which, unlike the American crime film were 'also concerned with atmospheric scenes which do not advance the plot to any extent' (Vincendeau 1992: 72).

One final link to the *cinéma du look* which also distances the film further from the American crime film is Kassovitz's tendency in *Les Rivières pourpres* to drift temporarily away in the realms of fantasy: specifically, horror and the supernatural.[25] The gothic atmosphere of the convent where Fanny and Judith's mother remains obscured from view in her stone 'cell' having taken the 'vow of the shadows' is deliberately exaggerated; when interviewed by Kerkerian, obscured by the darkness that has caused her to go half-blind, she speaks of demons and monsters having taken her child. Similarly, while the macabre *mise en scène* of Dr Cherneze's murder – where a flash of lightning reveals the surgeon's bloodied corpse suspended as if from a crucifix, with a message from the killer smeared in blood on the walls – can be read as an intertextual reference to *The Silence of the Lambs*,[26] the bloody and theatrical staging of the murder also brings to mind the films of cult Italian horror director Dario Argento (of whom Kassovitz was an avid fan during his teenage years). Moreover, as these references to both the *cinéma du look* and gothic horror indicate, in *Les Rivières pourpres* Kassovitz moves deliberately and decidedly away from the social realism traditionally associated with both the French *policier* and the American crime film.

25 These elements of fantasy in the *cinéma du look* are discussed by Austin (1996: 122–35).
26 The staging of Cherneze's murder recalls that of the police guard which leads to Hannibal Lector's escape in *The Silence of the Lambs*.

The *policier* in freefall: *Les Rivières pourpres* as generic simulacrum

If Kassovitz's film maintains continuity with the traditional post-war *policier*, it is largely through the genre's function as a means of exploring the relationship between French and American cinema/culture. *Les Rivières pourpres* does not, however, speak of a fear or ambivalence but rather a fascination with Americanisation (or we might even say the dangers of an *excessive* fascination with the Americanisation that is now embedded in French popular culture). Moreover, this dialogue with America is posited on a specifically cinematic level. *Les Rivières pourpres* is indicative of a broader shift in French production practices as they attempt to win back popular audiences from Hollywood, or what Ciment (2001: 1), in contrast to the *film d'auteur*, has labelled the resurgence in French cinema of a *cinéma des producteurs*: on the one hand, big-budget films with high-production values that are script-led and function as star vehicles (such as comedy or the heritage film); and, on the other, the youth-orientated *film d'action* or the spectacular genre film such as *Les Rivières pourpres*. Unlike the heritage film, whose identifiably French cultural and historical focus attempts a clear differentiation from Hollywood, the spectacular genre film – typically action, thriller and/or comedy hybrids, accompanied by spectacular set pieces and stunning visual effects – unashamedly takes many of its cues from American cinema, and thus problematises the notion of French cinema as a national cinema that traditionally defined itself *against* Hollywood.

By the end of *Les Rivières pourpres*, with its spectacularly staged avalanche sequence in the mountains, it appears that Hollywood finally holds sway over the narrative. Ultimately, however, Kassovitz's reverence for contemporary American cinema proves a restrictive rather than liberating influence. As Roy (2000: 61) suggests, it is as if the director tries too hard in *Les Rivières pourpres* to attract the attention of Hollywood.[27] Rather than transposing American influences into a specifically French context as he had done so successfully in both *Métisse* and *La Haine*, in *Les Rivières pourpres* Kassovitz attempts to forge an uncomfortable alliance between American and French/European production practices, narrative modes and film style. Consequently, the film appears to collapse under the weight of its

27 '...pour passer haut la main son examen d'entrée à Hollywood, il en met trop'/ 'in attempting to pass his entry exam into Hollywood he overdoes it'.

ultra-codified references to the action film and American crime thriller, which sit incongruously with the more French and European influences in the film. While *Les Rivières pourpres* maintains its sinister atmosphere through a carefully controlled *mise en scène*, the relentless pace of the narrative and ultimate emphasis on action mean that any impetus derived from the narrative's anti-Fascist subtext (the Neo-Nazi eugenics programme practised by the elite of the university) which might have given *Les Rivières pourpes* the socio-political edge of *La Haine* or *Assassin(s)*, is lost. With seemingly nowhere left to turn, Kassovitz imposes an ending on his audience that contains both excessive action–spectacle (the computer-generated avalanche) and an incredible revelation (the existence of Fanny's 'hidden' twin) leaving the film helplessly stranded between its American and French precursors (too overblown or bizarre for the American thriller; too focused on action and spectacle for the traditional *policier*) and verging on the ridiculous.

Such a reading of *Les Rivières pourpres*, bring us remarkably close to the position laid out by Hayward (1993: 289–91) more than ten years ago in relation to the French *policier* of the 1980s, which she describes as having fallen under the influence of the American thriller, void of its true subtlety and national specificity, with little more than an 'iconography of Frenchness'. For all his talk of creating an 'American thriller in the French way', and though audience figures of over three million in France might suggest otherwise, Kassovitz's approach in *Les Rivières pourpres* was perhaps less original than it had at first appeared. Whether or not this makes *Les Rivières pourpres* the exception that proves the rule of a popular French genre (the *policier*) in unarrested freefall, the film appears, in the final analysis, as a kind of generic simulacrum – bearing reference to the signs and iconography of both the American crime thriller and the *policier* but ultimately not sufficiently grounded in the representational 'reality' of either national generic form to be entirely credible.

Entering the Hollywood system: *Gothika* (2003)

In contrast to its success at the French box office, *Les Rivières pourpres* performed poorly abroad; another indication, perhaps, that rather than being a mere 'imitation' of Hollywood, the film was in fact too 'French' to attract foreign audiences. The film was, however, eventually seen by Joel Silver – for over two decades one of Hollywood's most commercially successful producers – and so served as the calling card to Hollywood that Kassovitz had hoped for. Silver was one of a number of American producers who had become interested in bringing Kassovitz to work in Hollywood since the early 2000s, though the director chose to hold out on the offers made to him until he received the script for *Gothika*, a mid-budget ($40 million) horror film, in spring 2003.

In many ways it is easy to dismiss *Gothika*, as virtually all French reviewers did, as an excursion into Hollywood genre cinema of no real significance. In common with *Les Rivières pourpres*, the film was commercially successful but poorly received by critics on both sides of the Atlantic. Equally, *Gothika* can be seen as a commissioned feature over which Kassovitz had even less creative control than Les *Rivières pourpres*: a film that is, therefore, of little importance to a study of the director as *auteur* in the context of contemporary French cinema. And yet, precisely for this reason the film is of interest, for it allows us to see whether, in the classic model of the American *auteurs* identified by the *Cahiers'* critics in the 1950s (Hillier 1985: 7), Kassovitz is able to stamp his mark as *auteur* on a film produced within the constraints of the Hollywood system. *Gothika* also provides further evidence of the transnational dimension to Kassovitz's filmmaking, and in particular the influence of American cinema that has marked all of his French releases to date. In a broader historical context, by venturing to North America, Kassovitz is following in the tradition of European filmmakers directing horror films in Hollywood: from James Whale's *Frankenstein* series in the 1930s to Polanski's seminal *Rosemary's Baby* (1968)).

Despite being a commissioned feature *Gothika* can, arguably, be read as a personal project insomuch as Kassovitz has always been an avid fan of American horror and exploitation films.[28] The earliest experiments with his parents' movie camera at home were in fact short spoof horror films – imitations of the classic American independent low-budget exploitation films such as *Halloween* (Carpenter, 1978) and *Evil Dead* (Raimi, 1981) that the director watched repeatedly on video

28 'À 15 ans j'ai passé 10 heures par jour à regarder des films comme *Gothika*. Même si j'aime aussi Costa-Gavras ou Werner Herzog' / 'Even if I also appreciate directors such as Costa-Gavras or Werner Herzog, at the age of 15 I spent ten hours a day watching films like *Gothika*' (Aubel 2003: 22).

as a teenager. *Gothika* thus reflects Kassovitz's own tastes as a spectator, as well as the realisation of his ambition to direct a horror movie (a genre that, until very recently with the emergence of what might be termed an *auteurist* 'cinema of the abject' had formed a structuring absence in French cinema). Indeed, the elements of the horror genre are already present to some degree in a number of Kassovitz's earlier French shorts and features; most obviously in *Les Rivières pourpres* but also in the explicit violence of *Assassin(s)* and as early as Kassovitz's second short film, *Cauchemar blanc* (1991), in which the narrative is structured around a nightmarish event that becomes imminent reality (in this case a racist attack by a gang of thugs); a frequently employed device in horror films.

Finally, *Gothika* is of significance in that it is the first of Kassovitz's films to foreground specifically a female protagonist in the lead role. Though not the author of the original screenplay, the decision to accept this female-centred narrative over the other scripts that were being offered to him at the time by Hollywood producers suggests an evolution on the part of Kassovitz the filmmaker – especially given criticism of his films in the past for ignoring or eliding female protagonists. For this reason alone, *Gothika* is worthy of serious consideration.

Gothika was released in America in November 2003 by Hollywood 'independent' Dark Castle Entertainment. The production company, created in 1999 as a sideline project by Joel Silver and A-list director Robert Zemeckis,[29] was designed to produce mid-budget horror films for Warner Brothers studios that would include both original scripts and remakes of the 1950s and 1960s films of cult 'schlock' horror director, William Castle. Castle's formula took standard horror narratives, made for very little money and combined them with ingenious marketing schemes (such as selling insurance for 'death by fright' at theatres showing his films) to attract audiences.

After the commercially successful remakes of Castle 'classics' such *House on Haunted Hill* (1999) and *13 Ghosts* (2001), the first Dark Castle production to be developed from an entirely original script, *Ghost Ship* (2002), fared less well at the box office. The poor performance of the third film in the Dark Castle series, with its computer-generated ocean liner filled with phantoms and rather predictable scares, suggested a

29 Silver is the producer behind the *Lethal Weapon*, *Die Hard* and *Matrix* franchises while Zemeckis has directed blockbusters such as *Back to the Future* (1985); *Who Framed Roger Rabbit* (1988); *Forrest Gump* (1994) and *Cast Away* (2000).

shift in audience tastes towards more sophisticated horror (Swanson 2003: 49). Silver and Zemeckis responded accordingly, by moving forward with *Gothika*, as much a supernatural suspense thriller as traditional horror, and a film that placed a strong female character at the centre of its narrative. The project was also given priority as Dark Castle had managed to secure the services of A-list star and Academy award winner Halle Berry for the lead, as well as signing Robert Downey Jr. and Penélope Cruz in supporting roles. Production costs escalated accordingly, with *Gothika*'s budget of almost $40 million being twice that of *House on Haunted Hill*, the first film in the Dark Castle horror series. With the increased financial risk involved, Joel Silver decided to revise his original choice of director from the relatively inexperienced director-screenwriter Sebastian Gutierrez – author of the original screenplay – in favour of Kassovitz, whom the producer felt would bring an edgier, European perspective to *Gothika* while understanding the essentially commercial nature of the film (*ibid.*: 50).

Kassovitz was, not surprisingly, enthusiastic to work with a producer of Silver's stature, as well as actors of the calibre of Berry, Downey Jr. and Cruz on his first Hollywood feature, and agreed to begin pre-production on the film less than two months after having received the script. The film was shot in Canada in forty-five days (half the time it took to film *Les Rivières pourpres*), in studios near Montreal, as well as on location in a former Victorian prison which provided both the gothic appearance and the institutional feel required for the fictional psychiatric prison in which the first half of the film takes place.

Gothika's narrative centres on Dr Miranda Grey (Berry) a talented young psychiatrist who works at Woodward Penitentiray, a prison for the criminally insane. One of her patients is Chloe (Cruz): a psychologically disturbed inmate, convicted of murdering her stepfather, whose claims of rape and molestation by 'devils' that visit her cell are dismissed as delusions. One night, driving home from work, Miranda is involved in an accident, swerving to avoid a distressed young woman who stands alone in the middle of the road. After blacking out at the scene of the accident, Miranda awakes in a cell at Woodward; this time as one of the inmates, charged with the violent murder of her husband and prison governor, Doug Grey (Charles Dutton), a crime that she has no recollection of committing. Despite claiming she does not believe in ghosts 'even if they believe in me', Miranda is repeatedly 'visited' in her cell by the young woman she encountered at the scene of the accident (who we eventually learn is the missing daughter of a colleague at the prison). With the intervention of the female spectre, Miranda escapes from Woodward and uncovers the truth behind her crime: the murder was committed after being possessed by Rachel Parsons, one of the victims in a series of rapes and murders carried out by Miranda's husband and the local sheriff (who is finally killed during a confrontation with Miranda, aided once again by the intervention of Rachel's ghost). The film ends on the streets of an unidentified city, with a meeting between Miranda and Chloe – whose allegations of sexual abuse in the prison have now been substantiated as part of the crimes committed by Doug and Sheriff Ryan. As Chloe departs, Miranda witnesses another apparition – this time a young boy – suggesting she is, in fact, a medium for these troubled spirits from the afterlife and (conveniently for Silver and Dark Castle) leaving the film's ending open for a sequel.[30]

As this synopsis of the film demonstrates, *Gothika* draws on existing tropes and narratives from the horror genre, while also continuing an established history of setting horror films in psychiatric institutions: from *Shock Corridor* (Fuller, 1963) and *Bedlam* (Robson, 1946), to more recent features such as *In the Mouth of Madness* (Carpenter, 1994) (Wheaton 2003a: 24). The film also employs a classic asylum-horror narrative, where an apparently sane individual is incarcerated with those deemed clinically insane – a plot that, equally, appears outside of the horror genre in films such as *One Flew over the Cuckoo's Nest* (Forman, 1975) and the Chris Marker-inspired science-fiction epic, *Twelve Monkeys* (Gilliam, 1995). Through its location and narrative focus, *Gothika* therefore questions the clearly defined boundaries between sanity and madness, 'truth' and delusion, and the ways in which such boundaries may be determined by those in authority (psychiatrists, prison governors, law enforcement officers, and so on) as a means of consolidating their positions of power.

In his interpretation of Gutierrez's original screenplay, Kassovitz shows a keen awareness of the horror genre's reliance on *mise en scène* to create atmosphere and suspense, as well as more traditional scares:

30 At the time of writing, no such plans for a sequel to *Gothika* have been disclosed. However, on the UK DVD commentary for the film, Kassovitz jokes that the ending allows for the creation of the franchise for a *Gothika*-style TV series.

'Horror movies are the best for a director because this is where one can work with the camera in the most efficient way...it's all about cam-erawork and timing'(Wheaton 2003b: 17–18). Kassovitz's reference here to the efficiency of the camera brings to mind his comments (discussed earlier in this chapter) on the control and movement of the camera in Spielberg's films. In *Gothika*, through a combination of Steadicam and state-of-the-art visual effects, the camera is seen to restlessly navigate the corridors of the prison. In certain scenes – for example, Miranda's escape from Woodward prison and the visitations of Rachel's ghost to Miranda's cell – the camera is apparently able to pass undetected through physical barriers such as glass doors and prison bars (as if adopting the perspective of a ghost). The tightly cho-reographed escape scenes also serve as further evidence of Kassovitz's talent for directing action cinema; first seen explicitly in *Les Rivières pourpres*, but apparent from the director's first short film *Fierrot le pou*, where the young director displayed an accomplished sense of timing in the edit and controlled movement of the camera to create a kinetic energy that has characterised his filmmaking style ever since. Indeed, the foregrounding of such scenes in *Gothika* suggests a generic hybrid of horror/action/suspense, given that the spectator can derive as much visual pleasure from the action sequences as from the scares themselves.

More specifically, through *Gothika*'s *mise en scène* Kassovitz applied the lessons he had learned from repeated viewings of horror films during his teenage years. This included borrowing directly from established horror classics – Kassovitz admits for example (Wheaton 2003b: 21) to 'stealing' a couple of moments from the films of cult Italian horror director Dario Argento. Therefore, while *Gothika* em-ploys state-of-the-art computer-generated effects that can be both spectacular (Miranda's possession by Rachel; Sheriff Ryan being burnt alive) and imperceptible (the reason the camera is able to pass seem-ingly unhindered through glass walls and prison bars is because these 'physical' barriers were digitally created in post-production) the film also relies heavily on camera movement and editing to create 'real' shocks and scares. Possibly the best example comes in the isolation cell where Miranda, shot in medium close-up, senses the presence of Rachel's ghost, and, as she moves out of the frame, the ghost behind her is revealed to the audience. This highly effective scare – one of the moments recycled from Argento's *Tenebre* (1982) – relies on little more than timing and the physical movement of the actors. It does not, therefore, 'cheat' its audience in the way that digitally enhanced monsters and computer-generated scares can be seen to do.

This combination of the more traditional mechanics of the horror genre (taken from both American and European cinema) and a willingness from Kassovitz to embrace more modern aesthetics and production practices is also reflected in *Gothika*'s set design. The prison location used in the film fuses the original Victorian structure with cold, clean surfaces of glass and steel, all of which lends the highly stylised *mise en scène* a more contemporary appearance; postmodern, we might even say, in its mixing and recycling of architectural styles. This conscious stylisation is extended to the mute palette of greys and blues found in both the prison décor and the inmates' costumes, which drain the *mise en scène* of much of its colour, while simultaneously highlighting the reds, oranges and yellows of the blood, bright lights and flames that appear at specific moments in the film. This deliberate manipulation of colour adds to the sense of an altered state of reality being presented on screen; mirroring the perspective of the heavily medicated patients in the prison, as well as further emphasising the discourse surrounding the dubious boundaries between truth and delusion, sanity and insanity found in the film.

Gothika as proto-feminist horror

As mentioned earlier, *Gothika* is of particular interest in relation to Kassovitz's development as filmmaker, in that it is the first time he has directed a film with a female lead at the centre of the narrative. Given the apparent lack of interest in exploring female subjectivities shown in his previous films, it is intriguing that Kassovitz should choose to make this change in a genre which is, precisely, notorious for its ambivalent and often misogynistic attitude to women. The intention here is not to make a claim for *Gothika* as a subversive feminist text, nor is it to suggest that Kassovitz has undergone some radical transformation in relation to gender politics post-*Les Rivières pourpres*. What is noticeable, however, is the extent to which *Gothika*'s narrative places an emphasis on female solidarity – not only between Miranda and her fellow female inmates such as Chloe, but also with the ghost of Rachel Parsons, the young murder victim. 'Not Alone', the phrase daubed in blood above Doug's dead body, which also appears as if written by an invisible hand on the misted glass of Miranda's cell door, as well as seeping through the bandage covering the lacerations on her arm sustained during the unseen attack on Miranda in the communal prison showers, indicates that there are more victims to be discovered, but also signifies the collective resistance of the female protagonists in the film to the male-dominated institutions that incarcerate them (literally and figuratively). The prison, both an extension and reflection of society in *Gothika*, is thus dominated by excessively obvious patriarchal signifiers – Doug describes himself on more than one occasion as 'God', while Miranda is routinely observed in her cell and in the exercise yard by the prison's male psychiatrists (Dr Grant and Dr Parsons) – with the camera mirroring the male protagonists' controlling gaze.

Not surprisingly, applying psychoanalytic theory to *Gothika* can help us begin to unpick the lines of feminist inquiry embedded within the filmic text. As Robin Wood suggests (2002: 30), the horror film can be read through psychoanalysis, not as escapism or an attempt to deny reality, but rather as a means of dealing with issues that society itself attempts to deny or repress. The genre offers, therefore, even in its most mainstream manifestations, a potentially subversive critique of the social world. *Gothika* is, precisely, concerned with the unspoken and the repressed – the classic strategy of the horror genre according to Wood – in that it deals with the phantoms of abuse and the silence or disbelief experienced by the female victims (Chloe and Miranda) within the narrative.

Following on from Mulvey's polemic surrounding the gaze and gender politics, Linda Williams (2002: 61–6), has argued that horror addresses a male spectator and is founded on the subjugation of women. Women's difference to the male norm is thus seen as monstrous, and she is punished for her difference. However, this is not the case in *Gothika*, where the abject is clearly not coded as feminine. The female ghost (Rachel) is, on the whole, a benevolent and protective spirit, while the 'demon' or monster surfaces in the narrative through the figures of Doug and, above all, Sheriff Ryan – the tattooed male rapist who visits Chloe in her cell. Indeed, despite the continual surveillance of Miranda by the male psychiatrists in the film, it is the female gaze (that of Rachel's ghost) which controls, and will eventually solve, the mystery of Miranda's 'insanity'. What is more, the women's 'madness' or 'delusions' are, in fact, proved to be sanity/truth; while Berry emerges, not as the defenceless victim or objectified sexual object, but as the resourceful and resilient star body who, in the final sequence, refuses to be beaten into submission by Sheriff Ryan. As such, *Gothika* takes its lead from low-budget American 'slasher' horror films of the 1970s and 1980s (*The Texas Chainsaw Massacre* (Hooper, 1974), *Halloween*). In these films, as Clover has demonstrated (2002: 77–90), it is the female, not the male, who emerges as the triumphant hero through the figure of the 'final girl'.

In this context, it is noticeable that Kassovitz refuses cheap opportunities – such as the communal shower scene in the prison – to objectify Berry as the eroticised female star whose body is put on display primarily for heterosexual male consumption or pleasure; a situation commonly found elsewhere in mainstream horror films, where women are presented as either helpless victims, or sexually available objects ready for slaughter (*ibid.*). Instead, both Cruz and Berry – female stars who are often cast precisely because of their physical attractiveness and sexual desirability – are deliberately de-eroticised through costume and make-up. While Berry's tied back hair, simple and (for a star with her physical appeal) modest clothing serves to normalise somewhat her physical appearance,[31] the transformation of Cruz from desirable star body to the emotionally scarred and physically unattractive Chloe is even more dramatic. *Gothika* therefore reflects developments that have taken place in mainstream American horror since the slasher films of the 1970s, which *potentially* provide the female protagonist with a more active and empowering role within the narrative. However, unlike the majority of postmodern slashers that have followed in the 1990s – for example *Scream* (Craven, 1996) and *I Know What You Did Last Summer* (Gillespie, 1997) – in *Gothika* Berry/Miranda's position as the 'final girl' is achieved without recourse to self-referential irony or sexual objectification of the female star.

While not particularly subversive or radical in terms of its representation of women or, indeed, its engagement with gender politics, *Gothika* nonetheless emerges, in many ways, as an empowering proto-feminist text. Though this outcome is due as much as anything to Gutierrez's original screenplay and Halle Berry's performance in

31 Compare with the revealing costumes worn by Berry in films such as *Die Another Day* (Tamahori, 2002) and *Swordfish* (Sena, 2001) where the clothing (or lack of it) is used to highlight her body and, thus, sexual desirability.

the film, it at least goes some way to redressing the lack of female protagonists and bias towards (young) male subjectivities found in Kassovitz's other films to date. Comments made by Kassovitz to French journalists (Aubel 2003: 23) suggest, moreover, that criticism of the gender bias (interpreted by some as casual sexism) in his earlier films partly informed his decision to direct this particular horror film. Although, in terms of influences and collaborators, Kassovitz remains largely ensconced in what is very much a cinematic 'boy's club', *Gothika* indicates the potential (unlikely as it may currently seem) for a more receptive approach to gender issues and the representation of female subjectivity in his subsequent films.

Conclusion: 'using Hollywood'

If, as Kassovitz suggested in his third feature film, *Assassin(s)*, 'every society has the crimes that it deserves', French critics have largely had the cinema they deserve from this director since the late-1990s, for having so relentlessly denigrated his attempts in *Assassin(s)* to establish himself as a polemical, popular *auteur*. Indeed, Kassovitz's decision post-*Assassin(s)* to immerse himself in largely impersonal and highly commercial genre cinema – the exact opposite of the territory occupied by the French *auteur* – was, in part, his response to such vitriolic criticism; and a move which, unsurprisingly, has further alienated the director from these same French critics. Although less engaged socio-politically than Kassovitz's first three features, *Les Rivières pourpres* and *Gothika* nonetheless maintain the director's focus on marginal protagonists (maverick detectives and the female inmates of a psychiatric prison, respectively) who inhabit an often violent society ill at ease with itself. In common with his earlier films, *Les Rivières pourpres* and *Gothika* also function (somewhat paradoxically, given their status as mainstream genre productions) as an expression of Kassovitz's mistrust of hegemonic institutions that exert control or influence over society – the police (*La Haine*); media (*La Haine* and *Assassin(s)*); an elitist university (*Les Rivières pourpres*);[32] a male-

32 Though it bears little resemblance to the majority of France's public universities, the fictional Guernon University in *Les Rivières Pourpres* could be seen to reflect the elitism of the French Grandes Écoles, and in particular L'ÉNA (L'École Nationale d'Administration) where the majority of France's political and diplomatic elite – tomorrow's political establishment – are trained.

dominated prison (*Gothika*) – a position that is entirely consistent with Kassovitz's public persona as an outspoken, anti-establishment director.

In spite of a poor reception from the critics, both *Les Rivières pour-pres* and *Gothika* proved popular with French audiences. *Les Rivières pourpres* was seen by over three million spectators in France, resulting in a sequel, the Besson-scripted and produced *Les Rivières pourpres 2: Les Anges de l'apocalypse* (Dahan, 2003), of which Kassovitz (wisely) declined the offer to direct. *Gothika* enjoyed similar success, grossing over $50 million on its original theatrical release in the USA and sub-sequently attracting more than one and a half million spectators in France.[33] The success of *Gothika* and *Les Rivières poupres* with a popular youth audience in France supports the argument presented earlier in this chapter that an affinity and familiarity with Hollywood is now (for better or worse) firmly embedded within French popular film culture. As O'Regan (1992: 334) reminds us, Hollywood's international appeal creates a kind of common mythological space (as powerful as it is problematic) which functions as an agent for the restratification of national cultural commodities. In doing so, Hollywood 'separates the élite from mass or popular taste and threatens the cultural hegemony enjoyed by national cultural élites' (ibid.). Kassovitz's films, and in particular his two most recent features address this issue of how national cinema in France is to be defined and promoted. What is more, they reveal the refusal within certain areas of the French film industry to acknowledge that this cultural resonance with Hollywood (especially amongst a youth audience and certain filmmakers) con-tributes to the identity of French cinema in the 2000s; nor the possi-bility that a popular youth-orientated cinema such as that produced by Kassovitz, Besson, Kounen and others may in fact occupy a legitimate space within French national cinema alongside the more established and 'accepted' practices of the *auteur* film and popular genres such as comedy and the heritage film. Such resistance can be explained both as a continuation of the ambivalent relationship between Hollywood and French cinema that has been played out across the past one hun-dred years, but also as a recourse from what is perceived in France as the increasingly homogenising political, economic and cultural

33 Source: CNC, 2004. Figures consulted at www.cnc.fr (site last consulted 18/9/05).

effects of globalisation (for which we can also read 'Europeanisation' and 'Americanisation').

In contrast, Kassovitz embraces the transnational as a potential source of enrichment in his cinema. And yet, although his films display an obvious passion for American cinema, Hollywood does not remain Kassovitz's sole point of reference in either *Gothika* or *Les Rivières pourpres*. Nor, indeed, are these influences from American cinema limited to the mainstream; alongside Spielberg, Kassovitz draws on the work of directors such as Scorsese and Spike Lee – filmmakers who occupy an uncertain position in relation to the Hollywood mainstream – as well as the mavericks of low-budget exploitation cinema such as Romero and Raimi. Both films, equally, owe a debt to European directors such as Argento and Besson.

Similarly, while Kassovitz understands the 'business' of American cinema, his relationship to Hollywood is not necessarily one of subservience and unquestioning loyalty that rejects the production practices and difference of French cinema. In fact, he has criticised Hollywood for its fetishisation of the star (resulting in overinflated salaries for often mediocre actors) and obsession with marketing and promotion – claiming that a film such as *Gothika* could have been made in France for half the cost of its $40 million budget (Aubel 2003: 24). Rather than becoming an exiled mercenary in Hollywood, Kassovitz has, instead, expressed a desire to alternate between big-budget (internationally funded) genre cinema – such as his current science-fiction project *Babylon AD* (to be shot in 2006) – and a more personal, experimental and even oppositional cinema produced mainly in France (Jeffries 2001). Evidence that the militant edge to Kassovitz's film practice has not been blunted by successive collaborations with Gaumont and Warner Brothers can be found in his role as co-producer (via Kasso Inc) of *Neg'Marron* (Flamond-Barney, 2005) a low-budget feature foregrounding the experiences of disenfranchised island youth in Guadeloupe and one of the few films since Palcy's *Rue Cases-Nègres* (1983) to give a voice to a director of French-Caribbean origin.

Rather than offering an empty imitation of Hollywood, Kassovitz thus 'uses' American cinema: as an important (though not unique) cinematic reference point, but also as an economic and industrial resource that will permit him in the future to make more ambitious, more personal films. This approach displays a keen understanding of what Maltby (2003: 7–14) refers to as Hollywood's 'commercial aesthetic', a symbiotic relationship between 'art' and 'business' that is essentially opportunistic in its economic practices, and that Kassovitz hopes will allow him to realise his global ambitions as a transnational filmmaker:

> je ne veux pas devenir un mercenaire à Los Angeles qui gagne beaucoup en faisant ce qu'on lui dit ... non plus être coincé en France ... je veux juste être un réalisateur international. (Kassovitz quoted in Aubel 2003: 16)[34]

References

Anon. (2000), 'Les Rivières pourpres' (review), Le Monde (27 September)
—— (2004), 'Sang aucun sens' L'Humanité (7 January)
Arroyo, José (2000) (ed.), Action/Spectacle Cinema: A Sight and Sound Reader, London: BFI
Aubel, François (2003), 'Kassovitz: Jusqu'ici tout va bien', Epok 42 (December–January), 16–25
Balio, Tino (1998), 'The art film market in the new Hollywood', in Nowell-Smith and Ricci (eds), Hollywood and Europe: Economics, Culture, National Identity 1945–95, London: BFI, 63–73
Belpêche, Stéphanie (2004), 'Mathieu Kassovitz, un Frenchie à Hollywood', Le Journal du Dimanche (4 January)
Bonnaud, Frédéric (2000), 'Made in France', Les Inrockuptibles (27 September)
Bourguignon, Thomas and Tobin, Yann (1995), 'Entretien avec Mathieu Kassovitz: les cinq dernières secondes', Positif, June, 8–13
Blumenfeld, Samuel (2000), 'Mathieu Kassovitz sur la piste d'un serial killer', Le Monde (27 September)
Cavrois, Jean Michel (2000), 'Les Rivières pourpres/The Crimson Rivers' (soundtrack review), Film Score Monthly, September/October, 42–3
Ciment, Michel (2001), 'Renouveau du cinéma français?', Positif, 487, 1
Clover, Carol J. (2002), 'Her body, himself: gender in the slasher film', in Mark Jancovich (ed.), Horror, The Film Reader, London and New York: Routledge, 77–90
Colombani, Florence (2004), 'Gothika' (review), Le Monde (9 January)
Constans, Marie-Ève (2004), 'Mathieu Kassovitz plonge dans le frisson hollywoodien', La Croix (7 January)
Conter, Elizabeth (2000), 'L'entretien du Film français: Mathieu Kassovitz', Le Film français, 2848 (22 September), 17

---

34 'I don't want to be a mercenary in Los Angeles making lots of money being told what to do ... nor do I want to be stuck in France ... all I want to be is an international filmmaker.'

De Bruyn, Olivier (2004), 'Gothika' (review), Le Point (9 January)
—— (2004a), 'Kassovision', Première, January, 102–5
Dupuy Julien et Guillomeau, Piéric (2000), 'Interview avec Mathieu Kasso- vitz', Starfix, 14 (September/October) consulted at www.mathieukassovitz. com/rivieres/interviews/starfix.htm (site last accessed 10/7/2005).
Ferenczi, Aurélien; Loiseau, Jean-Claude; and Remy, Vincent (1999), 'Cinéma français: ils ont fait la différence', Télérama, 2556 (6 January), 18–21
Forbes, Jill (1992), The Cinema in France after the New Wave, London: BFI
Frodon, Jean-Marie (1995), L'Âge moderne du cinéma français: de la Nouvelle Vague à nos jours, Paris: Flammarion
Ganne, Valérie (1998), 'Service Public et cinéma: je t'aime moi non plus', Écran Total, 244 (21 October), 15–16
Goudet, Stéphane (2000), 'Les Rivières pourpres: filles et fils de...', Positif, 477 (November), 50–1
Grantham, Bill (2000), Some Big Bourgeois Brothel. Contexts for France's Culture Wars with Hollywood, Luton: University of Luton Press
Hayward, Susan (1993), French National Cinema, London/New York: Routledge
—— (1999), 'Besson's mission elastoplast': Le Cinquième element (1997), in Powrie (ed.) French Cinema in the 1990s: Continuity and Difference, Oxford: Oxford University Press, 246–57
Hillier, Jim (ed.) (1985), Cahiers du Cinéma, the 1950s: Neo-Realism, Hollywood, New Wave, Cambridge (Massachusetts): Havard University Press
Higuinen, Erwan (2000), 'Que la montagne est belle', Cahiers du cinéma, 550 (October), 106
Jeancolas, Jean-Pierre (1998), 'From the Blum–Byrnes agreement to the GATT affair' in Nowell-Smith and Ricci (eds), Hollywood and Europe: Economics, Culture, National Identity 1945–95, London: BFI, 47–62
Jeffries, Stuart (2001), 'It's hard for me to play romantic. I come across as a bit of a jerk', Guardian (August 6), consulted at film.guardian.co.uk/ interview/interviewpages/0,,536181.html (site last accessed 16/9/05)
Kassovitz, Mathieu (1998), 'Les aventures de Mathieu Kassovitz' interview in Steadycam, consulted at www.mathieukassovitz.com/itw/steadycam.htm (site last accessed 19/7/05)
Katelan, Jean-Yves (2000), 'Les Rivières pourpres' (review), Première, 283 (October), 59
Kolker, Robert (2000), A Cinema of Loneliness, Oxford and New York: Oxford University Press
Labé, Jean (1999), 'Mathieu Kassovitz redonne de l'ambition au thriller français", Le film français, 284, December, 14
Lacomme, Jean Pierre (2000), 'Mathieu Kassovitz, la hargne: interview', Le Journal du Dimanche (24 September)
Maltby, Richard (2003), Hollywood Cinema (2nd edition), Oxford: Blackwell
O'Regan, Tom (1992), 'Too popular by far: on Hollywood's international popu- larity', Continuum, 5 (2), 302–47
Péron, Didier (2000), 'Ça rame sur Les Rivières pourpres', Libération (27 Sep- tember)
Powrie, Phil (1997), French Cinema in the 1980s: Nostalgia and the Crisis of

Masculinity, Oxford: Clarendon Press

—— (ed.) (1999), *French Cinema in the 1990s: Continuity and Difference*, Oxford: Oxford University Press

Reid, Mark A. (ed.) (1997), *Spike Lee's* Do the Right Thing, Cambridge: Cambridge University Press

Roy, André (2000), '*Les Rivières pourpres*' (review), *24 Images*, 106, 61

Stern, Lesley (1995), *The Scorsese Connection*, London: BFI

Strauss, Frédéric (2004), 'Gothika' (review), *Télérama*, 2817 (10 January)

Swanson, Tim (2003), 'Team Scream', *Premiere* (USA), 17/3 (November), 48–50

Tirard, Laurent (2000), 'Mathieu Kassovitz: la leçon de cinéma' *Studio*, no. 160, consulted at www.mathieukassovitz.com/rivieres/interviews/studio.htm (site last accessed 22/7/05)

Vincendeau, Ginette (1992), 'France 1945–65 and Hollywood: the *policier* as international text', *Screen*, 33/1 (spring), 50–80

Wheaton, Mark (2003a), 'Inmate of Gothika', *Fangoria*, 227 (October), 23–6

—— (2003b), 'Newly American Gothika', *Fangoria*, 228 (November), 17–21

Williams, Linda (2002), 'When the woman looks', in Mark Jancovich (ed.), *Horror, The Film Reader*, London/New York: Routledge, 61–6

Wood, Robin (2002), 'The American nightmare: horror in the 1970s', in Mark Jancovich (ed.), *Horror, The Film Reader*, London and New York: Routledge, 25–32

5

Kassovitz the actor/*auteur*

Comme comédien je ne possède pas les bases techniques. Jouer un petit mec avec une casquette, je sais le faire, je suis comme ça dans la vie. Être acteur ça ne m'intéresse pas, sauf à jouer des trucs différents. (Kassovitz in Bernard and Libiot 1996: 109)[1]

1993–2001: the emerging star?

Though *La Haine* may well have emphatically announced the arrival of Kassovitz the director to French cinema audiences, it was in fact two years earlier and as an actor that he was first officially recognised as one of French cinema's emerging young talents. As a result of his memorable performance as Félix in *Métisse* – for which he received a César nomination as most promising young actor – Kassovitz was cast in Jacques Audiard's idiosyncratic *noir* thriller *Regarde les hommes tomber* (1994) (Vachaud 1994: 40). In the film Kassovitz plays Johnny, an emotionally fragile, itinerant social misfit who is taken under the wing of Marx, an ageing, small-time criminal played by Jean-Louis Trintignant. Such was the critical impact of Kassovitz's performance in *Regarde les hommes tomber* that it won him a César for most promising actor. In 1995 he also became the recipient of the Prix Jean Gabin, a highly prestigious award presented each year by the Gabin museum to a young male screen actor viewed as showing outstanding potential.

1 'As an actor I lack the basics in terms of technique. I can play a small guy in a baseball cap, because I'm like that in real life. Acting doesn't interest me, unless it means playing a variety of roles.'

Therefore, by the mid-1990s, and before the media storm that surrounded *La Haine*, Kassovitz had been identified as an actor of considerable talent with, potentially, a significant screen career ahead of him. Moreover, as he progressed to more prominent roles in films such as *Un Héros très discret* (Audiard, 1996), *Le Fabuleux destin d'Amélie Poulain* (Jeuent, 2001) and *Amen* (Costa-Gavras, 2002), Kassovitz's rising celebrity profile (as both director and actor) and obvious on-screen charisma even suggested the possible emergence of a new French star. One of the issues this chapter will address is, precisely, whether or not we can think of Kassovitz in terms of stardom, that 'elusive quality', defined by Vincendeau (2005: 14), as the: 'amalgam of character type, performance style, looks and "aura" that allows a few actors, in Richard Dyer's words, to "crystalise and authenticate" social values and become emblematic of their time'.

There is a certain irony, however, that Kassovitz should have initially been recognised by the French film industry for his acting. Firstly because his earlier 'breakthrough' in *Regarde les hommes tomber* came in a film that is closer to an art-house *film d'auteur* than anything he has ever directed. But also, since Kassovitz has repeatedly claimed that he is not an actor, considering his screen performances as a mere sideline to directing. [2] This strategy of using the acting roles he plays as an outlet for what we might term his more '*auteurist* impulses', while at the same time denigrating his abilities as a screen actor in interviews, establishes a consistent pattern in an acting career that, for the most part, develops independently from Kassovitz's rise to fame as a director. In a number of his own films, however (*Métisse*, *La Haine*, *Assassin(s)*) these parallel careers collide: often resulting in a conflict between Kassovitz the *auteur* and Kassovitz the actor through performances that raise interesting questions concerning authorial control and agency within the filmic text.

While it is not unheard of for French actors to move into directing once they have established a reputation on screen (see, for example, the career of Josiane Balasko), few (if any) have managed to culti-vate successful parallel careers in both acting and directing from the outset. In this respect, as a director/actor Kassovitz is rather unique – and even more so given the differences between the films he chooses to act in and those he directs.

2 See, for example, comments made by Kassovitz in: Bernard and Libiot (1996) and Kassovitz (1998).

Furthermore, Kassovitz's approach to his acting career is uncon-ventional in the sense that he has been happy- even once his repu-tation had been established – to accept as many cameos as leading roles in films. While in some cases he has agreed to perform these secondary or cameo roles as a favour to family and friends – such as Nicolas Boukhrief's *Les Plaisir et ses petits tracas* (1998) or his father's Hollywood debut *Jakob the liar* (Peter Kassovitz, 1999) – these fleet-ing screen appearances have also been in films for directors whom Kassovitz particularly admires. He has thus taken cameos in *La Cité des enfants perdus* (Jeunet and Caro, 1994); *Mon homme* (Blier, 1996) and *Le Cinquième élément* (Besson, 1997). However, rather than functioning as some kind of sycophantic exercise through which to ingratiate himself with his cinematic heroes, Kassovitz in fact uses his performances in these films as an opportunity to learn from these filmmakers by observing their working practices on set (Kassovitz 1998).

As a director, Kassovitz also gains from his acting experience in the sense that it has (by his own admission) helped him better under-stand (and thus better direct) the actors working in his own films: be they seasoned veterans such as Michel Serrault or non-professional debutants such as Mehdi Benoufa, as was the case in *Assassin(s)*. This practice of cultivating a close working relationship with actors on set was noted by both Halle Berry and Robert Downey Jr. following their collaboration with Kassovitz on *Gothika* (Swanson 2003: 50). Experience on both sides of the camera further benefits Kassovitz's performances as an actor. Screenwriter and director Jacques Audiard, who cast Kassovitz in both *Regarde les hommes tomber* and *Un Héros très discret* , has commented (Bernard and Libiot 1996: 109) on how his knowledge as a director (both technical and creative) makes him an incredibly precise actor who appreciates more than most his place within the *mise en scène* and understands instinctively how the camera will move. (We shall return to a detailed discussion of this idea of Kassovitz as an instinctive actor later in the chapter, in the section on performance style, pp. 184–93).

Kassovitz may well dismiss his acting career as a mere sideline to directing – a means of observing other filmmakers and gaining experience in front of the camera that will help him as a director. It is, nonetheless, a 'sideline' that that has earned him considerable critical acclaim for his work with directors such as Audiard and Costa-Gavras, as well as with respected screen actors such as Serrault and

Trintignant. In terms of commercial exposure, the actor's most high-profile appearance to date came in Jeunet's *Le Fabuleux destin d'Amélie Poulain*, or *Amélie* as it is known outside of France. The French film event of 2001, *Amélie* attracted nine million spectators in France and an international audience of more than thirty-two million (a record for a French-language film); catapulted its female lead, Audrey Tautou, to stardom; was credited with spearheading a revival of popular cinema capable of competing with Hollywood; not to mention sparking a bitter and very public row between Jeunet and journalist Serge Kaganski over the potentially dubious ideological message sent by the film's digitally enhanced, retro-nostalgic representation of Paris, 'cleansed' of ethnic, cultural and sexual diversity (Bonnaud 2001: 36–8). Away from the controversy, Kassovitz's performance in *Amélie* as Nino Quincampoix, a naive and self-effacing eccentric who works as a part-time cashier in a Pigalle sex shop and emerges as the unlikely love interest of the film's eponymous heroine, endeared him to French audiences. Just as importantly, the film simultaneously introduced Kassovitz the actor to an international audience, so that when he arrived in Hollywood to direct *Gothika* has was better known to the American trade press as an actor rather than as the polemical *auteur* of such films as *La Haine* and *Assassin(s)*.

The association with the success of *Amélie* led, almost inevitably, to numerous offers of similar roles that cashed in on Kassovitz's new-found popularity as a quirky and unthreatening romantic lead with a self-effacing charm. To his credit, he eschewed these potentially lucrative deals for the opportunity to star in an altogether more challenging project: *Amen*. In *Amen* Kassovitz plays a young Jesuit priest whose attempts to expose the horrors of the Nazi concentration camps are met by a conspiracy of silence from within the Catholic church that leads all the way to the Vatican – a far more 'heroic' role than any of his previous roles, and a possible indication of his emerging star status as an actor.

Though in all his films to date (with the possible exception of *Amen*) he tends to play youthful outsiders, eccentrics and social misfits, Kassovitz's performances are nonetheless imbued with an often understated, but undeniable, charisma; an attribute that, when combined with his natural acting talent, could well point to that all elusive property of star quality. Given his slight frame and average looks, Kassovitz's on-screen attraction as an actor is fashioned from a mixture of wit and charm that is further combined with one of two elements. Either he is shown to possess a self-confidence that borders on arrogance (as in *Métisse* or *Le Plaisir (et ses petits tracas)*); or, more commonly, (as in *Regarde les hommes tomber*, *Un Héros très discret*, *Assassin(s)* and *Amélie*), he displays an awkwardness that manifests itself primarily through Kassovitz's physical performance, but which, rather than emerging as a fault or defect, is presented to the audience as an endearing trait or one that elicits sympathy.

A clear example of the way in which these elements combine to create the actor's unconventional on-screen charisma can be found in *Le Plaisir (et ses petits tracas)*, where Kassovitz plays Roland, a barman in a strip-club who dreams of a career in acting and stand-up comedy and who, upon learning that his fiancée has been unfaithful, embarks on a one-night stand with a stranger he meets in the metro. The character's status as something of an amiable, if eccentric, 'loser' is established before he even appears on screen through the discussion that ensues as Roland's fiancée and her family wait for him to arrive in a restaurant (he is late for the meal, it transpires, due to a casting audition for a bit part in a TV series). However, upon his arrival Kassovitz/Roland dominates the scene – the camera's gaze follows him in close-up as he moves his way around the table; greeting all the members of his fiancée's extended family with a kiss and flattering or comical remark, which endears him to the spectator and ensures that any animosity held by the other characters for his selfishly arriving late are instantly forgotten. The energy and inventiveness of his fifteen-minute performance in a somewhat unremarkable film based around an ensemble cast of eight actors was such that it prompted the following praise in an otherwise disparaging review of the film in *Télérama* (Murat 1998: 35): 'Consolation: Mathieu Kassovitz. Réalisateur contesté (par certains), c'est un acteur magnifique. À la présence étonnante. À l'inventivité permanente. Ses scènes avec Julie Gayet, puis avec Caroline Cellier, sont les seules à peu près regardables'.[3]

A more sustained example of the way in which Kassovitz's natural on-screen charisma is combined with a *mise en scène* that emphasises the actor as the unlikely object of desire of both the camera's gaze

---

3 'One consolation: Mathieu Kassovitz. A controversial director (for some), he is a magnificent actor, with surprising presence; and constantly inventive. His scenes with Julie Gayet and then with Caroline Cellier are about the only ones in the film worth watching.'

and that of the other characters within the diegesis can be found in Kassovitz debut feature, *Métisse*. Consider, for instance, the film's opening scene in which Félix (Kassovitz) and Jamal (Hubert Koundé), meet for the first time outside the apartment building where Lola (Julie Maudeuch), the woman with whom they are both romantically involved, lives. Stylishly dressed in an expensive suit and tie, Jamal/ Koundé is clearly the more conventionally attractive and physically imposing of the two actors. We would, therefore, logically expect him to occupy centre stage as the film's desirable and dominant male lead. In contrast, with his slight frame, pronounced nose, big glasses and clumsy cycling shoes, Félix/Kassovitz's presence in the opening scenes verges on the comic. This hierarchy also appears to be emphasised by the manner in which the two protagonists arrive at the apartment block. Jamal steps out of a taxi, leaving a generous tip for the driver and with a gift for Lola under his arm. Félix comes to a halt outside the building and, unable to release his feet in time from the pedals of his racing bike, crashes to the ground.

And yet, as the opening sequence develops, Félix's unrefined charm and bawdy wit places him on a level footing with his rival for Lola's affections. As Jamal patronisingly asserts his elevated status in terms of class and education by reminding Félix of the entry code to the flats: 'le jour le plus long, 6–J–44, le débarquement, c'est mnémotechnique' the latter refuses to be intimidated, retorting: 'mnémotechnique, mon cul'.[4] This contrast between Jamal's refined, educated pronouncements and Félix's coarse, carnivalesque humour is repeated later in the film when, commenting on Félix's attempt to dress more smartly, Jamal suggests: 'c'est pas la veste qui fait l'homme, c'est l'homme qui fait la veste' only for Félix to reply playfully: 'et mon pied dans ton cul: il fait quoi mon pied?'.[5] As an aspiring working-class youth from the *banlieue*, Félix thus refuses to be silenced by the traditional hierarchies of class and education. In many ways, then, and as he seems to intimate in the quote that opens this chapter, of all the characters he has played, Félix is the one that most closely resembles Kassovitz in real life: the 'little guy in the baseball cap' (though admittedly not from the working-class *banlieue*); an outspoken, quick-

---

4 'The longest day, 6–J–44, the D-day landings, it's mnemonic' / 'Mnemonic, my arse'.

5 'It's not the jacket that makes the man, but the man that makes the jacket' / 'And my foot up your arse, what does that make?'

witted personality with a self-belief that verges on arrogance, but an undeniable charisma, nonetheless.

Returning to our example from the opening sequence of *Métisse*, the equal status of the two male leads is, furthermore, implied by the camera's gaze. Both are accorded similar prominence in the medium shot as they walk from the lift to Lola's front door – a technique repeated throughout the film whenever Jamal and Félix appear on screen together. Similarly, Lola's intra-diegetic gaze in this scene (as elsewhere in *Métisse*) is meant to reinforce Félix's status as the unconventional but charismatic (desirable) male, and thus Jamal's equal. She therefore opens the door to greet the two men with the same adoring smile – a reaction that is equally meant to influence that of the spectator towards Félix. Kassovitz's use of the *mise en scène* to reinforce his/Félix's position as the co-lead in *Métisse* is further confirmed by the elaborate long take that follows the character through a hiphop nightclub: from the street as he bluffs his way past an unsatisfied customer to whom he earlier sold some dope; breezing past the bouncers and, finally, to the dance floor where he is enthusiastically greeted by friends and acquaintances. The elaborate camerawork in this sequence therefore has the effect of placing Félix/Kassovitz at the centre of the *mise en scène*: the focus both of the spectator's gaze and of the characters that surround him – and thus an indication of his potential identification as the film's emerging star.

'Kasso': the Seventh Art's young rebel

In addition to the critical and commercial recognition for his work and his undeniable on-screen charisma, offscreen Kassovitz has obtained celebrity status due to press and television interest in both his films and life outside of the cinema – the media being one of the key discourses that contributes to the construction of the star image beyond the filmic text. He has been the subject of numerous interviews in relation to his films (as both director and actor) appearing in the French dailies as well as film magazines such as *Première* and *Studio*. Kassovitz has also featured in lifestyle magazines such as *The Face* and *Epok*, as well as being the occasional subject of scrutiny in gossip magazines such as *Voici*.[6] He is, one would imagine, popular

6 See D'Elia (1995 14–15) for an example of *Voici*'s interest in Kassovitz's personal life following the success of *La Haine*.

with editors because his often frank and provocative opinions will always make good print. In the past he has spoken out against the French government and individual politicians – Le Pen, Pasqua, Chirac and, more recently, the current star of the centre right, Nicolas Sarkozy (Nivelle 2004: 40) – as well as igniting a wave of controversy with comments relating to 'failures' in the police system in interviews given following the release of *La Haine*. In February 1997, Kassovitz was one of the initial signatories of the 'appel des 59' – an open call to civic disobedience from a group of French filmmakers in support of the *sans-papiers* (undocumented immigrants residing in France) published in the French dailies *Le Monde* and *Libération*. Kassovitz not only targets the French political establishment, but also the country's cinematic establishment and has frequently expressed his opposition to the funding policies of the CNC, as well as speaking out against icons of French cinema such as Jean-Luc Godard (see Chapter 4).

The controversial persona that surrounds Kassovitz the film personality was further endorsed in February 2005, when he was arrested by Paris police as a result of motoring offences – speeding in a residential area, driving while speaking on a mobile phone and not wearing a seatbelt – as he rushed to collect his 5-year-old daughter from school. What attracted the media's attention was less the nature of the charges and more the circumstances surrounding the arrest: on being stopped by the police Kassovitz was alleged to have reacted in an abusive and verbally aggressive manner towards the arresting officers. The ensuing fracas saw the filmmaker taken to the police station in handcuffs, 'comme les héros de son film *La Haine*'[7] as one journalist remarked (Thibaudat 2005: 18). As the coverage of this incident shows, ten years on from the media storm surrounding *La Haine*, and despite his screen roles as both a romantic lead in *Amélie* and the anti-Nazi hero in Costa-Gavras's *Amen*, Kassovitz's public persona in France remains clearly defined by his status as the outspoken and rebellious director that was associated with his second and third feature films (*La Haine* and *Assassin(s)*).

In addition to his emergence as a controversial film and media personality in France, over the past decade Kassovitz has been a prominent figure (as actor and director) at both the Cannes Festival and the Césars awards ceremony – two annual events in the French

7 'Like the heroes from his film *La Haine*'.

film industry calendar that play an important part in the construction of stars in French culture (Vincendeau 2000: 17). With the official selection at Cannes of films such as *La Haine* and *Assassin(s)*,
he announced his presence in the mid-1990s as the young rebel of
French cinema. Later, in 2001, he featured as an outspoken member
of the festival jury, publicly criticising the festival's organisers for
failing to include *Amélie* in competition at Cannes (Bonnaud 2001:
37). At the Césars (the French equivalent of the Oscars) Kassovitz has
received a total of eight nominations as both actor and director since
1994 (most recently as best actor in 2003 for *Amen*), winning on two
occasions: for best film (*La Haine*) in 1996 and for most promising
male actor (*Regarde les hommes tomber*) in 1995. Despite this sustained
success since the mid-1990s, Kassovitz is largely conspicuous by his
absence from the Césars, having consistently declined since 1995
to attend the televised awards ceremony (Seguret 2000: 31). This
strategy is, in fact, entirely consistent with Kassovitz's public image
as an iconoclast who constantly positions himself against France's
cinematic establishment, and also with his attempts to sabotage his
own star trajectory (a point we shall return to shortly).

'Kasso',[8] as he is referred to in certain press articles and also,
significantly, by the young fans who contribute to internet discussion forums associated with the filmmaker, has gained a reputation through press interviews and the coverage of his public life as
a highly vocal and polemical personality. He is thus presented as a
rebellious figure, whose views and manner of expressing them aligns
him with a youth demographic – despite the fact that he is now in his
late thirties. This image appears to be confirmed by the controversies
that have surrounded many of the films Kassovitz has chosen to associate himself with as an actor: the unjudgmental depiction of hired
killers in *Regarde les hommes tomber*; an exploration of the myth of
France as a nation unified in its resistance to Nazi occupation during
the Second World War in *Un Héros très discret*; and the highly controversial, uncompromising portrayal of the effects of media violence
in his own film *Assassin(s)*. As we have already mentioned, even
the apparently innocent romantic comedy *Amélie* attracted negative

8 Vincendeau notes (2000: 19) that French stars are often called by a nickname
   and so perceived to be closer to audiences and fans than American stars. Kassovitz is often referred to in popular film magazines such as *Studio* and *Première*
   as 'Kasso' a nickname that is thus suggestive of his link to a youth audience.

attention for its digitally recreated vision of Paris that omitted to show the capital's ethnic, cultural and sexual diversity. In his characteristically outspoken manner, Kassovitz responded to comments by Serge Kaganski – the journalist who had levelled these accusations against *Amélie* – by menacingly claiming in an interview that, should their paths cross, he would be likely to 'smack him one' (Jeffries 2001).

Kassovitz thus emerges as a personality who attracts controversy rather than trying to avoid it in the way that stars normally tend to do. In many ways, though, this is a largely self-styled projection of 'Kasso the rebel', crafted from interview copy and press soundbites rather than the characters embodied by the actor on screen. Indeed, a closer inspection of the films concerned reveals that many of the roles Kassovitz has chosen as an actor are less controversial than they might at first appear. His performance as the social misfit turned hired killer in *Regarde les hommes tomber* falls within the realm of *auteur* cinema, where such morally ambiguous representations of social taboos or transgressive behaviour are more readily tolerated by audiences. Similarly, the polemic in *Un Héros très discret* concerning the myth of France as a nation united in its resistance to Nazi occupation during the Second World War was, undoubtedly, highly topical given the continued discussion in the mid-1990s of revelations relating to outgoing French President Mitterrand's links to the Vichy government during the occupation, as well as the trial a year after the film's release of former Paris police chief, Maurice Papon, for his involvement in the deportation of French Jews to Nazi concentration camps. Nevertheless, *Un Héros très discret*'s exposition of the 'great lie' of France as a nation resolutely united in resisting German occupation in fact formed part of a much wider and ongoing analysis of this period in twentieth-century French history that had begun as early as 1972 with the publication of *Vichy France* by American historian Robert Paxton and films such as *Lacombe Lucien* (Malle, 1974) (Lauten 1999: 58–9).

Even the controversies relating to *Amélie* were confined largely to the French press – the pages of *Libération* in particular – and thus not picked up by the majority of the film's foreign audience. Nor did the adverse coverage of *Amélie* deter French spectators from continuing to flock to cinemas to see the film. Indeed, the phenomenal international success of *Amélie* has made Kassovitz a recognisable face way beyond France, leading directly to the kind of deal with French parfumier Lancôme that we tend to associate with stars, not young rebels (and which has traditionally formed another extra-diegetic element of the star persona). As will be argued later in this chapter, the more 'authentic' elements that inform Kassovitz's image as a polemical film personality are actually to be found in relation to his output and activities as a director, which largely override the persona of the more fragile social misfit that emerges from the characters he has tended to play on screen.

Colluding against a star trajectory

Despite his increasing prominence as filmmaker and celebrity through the 1990s and early 2000s, critical and commercial success as an actor, as well as endorsement deals that would suggest a star celebrity, Kassovitz's star status as an actor is far from certain. Indeed, at a time where the reality format of *Loft Story*, *Popstars* and *Nouvelle Star* appears to dominate French television programming as much as in any other western culture – feeding directly into the proliferation and thus devaluation of 'celebrity' – we should be wary of labelling every young talented actor that appears as a star.

However, there are also other, more concrete, reasons for denying Kassovitz star status. Firstly, we must consider his output as an actor. Though he has appeared in seventeen feature films since 1991 (as well as two early films in the late 1970s and early 1980s as a child actor) more than half of these performances have comprised minor secondary roles or fleeting cameos. Many of these lesser roles are parts which Kassovitz has been willing to accept (as already noted) either for the opportunity to work with directors he admires, or else as a favour to friends and family. In the remaining eight or nine films, Kassovitz has been cast in a leading role six times: for *Métisse*, *Assassin(s)*, *Regarde les hommes tomber*, *Un Héros très discret*, *Amélie* and *Amen*. In only one of these films – namely *Un Héros très discret* – can he be unambiguously identified as the central protagonist around which the narrative revolves. It is, moreover, hard to justify Kassovitz as a star in terms of his capital value – as the name who will attract an audience to see a film, or attract investment in the early stages of production. His films with Audiard enjoyed critical acclaim but only modest box-office success; his role in *Amélie* was as the romantic foil to the film's true star, Audrey Tautou; while in *Amen*, though sharing the lead (and thus top-billing) with German actor Ulrich Tukur, the film was essentially an *auteur*-led production, and thus marketed accordingly as a 'Costa-Gavras film'.

Just as importantly, Kassovitz seems to have actively conspired *against* his own star trajectory as an actor. He has thus consistently prioritised his directing career over his acting. Moreover, he repeatedly plays down his abilities as a screen actor in interviews – despite the sustained positive response from critics to his performances as an actor (which has not always greeted his career as director) – to the extent that, on more than one occasion, he has claimed to be finished with acting altogether (Nivelle 2004: 40). Finally, Kassovitz has deliberately restricted his on-screen exposure by only accepting parts in a limited number of films, and often relegating himself to supporting roles or cameo appearances. This situation has come about partly due to Kassovitz's focus on his parallel career as a director. But it can also be read as an indication of the fact that because of his commercial success as a director Kassovitz is not bound by the same economic imperative as other French actors to appear more frequently in both *auteur* and mainstream films (Vincendeau 2000: 23–4). Consequently, though the success of Kassovitz's involvement in *Amélie* opened potentially lucrative doors for starring roles in mainstream French comedies (Jeffries 2001), the young filmmaker refused all such offers until the opportunity to act in Costa-Gavras's *Amen* presented itself. Moreover, during the early 2000s Kassovitz prioritised Hollywood over French cinema by focusing on his debut American feature *Gothika*, as well as appearing alongside Vincent Cassel in a supporting role as a hapless Eastern-European crook in the mid-budget Anglo-American comedy, *Birthday Girl* (Butterworth, 2001). Though in financial terms a relatively modest Hollywood production, the comedy was fronted by A-list star Nicole Kidman. *Birthday Girl* therefore provided further related exposure for Kassovitz with international film audiences, through association with a Nicole Kidman film, as well as evidence of his range as an actor – equally suited to comedy (first seen in *Métisse*) as to the idiosyncratic and more intense dramatic performances of films such as *Regarde les hommes tomber* and *Amen*.[9]

9 In fact in both *Regarde les hommes tomber* and *Un Héro très discret*, Kassovitz incorporates, at the appropriate moments, elements of comedy into his performances – something that further explains his popularity with audiences as an actor.

One further and significant way in which Kassovitz colludes against his own star trajectory is through the type of characters he has chosen to play on screen. Almost all the principal roles that he has accepted portray characters who are in some way flawed or fall short of the heroic norms we may expect of conventional stars: alienated, deviant, duplicitous characters who do not fit into society, and not necessarily in a heroic or attractive way as the maverick or rebel outsider. Even in *Amélie* where the potentially deviant elements of this character type are remodelled to render them more palatable for a mainstream audience, the protagonist still appears to some extent as an awkward outsider. Equally, Kassovitz will often collude in making himself the butt of the joke – as with his cameos in *Le Cinquième élément* and *Mon homme* – or else will emphasise a character's flaws through his own physicality (slight frame and unconventional looks) and performance style.

Performance style: 'instinctive naturalism'

Up to and possibly including *Amélie* a particular character type or on-screen persona therefore emerges in the acting roles selected by Kassovitz. Typically, he plays social misfits – youthful characters placed on the margins due to their dysfunctional background, socio-economic status, eccentricity or (ethnic/religious) difference. These characters are specifically linked to Kassovitz's own interest as a director in young (male) marginal protagonists found in *La Haine* and *Assassin(s)*. More generally, they appear as variations on the foregrounding of marginalised youth found in both French new realism (films such as *La Vie rêvée des anges* (Zonca, 1998) and *En avoir (ou pas)*, Masson, 1995) and the so-called *jeune cinéma* of the 1990s – two movements or moments in contemporary French cinema with which Kassovitz has been associated to varying degrees.[10] Kassovitz's performance type in these earlier films from the 1990s are thus, broadly speaking, consistent with his concerns as a director – even if the aesthetic or stylistic approach between, for example, *Regarde les hommes tomber* (Kassovitz as actor) and *La Haine* (Kassovitz as director) may differ considerably.

This decision by Kassovitz to embody a character type that is seemingly at odds with the heroic, extraordinary qualities of the typical star

10 For a summary of *jeune cinéma* and new realism, see Higbee (2005: 307–17)

also points towards possible challenges to the conventional French star system in the 1990s and 2000s . In particular, such challenges can be identified in the recent success at Cannes of non-professional actors whose performances challenge idealised representations of masculinity and femininity traditionally embodied by stars (Austin 2004: 251–64). They have also emerged through the participation of established female French stars such as Huppert and Dalle in what Orr (2004: 103–11) describes as the 'free-fall movie', where the star openly embraces the abject. By placing these disenfranchised marginal protagonists at the centre of the diegesis, Kassovitz is arguably contributing to an alternative star network in 1990s French cinema – comprising a group of young actors that includes Elodie Bouchez, Jeanne Balibar, Sami Boujahla, Jalil Lesperet and Roschdy Zem – that is closely associated with the promotion of a plurality of other-ed voices found in *jeune cinéma* of the 1990s and French new realism. An alternative star network, which, as Nacache also suggests in her analysis of Jeanne Balibar (2005: 49–53), has a more political than economic cachet.

In broader socio-cultural terms, the characters played by Kassovitz in films such as *Regarde les hommes tomber* and *Assassin(s)* are reflective of a substantial proportion of contemporary French youth who find themselves located on the margins of society; largely as a result of the high levels of youth unemployment that have persisted in France since the early 1980s. These protagonists also express a palpable sense of unease and pessimism felt by much of France's youth class (and shared by young people in many other western societies) towards the authorities and political establishment who seem hopelessly out of touch with their own values, ambitions and situations. Interestingly, though, characters such as Max and Johnny do not necessarily speak directly to a youth audience, but rather express the experiences of an alienated youth underclass to an older, more affluent art-house or *auteur*-focused audience.

At the core of this social misfit character type embodied by Kassovitz's are his performances in three films made between 1994 and 1997: *Regarde les hommes tomber*, where he plays Johnny, a damaged, easily influenced itinerant youth who ends up being taken under the wing of an ageing crook; *Un Héros très discret* in which he stars as Albert Dehousse, a bystander during the Nazi occupation of France during the Second World War who subsequently 'invents' a past for himself as a Resistance hero; and finally *Assassin(s)* where Kassovitz acts alongside Michel Serrault as Max, an unemployed, alienated youth from the suburbs who is cœrced into becoming a trainee assassin. These three characters are all, to varying extents, outcasts and drifters who are disillusioned or disenfranchised. As a consequence they are also easily influenced – Max says as much in the voice-over that accompanies the opening of *Assassin(s)*.[11] Their need for acceptance is so desperate that they are prepared to undergo radical transformation or commit extreme acts in order to secure the approval or acknowledgement they crave. Johnny even transforms his identity by changing his name from Frédérique to Johnny in an attempt to please Marx, who suggests that his real name is 'trop gonzesse'.[12]

Tellingly, all three characters in these films emerge from dysfunctional backgrounds; all three attempt to construct an alternative and previously lacking family unit with an older father-figure who acts as their mentor (Marx in *Regarde les hommes tomber*, Wagner in *Assassin(s)* and 'Le Capitaine' in *Un Héros très discret*). Consequently, through his portrayal of Johnny, Max and Albert, Kassovitz encourages not only sympathy from the audience but also a fascination for the unusual and, at times, threatening or deviant behaviour of the characters he plays. These are awkward social bodies, characters that provoke our interest as spectators. However, due to their threat to destabilise the social norm that comes from their deviance or dysfunctionality, these characters are also bodies that need to be kept at a distance. Consequently, they do not conform to the economies of desire that have traditionally governed the exchange between star and spectator.

As Audiard (quoted in Vachaud 1994: 40) has rightly identified, all of these characters present a combination of the juvenile or infantile with a more sinister potential for cruelty or malice. Johnny (*Regarde les hommes tomber*) and Max (*Assassin(s)*), both characters who are supposed to be in their early twenties, thus display a naivety towards the world of criminality and murder into which they enter. Max shoots at lines of empty beer cans for his own amusement with the gun used earlier by Wagner for a contract killing. Johnny purchases a dartboard with the money from his first 'job' with Marx, and is then shown alone, maniacally hurling the darts at the board that he has hung up on the

---

11 'Moi, je pense que j'étais comme tout le monde, ni bon, ni mauvais, juste influençable' / 'I think I was like all the rest, neither good nor bad, just easily influenced.'

12 'too girly'.

wall of his hotel room. Both characters are, equally, infantilised by a dependency on the proto-fathers who take them under their wing to train them as crooks and hired killers – a fact that is further reflected through their limited capacity to express themselves or explain their situation verbally. This desire to please their ageing tutors, reflects an obvious need to replace the absent father, but also points towards a need for recognition of their worth from a society that has overlooked them – a desperate desire to integrate into the social order of things that, unsettlingly, leads to acts of violence and cruelty.

The performance style that Kassovitz has developed in relation to the awkward social misfit type found in these three films from the mid-1990s, is perhaps best described as instinctive naturalism. Unlike most French film actors – who move easily between stage and screen (Vincendeau 2000: 7) – Kassovitz did not emerge from a theatrically trained background. Instead he drifted into acting after spending time on film and television sets where his parents worked, beginning at the age of 11 with an appearance in his father's debut feature film *Au bout du bout du banc* (Peter Kassovitz, 1978). Kassovitz has thus learned to act in much the same way he has learned to direct; not through formal training but rather through autodidactic observation, including repeated (re-)viewing of the films of his favourite actors' performances. As a result, he is more attuned to the specific demands and effects of screen acting than a formally trained actor who has arrived in screen acting from a background in theatre. In particular, Kassovitz understands better than most contemporary French actors the economy of screen acting; where, in performance terms, less is often more. His ability to portray emotion subtly through facial expression or by the understated corporeality of his on-screen performance is particularly evident in the films of Audiard – for example the penultimate scene of *Regarde les hommes tomber* where Johnny/Kassovitz framed in medium close-up struggles to contain his grief following the death of Marx.

We have established then that Kassovitz's performance style is naturalistic since he has had no formal training. It is 'instinctively' naturalistic in the sense that he is an actor who, by all accounts, requires very little input from his director, understanding intuitively the demands of the particular role he is playing. Audiard described preparatory discussions for Kassovitz's portrayal of Albert Dehousse in *Un Héros très discret* in the following way: 'on a discuté pendant des heures et à ce moment-là on a pris la décision de ne pas répéter trop, car Mathieu a peur – et moi aussi du reste – de s'user. Sur le plateau Mathieu est probablement l'acteur auquel j'ai le moins parlé' (Audiard in Herpe 1996: 21).[13] What Kassovitz came to realise, therefore, was that to overintellectualise or excessively ruminate as to the motivations, actions and gestures of his character was to lose the naturalism that provides his performances with such strength; where, in very subtle ways, he seems to inhabit the character he is playing. In the end, according to Audiard, Kassovitz merely asked his director whether he wanted him to play: 'un mec qui écoute, ou qui réfléchit' (Bernard and Libiot 1996: 108),[14] and elaborated the character of Dehousse from these basic indicators.

In keeping with his own film practice, and to accommodate Kassovitz's more naturalistic and instinctive performance style, Audiard agreed in *Un Héros très discret* to constantly adapt the approach to filming a particular scene or individual set-up. With each take, then, the intention was to try something different: not only in terms of camera movement and subtle variations in the *mise en scène*, but equally in relation to Kassovitz's own performance (ibid.: 109–10). Audiard has also hinted that another element in Kassovitz's acting technique which came to the fore in *Un Héros très discret,* was the actor's desire to 'bredouille le texte' (ibid.: 109).[15] On one hand, what Audiard is referring to here is Kassovitz's inclination to disrupt the text by changing the lines he has been given. However, this does not mean the actor gives himself over to an entirely free improvisational style. Rather, what Audiard describes is an approach from Kassovitz that may well disrupt or alter radically the direction of a given scene, but which, equally, responds and reacts to the original screenplay – and so does not succumb to the confused or exaggerated changes to a text that the director believes can sometimes occur with an excessively 'forced' improvisational approach.[16]

13 'we talked it over for hours and eventually took the decision not to over-rehearse, since, like me, Mathieu is afraid of overworking his performance. On set, Mathieu was probably the character with whom I had the least amount of discussion'.

14 'Someone who listens, or someone who is more reflective'.

15 The verb *bredouiller* literally means to stammer. Here, though, Audiard is expressing something closer to the notion of 'unsettling' the text.

16 'Le danger c'est l'improvisation vaseuse'/'The danger is sketchy, confused improvisation', Audiard in (Bernard and Libiot 1996: 109–10).

As we know, performance style is articulated, above all, through the actor's body. His or her physique and appearance will, more often than not, determine the type of roles they play (the dominating physical presence of Gérard Depardieu, or boyish good looks of Leonardo DiCaprio, for example). In this regard, Hollywood star Robert De Niro is one of a small number of actors who will go to the extent of dramatically altering their actual physique if required for a role (most famously in *Raging Bull*, where he subjected his body first to intense physical training and then significant weight gain in order to play Italian-American boxer Jake La Motta both in the prime of his professional career and as an ageing, retired fighter). Typically, the star body, in its first instance, is also an object of desire; and, more often than not, a thing of (conventional) beauty. In the case of French cinema, alongside the beauty of Delon (or, more recently, Olivier Martinez), a number of stars have emerged (Belmondo, Depardieu, Gabin) who despite their unusual or average looks have nonetheless established themselves as romantic leads and thus desirable star bodies (Vincendeau 2000: 21). With these more unconventional star bodies, looks are typically compensated for either with muscular athleticism (Belmondo), or else with an imposing physique (Gabin and Depardieu) that is set against their exposed or fragile masculinity. For 'beautiful' stars such as Delon, on the other hand, conventional or excessive masculinity acts as a means of concealing any potential weakness (emotional or otherwise) that may come from being the on-screen object of desire. Even in male French stars for whom a sense of masculinity in crisis is more readily visible – for example, Gabin and, more recently, Dewaere – these displays of emotional vulnerability are to an extent kept in check by a commanding physical presence (Gabin) or sex appeal (Dawaere).[17]

Kassovitz, on the other hand, is quite clearly not blessed with either the looks or the physique that connotes 'desirable' masculinity – another factor that would seem to prohibit him from emerging as a star in the proper sense of the word. The body nonetheless remains the key site of meaning, with the sense of fragility and awkwardness

17 The context of the star's crisis in masculinity is also, of course, dependent on the historical and socio-cultural moment in which those performances appear. For a detailed analysis of these male French stars and the various contexts in which their star personas need to be understood, see Austin (2003) and Vincendeau (2000).

found in the characters he plays expressed not through words, but rather through the corporeality of his performance: 'Kassowitz [*sic.*] a vingt-cinq ans mais il possède cette drôle d'alliance entre le juvénile crétin et la malice. Il fait aussi passer beaucoup de choses par son physique' (Audiard in Vachaud 1994: 40).[18] Though Audiard is talking specifically here of his interpretation of Johnny in *Regarde les hommes tomber*, these observations equally apply to the other roles played by Kassovitz in the late-1990s. In *Regarde les hommes tomber*, Johnny's physical awkwardness functions as a signifier of his marginalised status, but also reveals his damaged psychological state. This fact is established through the corporeality of Kassovitz's performance from the very first scene in which Johnny appears at the side of the road with Marx, trying to hitch a lift from the passing traffic. Kassovitz/ Johnny shuffles towards Marx with his hands in the pockets of his ill-fitting jacket – clothing that serves to further highlight his slight frame and awkward movement – and is repeatedly warned away by the ageing Marx. The scene is comic, but it also points to Johnny as a body ill at ease with himself and totally excluded from those around him (and thus marginalised from society in general).

However, behind the timid and naive character type hides a more sinister tendency towards violence that is also expressed through the body rather than in language. Indeed, like Max (from *Assassin(s)*) and even Nino in *Amélie*, Johnny actually does very little to verbalise his thoughts, feelings and motivations. His emotional fragility is instead articulated through extremes of physical action: be it the childish elation of playing with the dartboard bought for him by Marx, or the far darker and disturbing act of self-mutilation that comes earlier in the film. In *Assassin(s)*, though less extreme, Max similarly struggles to articulate his frustrations as part of an alienated youth underclass. The more expansive voiceover from Max that opens the film is soon replaced by the young man's inability to communicate his feelings of exclusion and hopelessness – which are eventually provided an outlet through the violence he commits as a hired killer.

The character of Albert in *Un Héros très discret* is somewhat different in the sense that he must learn to articulate and charm his way to acceptance (a place in the social norm) – and so transform

18 'Kassovitz is twenty-five years old but he possesses this strange combination of characteristics that fall between the juvenile cretin and a more malicious type. Much of this is expressed through his body'.

himself from the self-effacing figure of the opening scenes into the assured resistance hero found in the second half of the film. The sense of transformation that is so central to the narrative of *Un Héros très discret* is, nevertheless, also found in *Regarde les hommes tomber* and *Assassin(s)*. What we are presented with, then, in all three of these three key films are characters who create new and often extraordinary identities for themselves as hoodlums, hired killers and war heroes. Once again, the corporeality of Kassovitz's performance style comes into play here. It is precisely the unexceptional or seemingly unthreatening masculinity of the characters played by Kassovitz – or what we might describe as the greater *anonymity* of Kassovitz's body in performance which becomes less of a burden in comparison to stars like Delon or Belomondo – that allows these characters to transform themselves in the way that they do.[19]

This sense of transformation (and particularly in the way it is expressed through the body) is most extensively played out through performance-as-fabrication in *Un Héros très discret*. By fabricating a mythical past as a Resistance hero, Albert constructs a new identity for himself through rehearsal as much as performance: a number of scenes therefore present Albert alone in his room reciting the anecdotes and introductions he will use to ingratiate himself with former members of the Resistance. This idea of rehearsing an identity is repeated in *Regarde les hommes tomber*, through the short, jump-cut montage where Johnny practises his lines – and just as importantly the posture and gestures – of his hoodlum persona before he sets off with Marx to work as a debt collector. Johnny's playful approach to the these 'rehearsals' contrasts directly with the more sinister and unsettling actions they will lead to – and so further highlights the extremes of childish naivety and malicious violence contained within his character.

Despite the transformation effected by Kassovitz's characters in these three films, the awkward social outcast is never far from the surface and must constantly be controlled or contained. The extraordinary identities that these social misfits attempt to fashion for themselves are thus constantly under threat of being exposed – a further

19 In *Assassin(s)* Max/Kassovitz's anonymity is further emphasised through costume. Dressed in jeans, T-shirts, loosely fitting sweat-tops and trainers, Max is virtually indistinguishable from any other working-class male youth from the *banlieue*.

way in which a crisis of masculinity manifests itself through the characters played by Kassovitz. Max breaks down as he holds the gun to Mr Vidal's face, struggling to 'perform' as the hired killer when taken on his first contract killing with Wagner. Johnny self-harms with a razor, gruesomely playing out the role of violent hoodlum on his own body, rather than those around him.

In similar ways, the increasing psychological strain exacted on Albert through his attempts to maintain the pretence of the Resistance hero manifests itself on the body. One scene in particular towards the end of *Un Héros très discret*, where Albert (now a lieutenant in the army) is cœrced into a game of tennis with his fellow officers illustrates this sense of the actor's body/psyche on the verge of collapse. Not wanting to admit to his lower-ranked colleagues that he has never played tennis, Albert finds himself exposed as a fraud on court. As he flails about with the racket in a vain attempt to return the ball and thus salvage some respect from those watching, Albert's body (isolated in the frame in a medium shot) is placed under increasing strain: a visual metaphor for the pressures he is under to perform constantly the extraordinary identity he has fashioned for himself. Inevitably, then, it is Albert's body that eventually causes his downfall. He is exposed as an imposter by the fact that his torso contains no scar from the entry wound of the bullet he claims to have taken during active service (a fact that is revealed both when he takes a shower with his fellow officers but also when he lies naked in bed with his lover).

We could argue then that these three core films from the mid-1990s, and above all *Un Héros très discret*, serve as further evidence of Kassovitz conspiring against the traditional strategies of stardom – in this instance, the way in which the star authenticates through performance the on-screen illusion of the perfect or flawless persona to conceal that which is deviant, problematic or paradoxical (Dyer 1998: 23–8). Kassovitz elects to do the exact opposite, exposing the myth of performance as fabrication by openly parading the fragmented, damaged, ugly elements of the characters he plays and their attempts to rehearse or perform their new identities. Thus whereas most stars attempt to reconcile the unstable illusion of stardom through performance, Kassovitz appears to embrace such contradictions by placing them on screen. If an audience connects with anything in such a performance, then, it is with the apparent 'honesty' of Kassovitz's instinctively naturalistic performance style that allows for the fragility and vulnerability of the characters he plays to be exposed (often ruthlessly) on screen.

Grooming the social misfit for the mainstream: *Amélie*, and beyond

As the above analysis of his performance style in this trio of films from the late 1990s shows, Kassovitz establishes the actor-persona (as opposed to star persona) of an awkward outsider or social misfit, which incorporates association with youth and marginality (to which we might also add, in *Métisse* and *Un Héros très discret*, figures who desire to move beyond the confines of their working-class or provincial background). These marginal characters are not romantic figures; rather, they are presented to us as social outcasts who inspire or elicit sympathy, and in some cases (for example Johnny in *Regarde les hommes tomber*) a mixture of disquiet and fascination. A significant shift therefore takes places in relation to this actor–persona in *Amélie* in order to make the character acceptable to a mainstream audience. Kassovitz maintains his status as the quirky social misfit but elides or 'smoothes out' the more disturbing or threatening edges from the characters found in earlier films. This is made clear by Jeunet's approach to filming Amélie's initial encounters with Nino: on both occasions the film's heroine gazes down upon him as he scratches under photo-booths for unwanted pictures. He is thus shot from above, a camera position that typically identifies its subject as a submissive, unimposing or unthreatening figure. Nino is essentially an innocent – maintaining the appearance of childish naivety displayed by Johnny in *Regarde les hommes tomber* – but the underlying malice or potential for violence, cruelty or duplicity is completely evacuated from his character. He is thus able to project a similar air of (sexual) innocence as Amélie, even when employed as an assistant in a sex shop, or working as a 'scarer' on a fairground ghost train, without seeming dysfunctional or menacing.

Nino's eccentricities are presented as endearing rather than deviant. Amélie's attraction to Nino demands, moreover, that the audience read them as such. The photograph albums, in which Nino obsessively collects the shredded portraits discarded outside photo booths in train and metro stations around Paris by dissatisfied customers, are not therefore shown to be a sign of his dysfunctionality; instead they represent Nino's attempt to connect with the rest of society and construct a surrogate 'family album'. It is, therefore, the essentially unthreatening nature of Nino's idiosyncrasies that allows Amélie to find (safely) her soul-mate and thus sets up the film's happy ending.

The conscious grooming of Kassovitz's social misfit type in *Amélie* is clearly expressed through Nino's costume: the ill-fitting jacket of *Regarde les hommes tomber*, or fashionable sportswear of *Assassin(s)* and *Métisse* are replaced by an understated, but stylish wardrobe. Gone too is the stubble and unkempt, cropped haircut of these two earlier films. Kassovitz is thus styled in a similar way to Albert in the later scenes of *Un Héros très discret*, once he has established his persona as Resistance hero. The crucial difference between these two films, however, is that in *Un Héros très discret*, Albert is constantly threatened with exposure – and the pressure of concealment causes momentary slips in his performance, such as on the tennis court. Nino, on the other hand, is simply allowed to 'be' the eccentric outsider, with no pressure to either conform or transform. Consequently, he does not express the same physical awkwardness shown by either Johnny in *Regarde les hommes tomber* or Albert in moments of duress in *Un Héros très discret* – effecting an important change in the physicality of Kassovitz's performance style that (as we will see) would be refined even further in *Amen*.

In the wake of *Amélie*'s phenomenal international success, as well as the predictable offers of romantic leads in mainstream French comedies, came a far more unexpected contract for Kassovitz from parfumier Lancôme to promote its new male fragrance: Miracle for men. Photographs of Kassovitz dressed in a simple black shirt with stylishly cropped hair and designer stubble, staring pensively into the distance with the glow of the sunrise behind him, were placed in magazines and adorned advertising boards across the globe. The marketing synergy for the product was completed when Kassovitz agreed to direct the accompanying television advert for the Lancôme fragrance. Further promotional shots of Kassovitz, depicting the filmmaker as a confident, stylish and urbane 30-something, that appeared on Lancôme's American website, were accompanied by the following text: 'Now Lancôme has found the "Mircale" man: contemporary, artistic, bold, driven, a man who brings his dreams to life – a man who takes hold of his destiny and makes it happen'.[20]

20 See: www.lancome-usa.com/_us/_en/about/discoverlancome/lancomefaces/ mathieu/mathieu_beauty.aspx (site last accessed 10/9/05).

Despite the suggestion by Philippe Lançon (2001: 20) that 'Lancôme utilise moins le réalisateur de *La Haine* ou des *Rivières pourpres* que "Mathieu of Montmartre"'[21] – and, even if we accept the obvious promotional hyperbole – the personality described in the Miracle advertisement is entirely at odds with the self-effacing eccentric character played by the actor in *Amélie*. Instead, the apparent star image of Kassovitz that Lancôme appear to have bought into, and thus wished to promote, was one that capitalised on the global recognition afforded by *Amélie*'s success, but which then combined this exposure with the qualities and characteristics ('artistic', 'bold', 'driven') more immediately associated with Kassovitz the director. As with his court appearance in May 2005 for motor offences and the ensuing altercation with police, Kassovitz's public persona is determined far more by his image and reputation as director rather than his on-screen actor–persona.

The modification or 'grooming' of Kassovitz's marginal type that occurs in *Amélie* was further refined in *Amen*. Despite being directed by the iconic political *auteur* of 1970s civic cinema (Costa-Gavras), *Amen* has, in many ways, all the hallmarks of the French heritage film: a big-budget adaptation; star-named producer (Claude Berri, the principal exponent of the heritage film in the late 1980s and 1990s); high production values incorporating faithful reproduction of the period and numerous scenes involving elaborate décor or staging of real locations requiring substantial numbers of extras (such as the scenes in the Vatican) to create a sense of historical spectacle. The film thus served as a further indication of Kassovitz's cross-over to a mainstream audience as an actor following the success of *Amélie*.

In *Amen*, Kassovitz plays Riccardo Fontana, a young Jesuit priest who is compelled to take a stand against the Catholic church's conspiracy of silence over the Holocaust that eventually costs him his life. Kassovitz thus continues to play the young outsider caught up in events beyond his control. Riccardo is repeatedly warned by senior figures in the Vatican to desist in his attempts to expose the genocide taking place in Nazi concentration camps, and is often isolated (shot alone or placed apart in the frame) within the film's *mise en scène*. However, the moral ambiguity that surrounds the characters played by Kassovitz in his earlier films is completely expelled. Riccardo is a largely one-dimensional, idealised hero: a principled and ultimately noble figure

21 'less a case of Lancôme using the director of *La Haine* and *Les Rivières pourpres* than "Mathieu of Montmartre"'.

who refuses to bow in the face of Nazi aggression, and who is unable to countenance the sybaritic cardinals and diplomats attempting to justify their passivity towards the Holocaust around a dinner table in the Vatican while Jews are being transported to Auschwitz. He is also an agitator, a disruptive presence who refuses to accept the hypocrisy and political expediency of the Papacy's reluctance to acknowledge the Holocaust. And in this sense, as the wilful young militant, he is a character more closely aligned with Kassovitz's public persona as the outspoken rebel than any of his previous acting roles.

Kassovitz/Riccardo must, however, earn this position as the idealised hero, and is initially portrayed as something of a peripheral figure within the narrative of *Amen*. He first appears thirty minutes into the film as an onlooker to the discussion that takes place between his superiors and Kurt Gernstein (Ulrich Tukur), a German scientist enlisted by the SS whose Christian faith compels him to expose the horrors of the concentration camps to the world. Nevertheless, Riccardo/Kassovitz increasingly takes centre stage as the film's moral conscience, as the figure who articulates most consistently the outrage felt by both the audience and the film's director at the refusal of cardinals and diplomats to acknowledge the evidence of the Holocaust and intervene against Nazi deportation of the Jews. Devastated upon discovering that this conspiracy of silence extends as far as the Papacy, Riccardo finally makes a heroic and symbolic sacrifice; placing a yellow Star of David on his priest's robes and voluntarily boarding the trains carrying Jews to the concentration camps. This status as the hero/star is further reinforced by his refusal to accept attempts from both the Vatican and a last-minute intervention by Gerstein to rescue him from the gas chambers. In contrast to Riccardo's ascendancy from idealistic priest to idealised hero, Gernstein is presented as a broken man by the end of the film who deserts his family and turns himself over to the Allies at the end of the war, only to be wrongly accused of directing the murder of Jews in the concentration camps, finally committing suicide in his prison cell.

Therefore, in *Amen* Kassovitz plays a 'self-made hero', but not in the mould of Albert Dehousse. He is once again a character who transforms himself, but this time the metamorphosis is noble and courageous as opposed to duplicitous and self-serving. This more heroic dimension to Kassovitz's character in *Amen* is reflected in the scenes leading up to Riccardo's death in the concentration camp where he stands quite literally alone and defiant in the face of Nazi oppression. The awkward actor's body of *Regarde les hommes tomber* or *Un Héros très discret*, is transformed into something resembling the extraordinary star body; almost Christ-like as a site of sacrifice, suffering and purity.[22] Camerawork and framing in *Amen* adjust accordingly in comparison to the *mise en scène* of Kassovitz the actor in his previous films. He is dramatically lit in extreme-close up, traditionally the mode of unmediated access to the star's emotion and essence (described by Dyer (1986: 11) as an intimate, transparent 'window to the soul') as the camera's gaze contemplates Riccardo's courage and integrity in the face of Nazi brutality. What is lost in these scenes – undoubtedly the closest Kassovitz has so far come to colluding with a star trajectory in his career on screen – is the instinctive naturalism that in his films from the 1990s had served as a marker of authentication in the actor's performance style, as well as a point of audience identification with the actor–persona. The far more restrained and conventional performance in *Amen*, which earned Kassovitz a César nomination for best actor, was, of course, largely determined by the noble transformation and heroic dimension to the character he was playing. However, it also emerged from Costa-Gavras's more contained framing of Kassovitz in *Amen* – a process begun by Jeunet in *Amélie* – which has the effect of evacuating from the *mise en scène* both the spontaneity and moral ambiguity surrounding the youthful outcasts played by the actor in previous films.

The actor–director dialectic

Even though his performances in films such as *Regarde les hommes tomber* arguably present a type of marginalised male subjectivity analogous with the foregrounding of an alienated youth underclass found in *La Haine* and *Assassin(s)* there are, as we have already noted, a number of inconsistencies and tensions that emerge between Kassovitz the actor and the director. These contradictions can be accounted

22 This more heroic characterisation of Kassovitz as the anti-Nazi resister who sacrifices his life was first suggested by his cameo role in *Jakob the Liar*, where he appeared briefly as a Polish Jew imprisoned in the Warsaw ghetto, shot dead by Nazi guards while trying to pass information of the imminent arrival of the Russian army to a group of Jews in a train bound for the concentration camps.

for in relation to the idea of an 'actor–director dialectic', for reasons that will be explained below.

The first, and most obvious, of these tensions or inconsistencies is that Kassovitz's public persona as outspoken rebel is far closer to his persona as a director than as an actor. Equally, the impression given by the choices he has made in his acting career (above all his collaboration with Audiard) is of a filmmaker immersed largely in the *auteur*-led, art-house traditions of French cinema; whereas anyone who has paid even the slightest attention to Kassovitz's career as a director knows that he locates himself firmly within the sphere of youth-orientated cinema – and, more recently, popular genres such as the thriller and horror. Similarly, Kassovitz's consistent refusal in the 1990s as an actor to play the game of stardom – his choice of ambivalent often unpleasant characters, acceptance of a limited number of leading roles and repeated absence from the Césars awards ceremony, for example – appears to be at odds with a director who has clearly stated his commercial and artistic ambitions to reach a global audience with his films.

One way of explaining such tensions or differences, then, is to view Kassovitz's acting career as a creative outlet for the more eclectic, art-house tastes of a filmmaker who, in relation to his directorial career, has always played down such influences in favour of his links to popular genre cinema and Hollywood. His performance in *Regarde les hommes tomber* thus allowed him to experiment as a filmmaker (not just as actor, but also as a director, since, as we know, Kassovitz uses his acting career as an opportunity to observe the practices of other directors) in a film that was both more experimental in terms of its narrative structure, and more transgressive in its characterisation than Kassovitz's own debut feature, *Métisse* – essentially a popular postcolonial French comedy – released one year earlier. The influence of *Regarde les hommes tomber* on Kassovitz's subsequent films as director can be seen most clearly in *Assassin(s)* – the closest Kassovitz has come to a *film d'auteur* in his career to date. Notable similarities between the two films emerge both in relation to film form – a more fragmented elliptical narrative – but also the continuities between the two characters played by Kassovitz in the respective films. Equally both films focus on a relationship between alienated male youth and an ageing deviant proto-father who initiates the young man into a world of violence and criminality. In his later roles Kassovitz resolves the actor–director dialectic to an extent. He is able to do this by occupying a more mainstream position as an actor in romantic comedy (*Amélie*) and politicised-heritage cinema (*Amen*) respectively, and in a way that is consistent with most French actors and stars who alternate much less problematically than directors in France between *auteur* and mainstream productions (Vincendeau 2000: 23–4).

These tensions between Kassovitz as actor and director are most directly exposed in his first three feature films, where the filmmaker appears on both sides of the camera. When interviewed, Kassovitz has suggested that his presence as an actor in his first three films was largely motivated by financial necessity: 'J'ai joué dans mes propres films parce que ça simplifiait les choses, ça faisait des économies de budget et un acteur de moins à diriger! Je savais exactement ce que je voulais et je l'ai fait simplement.'[23] However, as the final part of this quote reveals, such decisions are also motivated by a desire for authorial control. It is more than that, though. For, in his own films, Kassovitz actively colludes to subvert his position as star. In *Métisse*, while the *mise en scène* establishes Félix/Kassovitz as the unconventional male lead and potential object of desire, he also emerges as a figure of ridicule. The repeated visual gag of Félix falling off his bike; his exaggerated appearance and anxiety as to whether he is the father of the baby (even when he knows the test results) therefore function as a means of the director keeping the ego of his on-screen persona in check. In *Assassin(s)* the director's control of the actor is more extreme, and leads Kassovitz to kill off, suddenly and unexpectedly, his own character half-way through the film. Even with his fleeting appearance in *La Haine*, where Kassovitz plays the skinhead who Vinz fails to kill to avenge the murder of a friend from the La Noë estate, this actor–director dialectic is maintained. In the scene Kassovitz establishes a clear hierarchy between actor and director. Not only does Kassovitz the actor appear in a fleeting cameo role, but he is also forced to adopt the position of a skinhead who is left entirely at the mercy of the black-*blanc*-beur trio. In contrast, the authorial presence of Kassovitz the director can be felt in every scene of *La Haine*'s tightly structured chronological narrative and consciously stylised

23 'I act in my own films to simplify things, to economise on the budget and give me one less actor to direct. I know exactly what I want and can do it more easily'., Interview with Kassovitz From *Amen* press release consulted at www.mathieu-kassovitz.com/amen/interviews/mathieu.htm (site last accessed 11/8/05).

mise en scène. Denigrating Kassovitz the actor by assigning him this minor role in the film as a repulsive and cowardly neo-Nazi skinhead becomes, therefore, a way of further emphasising the author(-ity) and thus valorising the control of Kassovitz the director.

As with so much in Kassovitz's filmmaking career, this actor–director dialectic can be seen as mirroring significant shifts taking place in contemporary French film. The inherent tension in the parallel (and occasionally overlapping) careers of Kassovitz the actor and Kassovitz the popular director could be seen as indicative of further divisions in the French film industry that seemed to become increasingly pronounced during the 1990s: namely, the gulf (in economic, creative and production terms) between the more artisanal *auteur*-led independent section of French cinema and that of the mainstream *cinéma des producteurs*. However, contained within this notion of an actor–director 'dialectic' should also, necessarily, be the idea of a synthesis emerging from an initial tension or conflict. Viewed more optimistically, then, we might consider the parallel careers of Kassovitz the actor–director as embodying the very diversity that marks French cinema as one of the few national cinema still able to compete with Hollywood while satisfying both mainstream and art-house audiences. When regarded in this way – as a collective whole – Kassovitz's output to date as actor and director encompasses this same broad spectrum of production practices and genres; from the low-budget *auteur* film, to militant youth cinema, mainstream comedy and the heritage film. It also helps to remind us that the divide (real and imagined) between independent, art-house cinema and the popular mainstream in France is not necessarily as absolute, nor impermeable, as certain critics and practitioners within the French film industry (including, at times, Kassovitz himself) would have us believe.

References

Austin Guy, (2004), 'The amateur actors of Cannes 1999: a shock to the (star) system' *French Cultural Studies*, 15(3), October, 251–64

——— (2003), *Stars in Modern French Film*, London: Arnold

Bernard, Jean-Jacques and Libiot, Éric (1996), 'Héros indiscrets' (interview with Audiard and Kassovitz), *Première*, 231 (June), 106–11

Bonnaud, Frédéric (2001), 'The *Amélie* effect', *Film Comment*, 37 (6), 36–8

Darke, Chris (1997), 'Monsieur memory', *Sight & Sound*, Arpil, 7(4), 24–26

D'Elia, Enzo (1995), 'Mathieu Kassovitz: Après "*La Haine*" le grand amour avec Juliette', *Voici*, (October 30), 14–15

Dyer, Richard (1986), *Heavenly Bodies: Film Stars and Society*, London: BFI/ Macmillan

—— (1998), *Stars*, (new edition) London: BFI

Jeffries, Stuart (2001), 'It's hard for me to play romantic. I come across as a bit of a jerk', *Guardian*, (August 6)

Herpe, Noël, (1996), 'Entretien avec Jacques Audiard: "je veux que tout soit faux"', *Positif*, May, 18–22

Higbee, Will (2005), 'Towards a multiplicity of voices: French cinema's age of the postmodern, part II – 1992–2004', in Hayward, *French National Cinema* (2nd edition), London and New York: Routledge

Kaganski, Serge (2001), '*Amélie*, pas jolie', *Libération*, (May 31)

Kassovitz, Mathieu (1998), 'Les aventures de Mathieu Kassovitz' interview in *Steadycam*, consulted at www.mathieukassovitz.com/itw/steadycam.htm (site last accessed 19/7/05).

Lançon, Philippe (2001), 'Pensez-y le goût des autres: parfum de fans', *Libération*, (21 December), 20

Lauten, Kathryn. M. (1999), "Dusting off' dehousse: *Un héros très discrèt* (Audiard, 1996)' in Powrie (ed.) *French Cinema in the 1990s: Continuity and Difference*, Oxford: Oxford University Press, 58–67

Murat, Pierre (1998), 'Le plaisir (et ses petits tracas)' (review), *Télérama*, 2534, (5 August), 34–5

Nacache, Jacqueline (2005), 'Group portrait with a star: Jeanne Balibar and French '*jeune* cinema', *Studies in French Cinema*, 5 (1), 49–60

Nivelle Pascale (2004), 'Profil: Mathieu Kassovitz', *Libération*, (7 January), 40

Orr, John (2004), 'Stranded: stardom and the free-fall movie in French cinema, 1985–2003', *Studies in French Cinema*, 4 (2), 103–11

Seguret, Olivier (2000), 'La 25e Nuit des Césars', *Libération* , (19 February), 31

Swanson, Tim (2003), 'Team Scream', *Premiere* (USA) 173(3), November, 48-50

Thibaudat, Jean-Pierre (2005), 'La mauvaise conduite de Kassovitz à la barre', *Libération* (May 18), 18

Vachaud, Laurent (1994), 'Entretien avec Jacques Audiard: du côté du cinéma', *Positif*, 407 (September), 36–40

Vincendeau, Ginette (2000), *Stars and Stardom in French cinema*, London: Continuum

—— (2005), 'Miss France', *Sight & Sound*, 15 (2), February, 12–15

Conclusion

This book has sought to argue for Kassovitz's importance in contemporary French cinema as a filmmaker whose work has engaged with (and, in some cases, helped shaped the direction of) key shifts in French cinema since the early 1990s, such as: new realism, the *banlieue* film and the 'post-look' spectacular genre film. In so doing, one of the central concerns in these chapters has also been to establish Kassovitz as a director who (in his various guises) consistently occupies the position of a 'popular' filmmaker, and whose films reflect the increasing prominence of youth at the heart of contemporary popular French culture. All his films are thus concerned with the popular – its form and function in contemporary French culture. His *fracture sociale* trilogy explores some of the socio-political realities affecting contemporary French society (racism, exclusion and violence) by presenting them in a cinematic vernacular that a youth audience can understand and engage with. And while his two most recent features interface more directly (and in some ways disappointingly) with Hollywood genre cinema, all his films display an affinity with an Americanised mass culture of the image that is now firmly embedded within contemporary popular culture (and cinema) in France.

Kassovitz is certainly not the first French director to engage with Hollywood in this way. As Forbes suggests (1992: 239–40), since 1945 successive generations of French filmmakers from both the independent *auteur*-led sector and the mainstream have attempted to 'come to terms with American cinema'. The problem that an increasing number of French critics seem to have with Kassovitz's particular brand of popular cinema, then, is not so much the fact that it looks to America as much as France for inspiration. Rather, it is the type of genres (the action thriller, horror and exploitation cinema) and individual directors (above all Spielberg) from within American cinema that Kassovitz chooses to valorise that provoke an often hostile response to his work.

In a national cinema that has made strategic use of the *auteur*'s cultural cachet in order to mark its difference from Hollywood (Powrie 1999: 8), Kassovitz is seen by many to side more closely with the American 'invaders' than the defenders of French cultural exception. This seems a somewhat odd position for him to be placed in, given his contribution to key developments in French cinema of the 1990s that we have already mentioned, but also the way he has used his acting career as a bridging point between *auteur* and popular cinema.

For his part, Kassovitz, in typically provocative fashion, has exacerbated the situation by repeatedly refusing to identify himself with what he considers the narrow definition of the 'French' *auteur* – which is to say one that is uniquely understood in terms of an intimate, introspective, and often intellectual cinema – preferring instead the idea of the contemporary American *auteur*:

> Depuis vingt ans, les États-Unis ont un bon cinéma commercial qui est un cinéma d'*auteur* ... un *auteur* ce n'est pas seulement quelqu'un qui se torture. C'est quelqu'un qui a des idées et crée un monde. *Matrix* c'est LE film d'*auteur* par excellence. (Aubel 2003: 24)[1]

Kassovitz's vision of the *auteur* therefore attempts to remove the 'wedge' driven between *auteur* and popular cinema in France since the late 1950s (Hayward and Vincendeau 2000: 6). In this way, we can put forward a case for Kassovitz as a new type of popular *auteur* of the 'posts' (postmodern, postcolonial, post-look). His films thus combine the visual spectacle and playful recycling of images and texts found in the *cinéma du look*, with a foregrounding of the network of global, national and local cultural positionings that inform the identities of a postcolonial French youth class, as well as (in his earlier films) a consideration of the effect that the modern mass media has on contemporary French society and the marginalised individuals who inhabit it.

Moreover, by employing this more flexible notion of the *auteur* as a filmmaker who can be found equally in mainstream and the

1 'For twenty years, the USA has had a good commercial cinema which is [also] an *auteur* cinema ... an *auteur* is not only a tortured artist. It is someone who has ideas and creates a world. *The Matrix* is THE *auteur* film, par excellence.'

independent sectors of cinema, and who can move, uninhibited, between genre cinema and more personal, militant or oppositional productions – as Kassovitz has intimated (Jeffries 2001) he would ultimately like to do – we can, perhaps, better understand the true diversity and vitality of contemporary French cinema, as well as Kassovitz's place within it as a popular *auteur*.

References

Aubel, François (2003), 'Kassovitz: jusqu'ici tout va bien', *Epok* 42, (December–January), 16–25

Forbes Jill (1992), *The Cinema in France after the New Wave*, London: BFI/Macmillan

Jeffries, Stuart (2001), 'It's hard for me to play romantic. I come across as a bit of a jerk', *Guardian*, (August 6)

Powrie, Phil (1999), 'Heritage history and new realism', in Powrie (ed.) *French Cinema in the 1990s: Continuity and Difference*, Oxford: Oxford University Press, 1–21

Hayward, Susan and Vincendeau, Ginette (2000), 'Introduction' in Ginette Vincendeau and Susan Hayward (eds), *French Film: Texts and contexts*, (2nd edition), London and New York: Routledge, 1–8

Filmography

(All films are produced in France unless otherwise stated)

Director

Gothika (USA), 2003, 94 mins

Production: Dark Castle Entertainment, Columbia Pictures
Screenplay: Sebastian Gutierrez
Photography: Matthew Libatique
Editor: Yannick Kergoat
Sound: Donna G. Walker
Original music: John Ottman
Main actors: Halle Berry (Miranda Grey), Penélope Cruz (Chloe Sava),
    Robert Downey Jr. (Pete Graham), Charles S. Dutton (Douglas
    Grey), John Carroll Lynch (Sheriff Ryan), Kathleen Mackey (Rachel
    Parsons), Bernard Hill (Phil Parsons)

Les Rivières pourpres, 2000, 101 mins

Production: Gaumont, Légende Entreprises (Alain Goldman), TF1
    Film Productions
Screenplay: Mathieu Kassovitz and Jean-Christophe Grangé
Photography: Thierry Arbogast
Editor: Maryline Monthieux
Sound: Vincent Tulli
Original music: Bruno Coulais
Main actors: Jean Reno (Niémans), Vincent Cassel (Kerkerian), Nadia
    Farès (Fanny Ferreira), Jean Pierre-Cassel (Dr Chernezé), Karim

Belkhadra (Captain Dahmane), Dominique Sandra (Sister Andrée)

Article premier, 1998, 1 min 30 sec

Short film commissioned by Amnesty International as part of Human Rights campaign

La Forêt, 1997, 3 mins

Short Film commissioned by Handicap International as part of an anti-landmine campaign

Assassin(s), 1997, 127 mins

Production: Lazennec (Christophe Rossignon), Studio Canal+, La Sept Cinéma, TF1 Film Productions, Kasso Inc.
Screenplay: Mathieu Kassovitz and Nicolas Boukhrief
Photography: Pierre Aïm
Editor: Mathieu Kassovitz and Yannick Kergoat
Sound: Bernard Aubouy
Original music: Carter Burwell
Main actors: Michel Serrault (Wagner), Mathieu Kassovitz (Max), Mehdi Benoufa (Mehdi), Robert Gendreu (Mr Vidal), Danièle Lebrun (Mrs Pujol), Nicolas Boukrief (Mehdi's brother)

La Haine, 1995, 95 mins

Production: Lazennec (Christophe Rossignon), Studio Canal+, La Sept Cinéma, Kasso Inc.
Screenplay: Mathieu Kassovitz
Photography: Pierre Aïm/ Georges Diane
Editor: Mathieu Kassovitz/ Scott Stevenson
Sound: Vincent Tulli
Original music: DJ Cut Killer
Main actors: Hubert Koundé (Hubert), Vincent Cassel (Vinz), Saïd Taghmaoui (Saïd), Karim Belkhadra (Samir), François Levantal (Astérix), Marc Duret (Inspector 'Notre Dame')

Métisse, 1993, 95 mins

Production: Lazennec (Christophe Rossignon), SFP Cinéma, Nomad Films
Screenplay: Mathieu Kassovitz
Photography: Pierre Aïm
Editor: Jean-Pierre Segal/ Colette Farrugia

Sound: Norbert Garcia
Original music: Assassin
Main actors: Hubert Koundé (Jamal), Mathieu Kassovitz (Félix), Lola
    (Julie Mauduech), Vincent Cassel (Max), Jany Holt (Félix's grand-
    mother), Tadek Lokcinski (Félix's grandfather)

Assassins, 1992, 10 mins

Production: Lazennec Tout Court
Screenplay: Mathieu Kassovitz
Photography: Pierre Aïm
Main actors: Marc Berman (the teacher), Mathieu Kassovitz (the stu-
    dent)

Cauchemar blanc, 1991, 10 mins

Production: Lazennec Tout Court
Screenplay: Corinne Bouvier (adapted from a Mœbius BD)
Photography: Georges Diane
Editor: Nathalie Geopfert
Sound: Jérome Thaillade
Music: Perez Prado, 'Mambo No. 5'
Main actors: Yvan Attal (René), Jean-Pierre Daroussin (J.P.), Roger Souza
    (Barjout), François Toumarkine (Berthon), Farouk (El Kebir)

Fierrot le pou, 1990, 8 mins

Production: Lazennec Tout Court
Screenplay: Mathieu Kassovitz
Photography: Georges Diane
Editor: Stéphane Foucault
Sound: Vincent Tulli
Original music: Rockin' Squat
Main actors: Mathieu Kassovitz (the B-boy), Alain Bréna-Labinski (the
    basketball player), Solange Labonne (the young woman)

Music Videos

2000 *'Y'a' Sayan Supa Crew*
1990 *Tanton David*

Adverts

2004 **SNCF** (public safety awareness campaign)
2001 **Miracle**, Lancôme
2000 **Printemps** ('Inventez vous!')

Actor (feature films)

Principal or supporting role

Amen, 2002, 130 mins

Director: Costa-Gavras
Production: Katharina Productions, Renn productions (Claude Berri),
    TF1 Films productions, Medien
Screenplay: Andra Barbuica
Photography: Patrick Blossier
Editor: Yannick Kergoat
Sound: Pierre Gamet
Original music: Armand Amar
Main actors: Ulrich Tukur (Kurt Gernstein), Mathieu Kassovitz
    (Riccardo Fontana), Ulrich Mühe (the Doctor), Michel Duchaussoy
    (The Cardinal), Ion Caramitru (Count Fontana), Marcel Iurès (the
    Pope), Friedrich von Thun (Gurnstein's father), Antje Schmidt
    (Mrs Gernstein)

Le Fabuleux destin d'Amélie Poulain, 2001, 120 mins

Director: Jean-Pierre Jeunet
Production: MCM Independent, France 3 Cinéma, Tapioca Films,
    Victoires Productions
Screenplay: Jean-Pierre Jeunet / Guillaume Laurant
Photography: Bruno Delbonnel
Editor: Céline Kélépikis
Sound: Jean Umanski
Original music: Yann Tiersen
Main actors: Audrey Tautou (Amélie), Mathieu Kassovitz (Nino),
    Rufus (Raphaël Poulin), Yolande Moreau (Madeleine Wallace),
    Artus de Penguern (Hipolito), Dominique Pinon (Joseph), Maurice
    Bénichou (Bretodeau), Michel Robin, (Collignon), Isabelle Nanty,
    (Georgette), Claire Maurier, (Suzanne), Clotilde Mollet (Gina), Serge
    Merlin (Dufayel), Jamel Debbouze (Lucien)

Le Plaisir (et ses petits tracas), 1998, 104 mins

Director: Nicolas Boukhrief
Production: Noé Productions
Screenplay: Nicolas Boukhrief
Photography: Jean-Max Bernard
Editor: Jacqueline Mariani
Sound: Carlo Thoss
Original music: Nicolas Baby
Main actors: Vincent Cassel (Michael), Francis Renaud (Raphael), Julie Gayet (Véra), Mathieu Kassovitz (Roland), Caroline Cellier (Hélène), Michele Placido (Carlo), Foued Nassah (Marcel), Florence Thomassin (Lise), Andréa Coftis (Rocco), Jean-Christophe Bouvet (Bob)

Assassin(s), 1997

See entry for this film under the section 'Director', p. 206.

Un Héros très discret, 1996

Director: Jacques Audiard
Production: Aliceleo, Lumière, France 3 Cinéma, M6 Films
Screenplay: Alain Le Henry and Jacques Audiard
Photography: Jean-Marc Fabre
Editor: Juliette Welfing
Sound: Jean-Pierre Duret
Original music: Alexandre Desplat
Main actors: Mathieu Kassovitz (Albert Dehousse), Anouk Grinberg (Servane), Sandrine Kiberlain (Yvette), Albert Dupontel (Dionnet), Jean-Louis Trintignant (Dehousse as old man)

Regarde les hommes tomber, 1994, 110 mins

Director: Jacques Audiard
Production: Bloody Mary Productions, France 3 Cinéma, CEC, Canal+
Screenplay: Alain Le Henry and Jacques Audiard
Photography: Gérard Stérin
Editor: Monique Dartonne/Juliette Welfling
Sound: François Waledisch, Dominique Gaborieau
Original music: Alexandre Desplat
Main actors: Jean Yanne (Simon Hirsch), Jean-Louis Trintignant

(Marx), Mathieu Kassovitz (Johnny), Bulle Ogier (Louise), Yvon Back (Mickey), Christine Pascal (Sandrine)

Métisse, 1993

See entry for this film under the section 'Director', pp. 206–7

Actor (minor or cameo role)

Astérix et Obélix: Mission Cléopiâtre, Chabat, 2002

Birthday Girl, Butterworth, 2001, UK/USA

Jakob the Liar, Peter Kassovitz, 1999, USA

Le Cinquième élément, Besson, 1997

Mon homme, Blier, 1996

La Haine, Kassovitz, 1995

Des nouvelles du bon Dieu, Le Pêcheur, 1995

Un été sans histories, Harel, 1992

Touch and Die, Solinas, 1991

L'année prochaine … si tout va bien, Hubert, 1981

Au bout du bout du banc, Peter Kassovitz, 1978

Select bibliography

See also the 'References' sections at the end of each chapter.

With the obvious exception of *La Haine*, there is a relative scarcity of critical work on Kassovitz as both actor and director at this stage in his career. For this reason, interviews and reviews form the majority of entries in this bibliography. Many of the French press reviews of Kassovitz's films are stored electronically at the BiFi, Paris, where they can be easily accessed.

Books

Vincendeau, Ginette (2005), *La Haine* (French Film Guide), London/
New York: I.B. Taurus. An engaging study of Kassovitz's breakthrough film as a director that considers *La Haine*'s stylistic sophistication and (apparent) ideological ambiguity, as well as explaining
the reasons for the film's considerable success with national and
international audiences. Analysis is located in relation to both the
French film industry of the 1990s and the broader socio-political
context from which the film emerged in France.

Book chapters and journal articles on Kassovitz's films

Higbee, Will (2005), 'The return of the political or designer visions of
exclusion? The case for Mathieu Kassovitz's *fracture sociale* trilogy'
Studies in French Cinema, 5 (2), 123–35

—— (2001), 'Screening the "other" Paris: cinematic representations of the French urban periphery in *La Haine* and *Ma 6–T va cracker*', *Modern & Contemporary France*, 9 (2), 197–208

Konstantarakos, Myrto (1999), 'Which mapping of the city? *La Haine* and the cinéma de banlieue', in Phil Powrie (ed.), *French Cinema in the 1990s: Continuity and Difference*, Oxford: Oxford University Press, 160–71

Loshitzky, Yosefa (2005), 'The post-Holocaust Jew in the age of postcolonialism: *La Haine* revisited', *Studies in French Cinema*, 5 (2), 137–47

Reader, Keith (1995), 'After the riot', *Sight & Sound*, November, 12–14

Reynaud, Bérénice, (1996) 'Le'hood: *Hate* and its neighbors', *Film Comment*, 32 (2), March/April, 54–58

Sherzer, Dina, (1999), 'Comedy and interracial relationships: *Romuald et Juliette* (Serreau, 1987) and *Métisse* (Kassovitz, 1993)', in Phil Powrie (ed.), *French Cinema in the 1990s: Continuity and Difference*, Oxford: Oxford University Press, 148–59

Tarr, Carrie (2005), *Reframing difference:* Beur *and* banlieue *filmmaking in France*, Manchester: Manchester University Press (see Chapter 3, 'Ethnicity and identity in Mathieu Kassovitz's *Métisse* and *La Haine*', 62–72)

Vincendeau, Ginette (2000), 'Designs on the *banlieue*: Mathieu Kassovitz's *La Haine* (1995)', in Susan Hayward and Ginette Vincendeau (eds), *French Film: Texts and Contexts*, London, Routledge

Interviews with Kassovitz

Aubel, François (2003), 'Kassovitz: Jusqu'ici tout va bien', 42, (December–January), 16–25

Belpêche, Stéphanie, (2004), 'Mathieu Kassovitz, un Frenchie à Hollywood', *Le Journal du Dimanche*, (4 January)

Bernard, Jean-Jacques and Libiot, Éric (1996), 'Héros indiscrets' (interview with Audiard and Kassovitz), *Première*, 231 (June), 106–11

Boulay, Anne and Colmant, Marie (1995), '*La Haine* ne nous appartient plus' (interview with Kassovitz), *Libération*, (31 May)

Bourguignon, Thomas and Tobin, Yann (1995), 'Entretien avec Mathieu Kassovitz: les cinq dernières secondes', *Positif*, June, 8–13

Conter, Elizabeth (2000), 'L'entretien du film français: Mathieu

Kassovitz', *Le Film français*, 2848 (22 September), 17

Ferenezi, Aurélien (1995), 'Je ne veux pas qu'on trouve mon film sympa...' (interview with Kassovitz), *Infomatin*, (31 May)

Les Frères K (1997), 'Kounen et Kasso se lâchent', *Première*, July, 51–4

Jeffries, Stuart (2001), 'It's hard for me to play romantic. I come across as a bit of a jerk', *Guardian*, (6 August)

Kassovitz (1998), 'Les aventures de Mathieu Kassovitz' interview in *Steadycam*, consulted at www.mathieukassovitz.com/itw/steadycam. htm (site last accessed 19/7/05)

Klifa, Thierry and d'Yvoire, Christophe (1993), 'Metteurs en scène: premiers pas', *Studio*, December, 108–12

Levieux, Michèle (1995), 'Le noir et blanc draine plus de réalisme' (interview with Kassovitz), *L'Humainté*, (29 May), 20

Lacomme, Jean Pierre (2000), 'Mathieu Kassovitz, la hargne: interview', *Le Journal du Dimanche*, (24 September)

Murat, Pierre (1997), 'Face à la violence, faut enfoncer le clou' (interview with Mathieu Kassovitz), *Télérama*, 2470, (14 May), 40–2

Nivelle Pascale (2004), 'Profil: Mathieu Kassovitz', *Libération*, (7 January), 40

Remy, Vincent (1995), 'Entretien avec Mathieu Kassovitz: "C'est pas interdit de parler aux mecs des banlieues"', *Télérama*, 2368, (31 May), pp. 42–6

Tirard, Laurent (2000), 'Mathieu Kassovitz: la leçon de cinéma' *Studio*, no. 160, consulted at www.mathieukassovitz.com/rivieres/interviews/studio.htm (site last accessed 22/7/05)

Wheaton, Mark (2003b), 'Newly American Gothika', *Fangoria*, 228, (November), 17–21

Reviews of Kassovitz's films:

Alexander, Karen (1995), 'La Haine', *Vertigo*, 5 (autumn/winter), 45–6

Anon (2000), '*Les Rivières pourpres*' (review), *Le Monde*, (27 September)

Anon (2004), 'Sang aucun sens' *L'Humanité*, (7 January)

Bonnaud, Frédéric (2000), 'Made in France', *Les Inrockuptibles*, (27 September)

Blumenfeld, Samuel (2000), 'Mathieu Kassovitz sur la piste d'un serial killer', *Le Monde*, (27 September)

Colombani, Florence (2004), 'Gothika' (review), *Le Monde*, (9 January)

Constans, Marie-Ève (2004), 'Mathieu Kassovitz plonge dans le frisson hollywoodien', *La Croix*, (7 January)

Goudet, Stéphane (2000),'*Les Rivières pourpres*: filles et fils de ...', *Positif*, 477 (November), 50–1

Higuinen, Erwan (2000), 'Que la montagne est belle', *Cahiers du cinéma*, 550, (October), 106

Jeancolas, Jean-Pierre (1997a), 'Assassin(s): êtres plats et petits écrans', *Positif*, no. 437/8, 119–20

Katelan, Jean-Yves (2000), '*Les Rivières pourpres*' (review), *Première*, 283 (October), 59

Lefort, Gérard (1997), '*Assassin(s)*' (review), *Libération* (18 May)

Léonardi, Jean Pierre (1997), 'Petite panoplie de zappeur pompier incendiaire', *L'Humainté*, (17 May)

Péron, Didier (2000), 'Ça rame sur *Les Rivières pourpres*', *Libération*, (27 September)

Rémy, Serge (1995), 'Banlieue haute tension', *L'Humainté*, (29 May), 20

Roy, André (2000), '*Les Rivières pourpres*', (review), *24 Images*, 106, 61

Rozenberg, G. (1993), 'Lola un peu autrement', *Le Quotidien de Paris*, (18 August).

Websites and related links:

All sites listed last consulted 10/10/05

www.mathieukassovitz.com/main.htm

Kassovitz's official website. Contains information on all his feature films to date, news on forthcoming features, as well as the various adverts and video clips directed by Kassovitz, which are available to view on the site. The site was redesigned in November 2005 and, as a result, pages containing press dossiers and interviews related to his films (including a number referenced in this book) have, unfortunately, been removed.

www.lescesarducinema.com/cesar/home.html

The Césars website (the French equivalent of the Oscars), where a dossier on Kassovitz is available with full details of his nominations and awards as both director and actor

www.cine-courts.com/cine4/UTILISATEUR/main.php?GOTO=ZONE2C
OURTS&PAGE=26&film=92
Link to short film website where it is possible to view Kassovitz's 1997 anti-landmine short *La Forêt*

www.bifi.fr
The BIFI (French Film library) website. Contains dossiers on all of Kassovitz's films with statistical information, and full details of cast and crew

www.cnc.fr
The official website of the Centre National de la Cinématographie (CNC) contains up to date statistical information on production, distribution and exhibition in France.

Index